DATE DUE

MAY 3 1994			

PRIVATE LIVES
AND PUBLIC POLICIES

Confidentiality
and Accessibility
of Government
Statistics

RECEIVED

George T. Duncan, Thomas B. Jabine, and
Virginia A. de Wolf, editors

Panel on Confidentiality and Data Access

Committee on National Statistics
Commission on Behavioral and Social Sciences and Education
National Research Council

and the

Social Science Research Council

NATIONAL ACADEMY PRESS
Washington, D.C. 1993

323.44
PAN

NATIONAL ACADEMY PRESS • 2101 Consitution Avenue, N.W. • Washington, D.C. 20418

NOTICE: The project that is the subject of this report was approved by the Governing Board of the National Research Council, whose members are drawn from the councils of the National Academy of Sciences, the National Academy of Engineering, and the Institute of Medicine. The members of the committee responsible for the report were chosen for their special competences and with regard for appropriate balance.

This report has been reviewed by a group other than the authors according to procedures approved by a Report Review Committee consisting of members of the National Academy of Sciences, the National Academy of Engineering, and the Institute of Medicine.

Funding for this project was provided by the National Science Foundation, the Bureau of the Census of the U.S. Department of Commerce, the Bureau of Labor Statistics of the U.S. Department of Labor, the Internal Revenue Service Statistics of Income Division of the U.S. Department of Treasury, the National Institute on Aging of the U.S. Department of Health and Human Services, the National Center for Education Statistics of the U.S. Department of Education, and, through their general contributions to the work of the Committee on National Statistics, several other federal agencies.

Library of Congress Cataloging-in-Publication Data

Panel on Confidentiality and Data Access (U.S.)
    Private lives and public policies : confidentiality and
accessibility of government statistics / Panel on Confidentiality
and Data Access [of the] Committee on National Statistics,
Commission on Behavioral and Social Sciences and Education, National
Research Council and the Social Science Research Council.
    p. cm.
    Includes bibliographical references and index.
    ISBN 0-309-04743-9
    1. Privacy, Right of—United States. 2. Public records—United
States—Access control. 3. United States—Statistical services.
I. National Research Council (U.S.). Committee on National
Statistics. II. Social Science Research Council (U.S.) III. Title.
JC596.2.U5P36 1993
323.448—dc20   93-31312
                                                               CIP

Printed in the United States of America

PANEL ON CONFIDENTIALITY AND DATA ACCESS

GEORGE T. DUNCAN (*Chair*) H. John Heinz III School of Public Policy and Management, Carnegie Mellon University
JAMES T. BONNEN, Department of Agricultural Economics, Michigan State University
JOE S. CECIL, Research Division, Federal Judicial Center
MARTIN H. DAVID, Department of Economics, University of Wisconsin
RUTH R. FADEN, Department of Health Policy and Management, The Johns Hopkins University
DAVID H. FLAHERTY, Social Science Centre, The University of Western Ontario, London, Ontario, Canada
F. THOMAS JUSTER, Survey Research Center, University of Michigan
GARY T. MARX, Department of Sociology, University of Colorado at Boulder
WILLIAM M. MASON, Department of Sociology, University of California, Los Angeles
DONALD B. RUBIN, Department of Statistics, Harvard University
ELEANOR SINGER, Center for the Social Sciences, Columbia University
WILLIAM H. WILLIAMS, Department of Mathematics and Statistics, Hunter College

Virginia A. de Wolf, *Study Director*
Thomas B. Jabine, *Consultant*
Wlodzimierz Okrasa, *Staff Liaison*, Social Science Research Council
Robert W. Pearson, *Staff Liaison*, Social Science Research Council
David L. Szanton, *Staff Liaison*, Social Science Research Council
Michele L. Conrad, *Senior Project Assistant*

The National Academy of Sciences is a private, nonprofit, self-perpetuating society of distinguished scholars engaged in scientific and engineering research, dedicated to the furtherance of science and technology and to their use for the general welfare. Upon the authority of the charter granted to it by the Congress in 1863, the Academy has a mandate that requires it to advise the federal government on scientific and technical matters. Dr. Bruce M. Alberts is president of the National Academy of Sciences.

The National Academy of Engineering was established in 1964, under the charter of the National Academy of Sciences, as a parallel organization of outstanding engineers. It is autonomous in its administration and in the selection of its members, sharing with the National Academy of Sciences the responsibility for advising the federal government. The National Academy of Engineering also sponsors engineering programs aimed at meeting national needs, encourages education and research, and recognizes the superior achievements of engineers. Dr. Robert M. White is president of the National Academy of Engineering.

The Institute of Medicine was established in 1970 by the National Academy of Sciences to secure the services of eminent members of appropriate professions in the examination of policy matters pertaining to the health of the public. The Institute acts under the responsibility given to the National Academy of Sciences by its congressional charter to be an adviser to the federal government and, upon its own initiative, to identify issues of medical care, research, and education. Dr. Kenneth I. Shine is president of the Institute of Medicine.

The National Research Council was organized by the National Academy of Sciences in 1916 to associate the broad community of science and technology with the Academy's purposes of furthering knowledge and advising the federal government. Functioning in accordance with general policies determined by the Academy, the Council has become the principal operating agency of both the National Academy of Sciences and the National Academy of Engineering in providing services to the government, the public, and the scientific and engineering communities. The Council is administered jointly by both Academies and the Institute of Medicine. Dr. Bruce M. Alberts and Dr. Robert M. White are chairman and vice chairman, respectively, of the National Research Council.

* * *

Founded in 1923, the Social Science Research Council is an autonomous, nongovernmental, not-for-profit organization composed of social scientists from all over the world. The Council's primary purpose is to advance the quality, value, and effectiveness of social science research. It seeks to encourage scholars in separate disciplines—e.g., anthropologists, psychologists, sociologists, statisticians, and others—to work together on important topical, conceptual, and methodological issues that can benefit from interdisciplinary collaboration. Natural scientists, geographers, linguists, and scholars in the humanities also participate in many of the Council's activities. The Council's work is carried out through a wide variety of workshops and conferences, fellowships and grants, summer training institutes, research consortia, scholarly exchanges, and publications.

Acknowledgments

The Panel on Confidentiality and Data Access is grateful to the many organizations and individuals who contributed to its work.

Support for the study was provided by the National Science Foundation, the Bureau of the Census of the U.S. Department of Commerce, the Bureau of Labor Statistics of the U.S. Department of Labor, the Internal Revenue Service Statistics of Income Division of the U.S. Department of Treasury, the National Institute on Aging of the U.S. Department of Health and Human Services, the National Center for Education Statistics of the U.S. Department of Education, and, through their general contributions to the work of the Committee on National Statistics, several other federal agencies. We also thank the National Highway Traffic Safety Administration of the U.S. Department of Transportation for granting time, through the Intergovernmental Personnel Act, for Virginia A. de Wolf to serve as the panel's study director.

We thank the many federal government officials who gave generously of their time to attend panel meetings, provide documentation necessary for the panel's work, and answer our many questions: they provided an invaluable sense of the structure and needs of the federal statistical system. We also appreciate the help of researchers, privacy advocates, and others who provided useful insights into nongovernment perspectives on data confidentiality and accessibility issues.

We are grateful to the Committee on National Statistics (CNSTAT) and the Social Science Research Council (SSRC) for their efforts in developing and collaborating on this study. Without the guidance and encouragement of CNSTAT director Miron Straf, SSRC president David Featherman, and former SSRC staff associate Robert Pearson, the work of this panel would not have been possible. We also thank David Szanton and Wlodzimierz Okrasa, who ably maintained SSRC's active role in the study after the departure of Robert Pearson.

We thank the participants and chairs of two workshops that preceded the panel's formation for their contribution to our work. We thank Richard Suzman and other staff of the National Institute on Aging, as well as staff of the Census Bureau and the National Center for Health Statistics for their support of the Workshop on the Longitudinal Retirement History, held in September 1987. We thank Charles Dickens, former head of the Surveys and Analysis Section, and other staff of the National Science Foundation for their support of the Workshop on Confidentiality of and Access to Doctorate Records, held in November 1988. We also thank the U.S. Department of Education, the National Endowment for the Humanities, the National Institutes of Health of the U.S. Department of Health and Human Services, the U.S. Department of Agriculture, the U.S. Department of Energy, the Office of Scientific and Engineering Personnel of the National Research Council, and their staffs for their cooperation in making possible the Workshop on Confidentiality of and Access to Doctorate Records. Both of the workshops identified important issues for the panel.

We also thank the participants and chair of the Workshop on Confidentiality of and Access to National Center for Education Statistics Data, and we thank the National Center for Education Statistics for its support of the workshop. We thank the participants of the Conference on Disclosure Limitation Approaches and Data Access. Both of these panel-sponsored activities outlined issues for the panel's consideration.

Jean Shirhall helped to strengthen the presentation of our report through her skillful editing; we thank her for her efforts. We are indebted to Eugenia Grohman, associate director for reports, Commission on Behavioral and Social Sciences and Education, for her role in guiding our report through the review and publication process.

We especially thank the panel's staff. They not only functioned as a harmonious team in drawing out the best in the panel members, but also contributed individually in noteworthy ways. Virginia A. de Wolf, study director, was especially helpful in contributing her organizational talents and energies to the conference, meetings, and workshop that the panel sponsored. Thomas B. Jabine, consultant, contributed his expository skill, experience with statistical agencies, and uncommon wisdom. Robert H. Mugge, consultant, helped with the analysis of background materials submitted by statistical agencies and prepared a useful background paper on informed consent and notification statements used by federal statistical agencies. Michele L. Conrad, senior project assistant, the panel's communication center, ensured that the project functioned both efficiently and effectively.

Finally, I thank the panel members, who gave generously of their time and wisdom to the deliberations of the panel and the production of this report. It has been rewarding to work with such a distinguished group of people.

George T. Duncan, *Chair*
Panel on Confidentiality
and Data Access

Contents

Executive Summary

The Panel on Confidentiality and Data Access was charged by the Committee on National Statistics and the Social Science Research Council with developing recommendations that could aid federal statistical agencies in their stewardship of data for policy decisions and research. Three areas were of paramount concern in the panel's deliberations: protecting the interests of data subjects through procedures that ensure privacy and confidentiality, enhancing public confidence in the integrity of statistical and research data, and facilitating the responsible dissemination of data to users.

STUDY GOALS AND SCOPE

Deciding on the exact scope of our investigation was not easy, for the federal statistical system is complex and far reaching, and its boundaries are not clearly defined. More than 70 federal agencies have a role in collecting data from individuals, households, farms, businesses, and governmental bodies and disseminating those data for a variety of statistical purposes. Federal statistical activities include the development and dissemination of large, general-purpose data sets based on censuses, surveys, and administrative records. They also include the collection and analysis of personal data in experimental research with human subjects. A few federal statistical agencies conduct general or multipurpose programs (e.g., the Bureau of the Census), but many others conduct specialized programs or activities (e.g., the Bureau of Labor Statistics and the National Center for Education Statistics). In addition, some basically programmatic agencies conduct some statistical activities (e.g., the Federal Aviation Administration and the Internal Revenue Service). Finally, the data subjects and units of analysis for statistical programs include persons and organizations, but when the concepts of privacy and confidentiality are applied to organizations, they have quite different meanings than they do when applied to persons.

Given the complexity of the federal statistical system, designing an ideal configuration to address confidentiality and data access issues throughout the system, or even in any one federal statistical agency, was too daunting for this panel. Instead, we sought to contribute to a long tradition in the statistical community of periodically reconsidering current institutional structures and practices. Fundamentally, we seek to spur this ongoing process by articulating and applying three tenets of an ethic of information in a free society: democratic accountability, constitutional empowerment, and individual autonomy. We believe this attention to underlying principles can have a more beneficial and lasting impact than would an attempt to provide detailed recommendations for micromanagement of agency procedures for confidentiality and data access.

Although we recognize the inherent tension between data protection and data access we do not advocate a specific trade-off between the two. The dynamics of such a trade-off would be complicated and heavily influenced by the missions and operational environments of individual agencies, so that a single solution would not work for every agency. Nevertheless, we see some opportunities to enhance data access without decreasing data protection, and some opportunities to increase data protection without diminishing data access.

GUIDING PRINCIPLES

The panel's analysis and recommendations are based on an ethic of information formed of the three principles referred to above: democratic accountability, constitutional empowerment, and individual autonomy. The ethical guidance these principles provide for the structure and practice of statistical agencies is often reinforcing, but not always harmonious.

DEMOCRATIC ACCOUNTABILITY

Functionally, *democratic accountability* recognizes the responsibilities of those who serve on behalf of others. It requires that the public have access to comprehensive information on the effectiveness of government policies. Government statistical agencies play a pivotal role in ensuring democratic accountability by obtaining, protecting, and disseminating the data that allow the accurate assessment of the influence of government policies on the public's well-being. Furthermore, they themselves are accountable to the public for two key functions in this process: (1) protecting the interests of data subjects through procedures that ensure appropriate standards of privacy and confidentiality and (2) facilitating the responsible dissemination of data to users.

CONSTITUTIONAL EMPOWERMENT

Constitutional empowerment refers to the capability of citizens to make informed decisions about political, economic, and social questions. In the United States, constitutional theory emphasizes that ultimate power should reside in the people. In order to advance the common welfare, certain specific powers are delegated to a representative government (Article X, U.S. Constitution). Constitutional practice emphasizes restraints on executive excess and broad access to the political process through the direct election of representatives as well as through separation and balance of power.

INDIVIDUAL AUTONOMY

Individual autonomy refers to the capacity of members of society to function as individuals, uncoerced and with privacy. Protection of individual autonomy is a fundamental attribute of a democracy. If excessive surveillance is used to build data bases, if data are unwittingly dispersed, or if those who capture data for administrative purposes make that information available in personally identifiable form, individual autonomy is compromised.

KEY FINDINGS AND RECOMMENDATIONS

Most of the panel's findings and recommendations can be grouped into five categories, each of which represents a key aspect of the trade-offs between confidentiality and data access. In this section we provide a brief summary of the major problems associated with each category and identify the broad principles underlying the solutions we suggest in the recommendations. We also refer to additional recommendations in the body of the report that augment the recommendations presented here. At the end of the section we present three cross-cutting recommendations bearing on the general management of confidentiality and data access functions in federal statistical agencies. (The numbering of the recommendations below follows that of the full report.)

STATUTORY PROTECTION AGAINST MANDATORY DISCLOSURE OF
INDIVIDUALLY IDENTIFIABLE DATA

For federal statistical agencies, pertinent statutes determine who can have access to individually identifiable information collected for statistical and research purposes, the conditions of access, and the penalties for unlawful use and disclosure of the information. Statutes also determine who can have access to administrative records for statistical and research purposes.

Two kinds of legislation provide the framework for federal policies and practices with respect to confidentiality and data access: government-wide and agency-specific legislation. In the former category, the Privacy Act of 1974 (P.L. 93-579) is most important, and the Freedom of Information Act of 1966 (P.L. 89-487) and the Paperwork Reduction Act of 1980 (P.L. 96-511) are also relevant. In the latter category, several federal statistical agencies have laws that further specify the confidentiality and data access policies they must follow (e.g., the Bureau of the Census and the National Center for Health Statistics). The procedures of some agencies, however, are not backed by statutory provisions. Instead, they must rely on persuasion, common-law tradition, and other means to protect identifiable statistical records from mandatory disclosure for nonstatistical uses. But there is no guarantee that such means will always be successful.

The basic distinction between statistical and administrative data is important. To carry out their basic functions, government agencies collect enormous amounts of data, most of which are used directly for various administrative purposes. Those data collected exclusively for statistical and research purposes form a tiny fraction of the total. Data collected for administrative purposes are often useful and appropriate for statistical purposes, as when patterns of Food Stamp applications are used to trace the effects of program changes. In contrast, data collected for research and statistical purposes are inappropriate for administrative uses.

These ideas are summarized in the concept of functional separation: Data collected for research or statistical purposes should not be made available for administrative action about a particular data subject. This concept was enunciated in a recommendation of the Privacy Protection Study Commission (1977a:574):

> That the Congress provide by statute that no record or information contained therein collected or maintained for a research or statistical purpose under Federal authority or with Federal funds may be used in individually identifiable form to make any decision or take any action directly affecting the individual to whom the record pertains, except within the context of the research plan or protocol, or with the specific authorization of such individual.

In part to ensure that statistical data are not used for administrative purposes, agencies give data providers pledges of confidentiality, both explicit and implicit. Unless those pledges are backed by legal authority, however, they provide an inadequate shield against administrative uses.

Recommendation 5.1 [parts a and b] Statistical records across all federal agencies should be governed by a consistent set of statutes and regulations meeting standards for the maintenance of such records, including the following features of fair statistical information practices:

(a) a definition of statistical data that incorporates the principle of functional separation as defined by the Privacy Protection Study Commission
(b) a guarantee of confidentiality for data.

Recommendation 7.2 Legislation that authorizes and requires protection of the confidentiality of data for persons and organizations should be sought for all federal statistical agencies that do not now have it and for any new federal statistical agencies that may be created.

The panel believes that the principle of functional separation should apply equally to data on persons and data on organizations (Recommendation 7.1). In addition, the panel recognizes that there may have to be some exceptions to the principle of functional separation, but it stresses that data providers participating in statistical surveys and censuses must be told of any planned or potential nonstatistical uses of the data they provide (see Recommendation 3.2 below).

BARRIERS TO DATA SHARING WITHIN GOVERNMENT

Some of the laws that govern the confidentiality of statistical data prohibit or severely limit interagency sharing of data for statistical purposes. Laws that control access to administrative records, such as reports of earnings covered by Social Security, restrict their use for statistical purposes. These barriers to data sharing for statistical purposes have led to costly duplication of effort and excessive burden on individuals and organizations who are asked to supply information. They have also made it difficult or impossible to develop data sets needed for policy analysis on topics of major interest to the public.

Not all barriers to data sharing are necessarily statutory, however. Within agencies, organizational inertia and excessive concern for bureaucratic turf can also impede data sharing.

> **Recommendation 4.1** Greater opportunities should be available for sharing of explicitly or potentially identifiable personal data among federal agencies for statistical and research purposes, provided the confidentiality of the records can be properly protected and the data cannot be used to make determinations about individual data subjects. Greater access should be permitted to key statistical and administrative data sets for the development of sampling frames and other statistical uses. Additional data sharing should only be undertaken in those instances in which the procedures for collecting the data comply with the panel's recommendations for informed consent or notification (see Recommendation 3.2 below).

In part (f) of Recommendation 5.1 (parts (a) and (b) appear above), the panel further recommends that "a provision that permits data sharing for statistical purposes under controlled conditions" be included in the "consistent set of statutes and regulations" governing the maintenance of federal statistical records. The panel also believes interagency sharing of data for statistical purposes should include the sharing of lists of businesses by federal and state agencies (Recommendation 7.4).

ACCESS TO DATA BY NONGOVERNMENT USERS

Some data users complain that federal statistical agencies are not always adequately responsive to their requests for access to data. Others appear to be dissuaded from attempting to use federal statistical data because of perceptions of difficulty of access. Because of legitimate concerns about the possibility of disclosure of individual information, statistical agencies have limited the amount of detailed data provided to nongovernment users in tabulations and public-use microdata files. This lack of detail restricts the ability of users to do analyses that could contribute to the understanding of significant economic, social, and health problems. Some agencies have developed mechanisms for providing access to more detailed information on a restricted basis (e.g., on-site access at an agency office, licensing agreements, remote on-line access for registered users, data release in encrypted CD-ROM format), but current arrangements do not meet all legitimate needs.

Recommendation 6.4 Statistical agencies should continue widespread release, with minimal restrictions on use, of microdata sets with no less detail than currently provided.

Recommendation 4.2 Federal statistical agencies should seek to improve the access of external users to statistical data, through both legislation and the development and greater use, under carefully controlled conditions, of tested administrative procedures.

The panel believes that, through a combination of legislation and administrative procedures, this can be done without sacrificing confidentiality protections for data subjects and data providers.

Recommendation 5.3 There should be legal sanctions for all users, both external users and agency employees, who violate requirements to maintain the confidentiality of data.

Under appropriate safeguards, statistical agencies should experiment with innovative ways of providing restricted access to data (Recommendation 6.6). In addition, federal statistical agencies that collect data on organizations should make a special effort to make that data more accessible to users (Recommendation 7.7). The panel notes that it is difficult to define the problems that inhibit data access without better access to information on the numbers and types of user requests that are being denied for confidentiality reasons. Thus, federal statistical agencies should establish systematic procedures for capturing and reviewing such information (Recommendation 4.3).

PRIVACY CONCERNS AND DECLINING COOPERATION IN SURVEYS

Many citizens believe increasingly and with some justification that their privacy is being eroded by organizations that develop and control the use of large data bases that contain detailed information about them. They see the linkage of data from different sources as a particular threat. For these and other reasons, statistical agencies are finding it more difficult to persuade persons and organizations to participate in statistical surveys, whether voluntary or mandatory.

Ethics and law demand that data providers be told about the conditions under which they are asked to supply information that will be used for statistical and research purposes. If participation is voluntary, data collectors must let data providers know this and give them enough information to make an informed decision about whether to provide the information requested.

Recommendation 3.2 Basic information given to all data providers requested to participate in statistical surveys and censuses should include

(a) for data on persons, information needed to meet all Privacy Act requirements. Similar information is recommended for data on organizations, except that the requirement to inform providers about routine uses (as defined by the Privacy Act) is not applicable.

(b) a clear statement of the expected burden on the data providers, including the expected time required to provide the data (a requirement of the Office of Management and Budget) and, if applicable, the nature of sensitive topics included in the survey and plans for possible follow-up interviews of some or all respondents.

(c) no false or misleading statements. For example, a statement that implies zero risk of disclosure is seldom, if ever, appropriate.

(d) information about any planned or potential *nonstatistical* uses of the information to be provided. There should be a clear statement of the level of confidentiality protection that can be legally ensured.

(e) information about any planned or anticipated record linkages for statistical or research purposes. For persons, this notification will usually occur in conjunction with a request for the data subject's Social Security number.

(f) a statement to cover the possibility of unanticipated future uses of the data for statistical or research purposes.

(g) information about the length of time for which the information will be retained in identifiable form.

The goal should be to give each data provider as much information as is necessary to make his or her consent as informed as he or she wishes it to be. A multistaged procedure is recommended: Those who want more information should have the opportunity to obtain it directly from the interviewer or by other means (Recommendation 3.1).

In addition, statistical agencies need to "know their respondents." How do they interpret concepts like privacy, confidentiality, disclosure, data sharing, and statistical purposes? Do they understand the informed consent and notification statements they are given? What information about themselves do they consider to be most sensitive? How are their decisions on survey participation influenced by different formats and modes of presentation? How do their reactions vary by race-ethnicity, gender, and socioeconomic status?

Recommendation 3.4 Statistical agencies should undertake and support continuing research, using the tools of cognitive and survey research, to monitor the views of data providers and the general public on informed consent, response burden, sensitivity of survey questions, data sharing for statistical purposes, and related issues.

The panel believes that the risks of major or deliberate violations of privacy or confidentiality are extremely low in the federal statistical system. The risks are somewhat higher for federal administrative records, and probably highest of all for private sector record systems. Because the public does not always distinguish among these different types of records, there is a danger that violations not involving statistical data bases can engender public indignation and have damaging spill-over effects on federal statistical programs. Thus, the panel further recommends that federal statistical agencies develop systematic public information activities, be prepared to deal quickly and candidly with actual or perceived violations of pledges of confidentiality, and as part of the communication process, work closely with appropriate advocacy groups (Recommendations 3.5-3.7).

STATISTICAL PROCEDURES TO PROTECT CONFIDENTIALITY

Technological advances in computers and communications offer opportunities and threats: opportunities to process, access, and analyze large data sets more efficiently and threats of unauthorized access to individually identifiable data. Statistical disclosure limitation procedures (e.g., cell suppression, random error, topcoding) are used to transform data to limit the risk of disclosure. Use of such a procedure is called masking the data, because it is intended to hide personal characteristics of data subjects. Some statistical disclosure limitation techniques are designed for data accessed as tables, and some are designed for data accessed as records of individual data subjects (microdata).

Many federal statistical agencies have standards, guidelines, or formal review mechanisms that are designed to ensure that (1) adequate analyses of disclosure risk are performed and (2) appropriate statistical disclosure limitation techniques are applied prior to release of tables and public-use microdata files. Those standards and guidelines, however, vary widely in their specificity: Some contain only one or two simple rules; others are much more detailed. This variation across agencies in the comprehensiveness of disclosure review has little justification in terms of agency mission. Further, unfulfilled opportunities exist for agencies to work together and learn from one another, perhaps pooling resources to investigate the strengths and weaknesses of various statistical disclosure limitation techniques.

Every federal statistical agency should develop standards and procedures for the application of effective statistical disclosure limitation techniques to all forms of data dissemination, taking advantage of relevant features of standards and procedures that have worked well for other agencies. Particular care should be taken in the review of proposals for the release of new public-use microdata files. In choosing among different disclosure limitation techniques, agencies should take account of the level of protection provided and the effects on the ability of users to draw valid inferences.

Based on its findings, the panel endorses the Federal Committee on Statistical Methodology's recommendation that "All federal agencies releasing statistical information, whether in tabular or microdata form, should formulate and apply policies and procedures designed to avoid unacceptable disclosures" (*Report on Statistical Disclosure and Disclosure-Avoidance Techniques*, Statistical Policy Working Paper 2, 1978:41-42, Recommendation B1). Since this panel convened, the federal statistical agencies have initiated some activities consonant with the above recommendation. In particular, in 1991 the Office of Management and Budget's Statistical Policy Office took the lead in organizing an interagency committee to coordinate research on statistical disclosure analysis.

Recommendation 6.1 The Office of Management and Budget's Statistical Policy Office should continue to coordinate research work on statistical disclosure analysis and should disseminate the results of this work broadly among statistical agencies. Major statistical agencies should actively encourage and participate in scholarly statistical research in this area. Other agencies should keep abreast of current developments in the application of statistical disclosure limitation techniques.

Statistical disclosure limitation methods can hide or distort relations among study variables and result in analyses that are incomplete or misleading. Further, data masked by some disclosure limitation methods can only be analyzed accurately by researchers who are highly sophisticated methodologically.

Recommendation 6.2 Statistical agencies should determine the impact on statistical analyses of the techniques they use to mask data. They should be sure that the masked data can be accurately analyzed by a range of typical researchers. If the data cannot be accurately analyzed using standard statistical software, the agency should make appropriate consulting and software available.

The panel believes that no one procedure can be developed for all statistical agencies. Furthermore, confidentiality laws governing particular agencies differ, as do the types of data collected and the needs of data users. Thus, the panel also endorses the following recommendations contained in Statistical Policy Working Paper 2:

> In formulating disclosure-avoidance policies, agencies should give particular attention to the sensitivity of different data items. . . . Agencies should avoid framing regulations and policies which define unacceptable statistical disclosure in unnecessarily broad or absolute terms. Agencies should apply a test of reasonableness, i.e., releases should be made in such a way that it is reasonably certain that no information about a specific individual will be disclosed in a manner that can harm that individual (p. 42, part of Recommendation B1).

Given the potential difficulties that certain statistical disclosure limitation techniques can cause for analysts, it is important that federal statistical agencies involve data users in selecting such procedures. In the past, agency staffs have often been the sole determiners of which statistical disclosure limitation techniques are to be used prior to releasing tables and microdata files.

Recommendation 6.3 Each statistical agency should actively involve data users from outside the agency as statistical disclosure limitation techniques are developed and applied to data.

CROSS-CUTTING RECOMMENDATIONS

Three recommendations of the panel refer to the general management of the confidentiality and data access functions of federal statistical agencies.

Recommendation 8.1 Each federal statistical agency should review its staffing and management of confidentiality and data access functions, with particular attention to the assignment within the agency of responsibilities for these functions and the background and experience needed for persons who exercise these responsibilities.

Recommendation 8.2 Statistical agencies should take steps to provide staff training in fair information practices, informed consent procedures, confidentiality laws and policies, statistical disclosure limitation procedures, and related topics.

Recommendation 8.5 The panel supports the general concept of an independent federal advisory body charged with fostering a climate of enhanced protection for all federal data about persons *and* responsible data dissemination for research and statistical purposes. Any such advisory body should promote the principle of functional separation and have professional staff with expertise in privacy protection, computer data bases, official statistics, and research uses of federal data.

1

Principles and Problems

Privacy is the most comprehensive of all rights and the right most cherished by citizens of a free nation.

Justice Louis Brandeis
Olmstead v. United States, 1928

A people who mean to be their own Governours, must arm themselves with the power to which knowledge gives.

James Madison, 1822

THE TENSION BETWEEN PRIVATE LIVES AND PUBLIC POLICIES

Private lives are requisite for a free society. To an extent unparalleled in the nation's history, however, private lives are being encroached on by organizations seeking and disseminating information. In their stewardship of data collection and data dissemination, federal statistical agencies have had a long-standing concern for the privacy rights of their data providers, but they now face mounting demands for privacy in the wake of such external developments as telemarketing through random digit dialing and computerized capture of data on everyday activities, like supermarket purchases by credit card.

In a free society, public policies come about through the actions of the people. Those public policies influence individual lives at every stage—financing of prenatal care, state aid to school districts, job training and placement, law enforcement, and determining retirement benefits. Data provided by federal statistical agencies, such as the Bureau of Justice Statistics, the Bureau of Labor Statistics, the National Center for Education Statistics, and the National Center for Health Statistics, are the factual base needed for informed public discussion about the direction and implementation of those policies. Further, public policies encom-

15

pass not only government programs but all those activities that influence the general welfare, whether initiated by government, business, labor, or not-for-profit organizations. Thus, the effective functioning of a free society requires broad dissemination of statistical information.

Juxtaposing the Brandeis and Madison quotations above reveals a basic tension in the stewardship of federal statistical agencies. Such agencies seek, on the one hand, to ensure private lives for the citizenry. On the other hand, they seek to provide the data on which public policies are based. Yet, because of concerns about data confidentiality, there is a large unmet need for greater access to data. Data users, whether in federal agencies (including policy research units), state or local governments, academe, trade associations, businesses, market research organizations, political interest groups, or the media, have persistently asked for increased access to data.

How can federal statistical agencies serve data users better by providing more access to useful data and at the same time serve data providers by better ensuring privacy and confidentiality? What principles must guide their actions? What are the key problems? Because facts are the lifeblood of a free society, answers to these questions concern many people—not just government statisticians. In particular, they are of concern to data users and data providers.

Answers to fundamental questions of confidentiality and data access affect many *data users*. Included in this category are researchers (e.g., university researchers investigating the affordability of housing), policy analysts (e.g., staff of an educational policy group assessing the influence of federal student loans on degree completion rates), and legislators and congressional staff (e.g., members of the Joint Committee on Taxation who are modeling the effects of proposed changes in the tax code).

Answers to questions of confidentiality and data access also affect many *data providers*. Included in this category are individuals (e.g., those in households throughout the country who respond to decennial censuses), institutions (e.g., nursing homes that provide data to the National Center for Health Statistics), and enterprises (e.g., car manufacturers that respond to the Energy Information Administration's Manufacturing Energy Consumption Survey).

In addition, many other individuals and groups are concerned with data use and data supply. Included in this category are legislators (e.g., members of the House Committee on Government Operations); lawyers (e.g., attorneys trying to build a class action case for Medicaid clients turned out of nursing homes or representing a client whose research files on a project funded by the National Institutes of Health have been subpoenaed); journalists (e.g., a reporter writing about freedom of information or privacy issues involving AIDS); and business executives, who simultaneously are asked for data on their operations and are seeking information on their business environment.

Finally, advocacy groups represent various positions on these issues. Groups such as Computer Professionals for Social Responsibility are concerned with computer-related privacy issues. And professional organizations such as the Association for Public Data Users are concerned with issues like access to health data on minority populations.

STUDY GOALS AND SCOPE

The federal statistical system is complex and far reaching. It encompasses more than 70 federal agencies having a role in collecting data from individuals, households, farms, businesses, and governmental bodies and disseminating data for statistical purposes. Those statistical purposes include description, evaluation, and research. Although it may collect data from individual respondents, administrative records, or organizations, a statistical agency does not do so in order to take administrative, regulatory, or enforcement action toward a particular individual or organization.[1] Indeed, it is not concerned with identifying the respondent with particular information, but rather with describing and inferring patterns, trends, and relationships for groups of respondents (National Research Council, 1992b).

The Panel on Confidentiality and Data Access was charged by the Committee on National Statistics and the Social Science Research Council with developing recommendations that could aid federal statistical agencies in their stewardship of data for policy decisions and research. Three areas were of paramount concern in our deliberations: protecting the interests of data subjects through procedures that ensure privacy and confidentiality, enhancing public confidence in the integrity of statistical and research data, and facilitating the responsible dissemination of data to users.

Deciding on the exact scope of our investigation was not easy, for the boundaries of federal statistical activities are not clearly defined. Federal statistical activities include the development and dissemination of large, general-purpose data sets based on censuses, surveys, and administrative records. They also include

the collection and analysis of personal data in experimental research with human subjects. A few federal statistical agencies
conduct general or multipurpose programs, but many others conduct specialized statistical programs or activities. In addition,
some basically programmatic agencies, like the Federal Aviation
Administration, the Health Care Financing Administration, and
the Internal Revenue Service, conduct some statistical activities.
Moreover, many federally supported statistical activities are carried out by contractors and grantees, and some statistical activities depend heavily on federal-state cooperative arrangements of
long standing. Finally, the data subjects and units of analysis for
statistical programs include persons and organizations, but when
the concepts of privacy and confidentiality are applied to organizations, they have quite different meanings than they do when
applied to persons.

To make our task manageable, we decided to concentrate our
attention on major federal statistical programs and to look beyond
them only to the extent that seemed necessary to provide adequate coverage of confidentiality and data access questions related to those programs. In addition, given the basic nature of the
issues and our backgrounds and experience (see Appendix B), we
were more comfortable dealing with our charge as it applied to
personal, rather than organizational, data. Nevertheless, input
from statistical agencies and events that occurred during our deliberations made it clear that there are major issues relating to
data for organizations that cannot be ignored. Accordingly, we
lay out a framework for the treatment of data on organizations in
Chapter 7. We also refer to organizations in other chapters, especially Chapter 5, which deals with legislation. We believe that
confidentiality and data access questions for organizations warrant more attention than they have received in the past and more
than we have been able to give. We hope that the federal statistical agencies and others will pursue them through systematic studies.

Given the complexity of the federal statistical system, designing an ideal configuration to address confidentiality and data access issues throughout the system, or even in any one federal
statistical agency, is too daunting for this panel. Instead, we seek
to contribute to a long tradition in the statistical community of
periodically reconsidering current institutional structure and practice.
Fundamentally, we seek to spur this ongoing process by articulating and applying three tenets of an ethic of information in a free
society: democratic accountability, constitutional empowerment,
and individual autonomy. These tenets are consistent with the

ethos of American society and are the basis for trustworthy operation of federal statistical agencies. We believe that this attention to underlying principle can have a more beneficial and lasting impact than would an attempt to provide detailed recommendations for micromanagement of agency confidentiality and data access procedures.

Although we recognize the inherent tension between data protection and data access, we do not advocate a specific trade-off between the two. The dynamics of such a trade-off would be complicated and heavily influenced by the missions and operational environments of individual agencies, so that a single solution would not work for every agency. Nevertheless, we see some opportunities to enhance data access without decreasing data protection, and some opportunities to increase data protection without diminishing data access. Accordingly, society faces win/no loss situations, arguably because current institutional arrangements are inadequate. To develop this theme and inductively build a better understanding of the broad principles, we use as illustrations particular circumstances that individual agencies currently confront.

Many topics that fall under the rubric of societal concerns for effective, efficient, and ethical collection and use of information are largely outside the scope of this report. We are mindful of the burgeoning information industry in the private sector, including marketing firms and consumer credit bureaus. While we have concerns about this industry's impact on individual privacy, those concerns are outside the scope of this report. Nor do we address the paperwork and privacy burden imposed by government in administering its programs.

Directly within the scope of this report is the functioning of the federal statistical system as it grapples with confidentiality and data access issues. Specifically, we have a concern for how a federal statistical agency relates to its three diverse and overlapping constituencies: data providers, government itself, and data users.

We direct this report to all concerned with confidentiality and data access issues. We hope that the ideas and recommendations we put forth will stimulate consideration of these critical issues by all concerned and make each interested party more aware of the legitimate concerns of the other parties. Further, we hope that this report will stimulate discussion of confidentiality and data access issues across levels of government and across geographical boundaries.

HOW DOES THE FEDERAL
STATISTICAL SYSTEM FUNCTION?

The federal statistical system is a largely decentralized agglomeration of agencies. Each agency functions under the guidance of officials in a government department, as the Bureau of the Census does in the Department of Commerce and the National Center for Education Statistics does in the Department of Education. The agencies operate with various legal authorizations to compile, analyze, and disseminate statistical data. According to the Office of Federal Statistical Policy and Standards (1978:413),

> The ultimate purpose of all Federal statistical collection activities is to develop statistical material for use by Government agencies, policymakers, and the public. The ultimate test of the Federal Statistical System is the availability of relevant information; therefore, the question of data access must continually receive a high level of attention.

Identifying seven of the larger federal statistical agencies illustrates the reach of the system's activities:

- Bureau of the Census
- Bureau of Justice Statistics
- Bureau of Labor Statistics
- Energy Information Administration
- National Agricultural Statistics Service
- National Center for Education Statistics
- National Center for Health Statistics

Some of these agencies have purposes that are not purely statistical. The Energy Information Administration (EIA), for instance, is in some cases required to provide identifiable data in support of regulatory and program needs of the Department of Energy.

Each of the existing federal statistical agencies was founded in response to needs for data bearing on critical areas of public policy. A recent addition is the Bureau of Transportation Statistics, which was established by Congress in 1991 to compile and analyze data related to such issues as the environmental impact of mass transit, the factors affecting choice of transportation mode, and the nature of vehicular accidents. Congressional support has been voiced for the establishment of specialized statistical agencies in other crucial policy areas, as well.

In collecting data, as noted, the agencies of the federal statistical system obtain data from individual respondents (e.g., the U.S. Fish and Wildlife Service's Survey of Fishing, Hunting, and

Wildlife Related Recreation elicits data from outdoor enthusiasts on their recreational activities), households (e.g., the Census Bureau conducts the Consumer Expenditures Survey for the Bureau of Labor Statistics), organizations (e.g., the National Agricultural Statistics Service collects information from farm operators on some 120 crops and 45 varieties of livestock), and governmental subunits (e.g., the Census Bureau collects data from state and local governments).

In disseminating data, federal statistical agencies provide information to a range of clients. Within the government, clients include researchers within the same department (e.g., the National Agricultural Statistics Service provides data to the Economic Research Service in the Department of Agriculture), other federal agencies (e.g., the Internal Revenue Service's Statistics of Income Division furnishes data to the Bureau of Economic Analysis in the Department of Commerce), state and local governments (e.g., the National Center for Education Statistics supplies data to the Commonwealth of Pennsylvania's Department of Education), business firms (e.g., the National Center for Health Statistics makes data available to the Kaiser Permanente Health Maintenance Organization), Congress (e.g., the Bureau of Economic Analysis calculates the gross domestic product, which informs the Congressional Budget Office), and the Executive Office of the President (e.g., the Census Bureau gives information on job seeking by the unemployed to the Council of Economic Advisers). Outside the government, clients include the media (e.g., the *New York Times*, September 23, 1990:Section 3, p. 11, reported on investment in farms using Department of Agriculture figures), individual members of the public (e.g., the 1990 *World Almanac*, which sold over 54 million copies, is replete with government statistics), and academic researchers (e.g., Babcock and Engberg, 1990, use Bureau of Labor Statistics data as a reference point for their survey of local labor market conditions).

With limited authority and resources, the Office of Management and Budget, through its Statistical Policy Office, provides long-range planning for statistical programs and coordinates statistical policy within the federal government. The Statistical Policy Office does not have direct administrative responsibility for federal statistical agencies, however.

KEY DEFINITIONS

A lack of general agreement on terminology has caused some confusion in discussions of the issues involved in data protection and data access. The panel found the following definitions for certain key terms to be helpful. They are used consistently in this report.

DATA SUBJECTS AND DATA PROVIDERS

Data subjects are persons, households, or organizations for which data are obtained and presented in statistical form. The data subjects are not always the *data providers*, however. One person in a household may respond to a survey questionnaire that asks for information about all members of that household. Data providers are often called *respondents*. When respondents provide information for data subjects other than themselves, they are called *proxy respondents*.

INFORMATIONAL PRIVACY

Privacy has multiple definitions depending on what aspect of this broad concept is being stressed. We take the following as our working definition:

> *Informational privacy* encompasses an individual's freedom from excessive intrusion in the quest for information and an individual's ability to choose the extent and circumstances under which his or her beliefs, behaviors, opinions, and attitudes will be shared with or withheld from others.

CONFIDENTIALITY AND DATA PROTECTION

Confidentiality refers broadly to a quality or condition accorded to information as an obligation not to transmit that information to an unauthorized party (National Research Council, 1991:289). This has implications that range over religious confessionals, national security, private business "whistleblowing," and disclosures of crimes. Our concern is, more narrowly, with the promises, explicit or implicit, made to a data provider by a data gatherer regarding the extent to which the data provided will allow others to gain specific information about the data provider or data subject. Confidentiality has meaning only when the promises made to a data provider can be delivered, that is, the data gatherer must have the will, technical ability, and moral and legal authority to protect the data.

Our definition of confidential data is consistent with the position of the President's Commission on Federal Statistics (1971:222):

> [*Confidential* should mean that dissemination] of data in a manner that would allow public identification of the respondent or would in any way be harmful to him is prohibited and that the data are immune from legal process.

Data protection refers to the set of privacy-motivated policies and procedures that ensure minimal intrusion by data collection and maintenance of data confidentiality. The term is generally used in the context of protecting personal information (Flaherty, 1989). Unlike privacy, however, which is an individual right, confidentiality is not restricted to data on individuals and is often extended to data on organizations.

INFORMED CONSENT AND NOTIFICATION

Informed consent and *notification* are related, but distinct, ethical and legal concepts. From our perspective, informed consent refers to a person's agreement to allow personal data to be provided for research and statistical purposes. Agreement is based on full exposure of the facts the person needs to make the decision intelligently, including any risks involved and alternatives to providing the data (derived from Black et al., 1990:779). Informed consent describes a condition appropriate only when data providers have a clear choice. They must not be, nor perceive themselves to be, subject to penalties for failure to provide the data sought.

Notification also involves a condition of data provision under full exposure of pertinent facts. Unlike with informed consent, however, the elements of choice and agreement are absent. Notification is the more appropriate concept when data provision for stated purposes is mandatory, as it is in the decennial census of population.

DISCLOSURE

Disclosure relates to inappropriate attribution of information to a data subject, whether an individual or an organization. Disclosure occurs when a data subject is identified from a released file (*identity disclosure*), sensitive information about a data subject is revealed through the released file (*attribute disclosure*), or the released data make it possible to determine the value of some characteristic of an individual more accurately than otherwise would have been possible (*inferential disclosure*).

Inferential disclosure is the most general of the types of disclosure. The definition above was suggested by Dalenius (1977) and supported by Statistical Policy Working Paper 2 (Federal Committee on Statistical Methodology, 1978:41). Underlying that support was the belief that it offers the best basis for (1) identifying all potential disclosures in connection with proposed releases, (2) deciding which of the potential disclosures are *unacceptable*, and (3) using appropriate techniques to prevent unacceptable disclosures.

ADMINISTRATIVE AND STATISTICAL DATA

One purpose of data collection concerns a course of action that affects a particular person or business. The purpose can be regulatory, administrative, legislative, or judicial. Examples include tax audits of a person, couple, or corporation; a criminal investigation into a report of arson; license renewal for a liquor store; and determination of welfare benefits. We refer to these purposes generically as *administrative*.

Another purpose of collecting data is to generate an aggregate description of a group of persons or businesses. No direct action is taken for or against a specific individual or business, although as a result of the information, policy changes based on such information could result in benefits or costs to persons or businesses. Examples include development of a formula for determining which tax returns should be audited, investigating geographical patterns of arson in a large city, and researching the relationship between the incidence of liquor law violations by stores and store characteristics or how the duration of welfare benefits varies with the educational level of the recipient. We refer to these purposes generically as *statistical*. Consistent with the distinction between administrative and statistical data, the Privacy Act of 1974 (P.L. 93-579) defines a statistical record to be

> a record in a system of records maintained for statistical research or reporting purposes only and not used in whole or in part in making any determination about an identifiable individual, except as provided by Section 8 [which authorizes certain kinds of data access, including for research activities by the Bureau of the Census] of Title 13.

WHAT PRINCIPLES SHOULD GUIDE
STATISTICAL AGENCIES?

As creations of government, statistical agencies mirror, with varying shadings, the ethos of their society. For the United States, and a growing list of other countries, this ethos embraces a freedom that recognizes pluralism, public decision making based on representative democracy, and a market-oriented economy. Statistical agencies reflect those themes through a remarkably intricate configuration of institutional structure and practice.

As noted above, the principles of democratic accountability, constitutional empowerment, and individual autonomy maintain the ethos of American society and provide valuable ethical guidance for the structure and practice of federal statistical agencies. Recognizing that the guidance they provide is often reinforcing but is not always harmonious, we examine each principle in turn. When we apply the principles in subsequent chapters, we either explore ways that they can be reconciled or note that difficult trade-offs must be made.

DEMOCRATIC ACCOUNTABILITY

Functionally, *accountability* recognizes the responsibilities of those who serve on behalf of others. With position and involvement in manifold areas of life, government in a democracy should serve the public—collectively, individually, and in assorted assemblages—and be accountable to it. As John Locke (1690/1988:426-427) said in his *Two Treatises of Government*,

> Who shall be Judge whether the Prince or Legislative act contrary to their Trust . . . The People shall be Judge; for who shall be Judge whether his Trustee or Deputy acts well, and according to the Trust reposed in him, but he who deputes him.

In implementation, accountability requires that the public obtain comprehensive information on the effectiveness of government policies. Prewitt (1985) addresses this relationship between government and citizens as "democratic accountability." Federal statistical agencies play a pivotal role in ensuring democratic accountability—they obtain, protect, and disseminate the data that allow accurate assessment of the influence of public policies on individual well-being. Further, they themselves are accountable to the public for two key functions in this process: (1) protecting the interests of data subjects through procedures that ensure appropriate standards of privacy and confidentiality and (2) facilitating the responsible dissemination of data to users, including those to whom democratic government is accountable—the country's citizens.

CONSTITUTIONAL EMPOWERMENT

Constitutional empowerment, as a cornerstone of an information ethic, is the capability of citizens to make informed decisions about political, economic, and social questions. In the United States, constitutional theory emphasizes that ultimate power resides in the people. For reasons of advancing the common welfare, certain specific powers are delegated to a representative government. However, "the powers not delegated to the United States by the Constitution, nor prohibited by it to the states, are reserved to the states respectively, or to the people" (Amendment X, U.S. Constitution). Constitutional practice emphasizes restraints on executive excess and broad access to the political process through the direct election of representatives, as well as through separation and balance of power.

Knowledge is a prerequisite to the ethical exercise of power. As Supreme Court Justice Felix Frankfurter (1930:127) observed,

> We now realize that democracy is not remotely an automatic device for good government. . . . We now know that it is dependent on knowledge and wisdom beyond all other forms of government. . . . [Democracy] seeks to prevail when the complexities of life make a demand upon knowledge and understanding never made before.

The principle of constitutional empowerment is increasingly important today as federal statistical agencies struggle to obtain and protect data needed for a factual understanding of a fast-changing, complex world. "Electoral power per se is the mechanical guarantee of the system, but the substantive guarantee is given by the conditions under which the citizen gets the information" (Sartori, 1962/1972:74).

As the Office of Technology Assessment (1989:1) notes in *Statistical Needs for a Changing U.S. Economy,*

> Good public policy demands good information. There may be disagreement about the wisdom of different Federal programs but there is little dispute over the need for adequate data to inform the debate. The information generated by the $2 billion spent this year by Federal agencies on statistical programs is a key

resource for government policymakers as well as for private investors, public interest groups, academic researchers, and labor organizations. . . . Government statistics play a key role in evaluating and implementing legislation and are often used as indexes in private contracts.

Individually, empowerment of the citizenry through access to data can heighten fairness. Moreover, it can lessen inefficiencies ascribable to imbalances in information. A sugar beet farmer, for example, without knowledge of current market prices is vulnerable when negotiating a contract with a knowledgeable sugar beet processor. Collectively, empowerment through access to data can create benefits to parties acting cooperatively. In salary negotiations between a school board and teachers union, for example, both sides might turn to a common, legitimated base of statistical information about population and property tax assessment trends to help resolve negotiations. In order to function properly, both a political democracy and a market economy require that voters and consumers make informed choices.

As part of their basic mandate, federal statistical agencies are instructed to provide data that can be used to evaluate the efficiency and effectiveness of government programs. In 1967, Congress affirmed the principles of constitutional empowerment and democratic accountability by passing the Freedom of Information Act to serve democratic values by (1) creating a more fully informed public debate on important issues and (2) counteracting political corruption.

INDIVIDUAL AUTONOMY

Individual autonomy refers to the capacity of the individual to function in society as an individual, uncoerced and cloaked by privacy. Protection of individual autonomy is a fundamental attribute of a democracy. Individual autonomy is compromised by the excessive surveillance sometimes used to build data bases (Flaherty, 1989), unwitting dispersion of data, and a willingness by those who collect the data for administrative purposes to make them readily available in personally identifiable form. Illustrating this latter issue is the following, reported by Desky (1991:1):

For five cents a name, the Maryland Motor Vehicles Administration (MVA) will sell the names of 3.3 million licensed drivers to vendors who request them, with a minimum nonrefundable deposit of $500. All information on a driver's license including height, weight, gender, address and driving record from the previous three years is being sold by the state.

While some may argue that governmental bodies appropriately use administrative records as a source of revenue, most federal statistical agencies are acutely aware of the importance of maintaining respect for an individual's autonomy. The National Center for Health Statistics, for example, has legislative authority to protect its records under the Public Health Service Act (42 U.S.C. 242m), which provides that

> no information obtained in the course of activities undertaken or supported under Section 304, 305, 306, or 307 (the sections authorizing the programs of NCHS and of the National Center for Health Services Research) may be used for any purpose other than the purpose for which it was supplied unless authorized under regulations of the Secretary; and (1) in the case of information obtained in the course of health statistical activities under Section 304 or 306 (which authorize the program of NCHS), such information may not be published or released in other form if the particular establishment or person supplying the information or described in it is identifiable unless such establishment or person has consented (as determined under regulations of the Secretary) to its publication or release in other form.

Federal statistical agencies have ethical and pragmatic reasons to be concerned about individual autonomy.[2] From an ethical standpoint,

   •   agencies are obligated by the imperatives of our society to respect individual dignity,
   •   agencies should protect the personal information that has been entrusted to them, and
   •   intrusive data collection by agencies can disturb an individual's chosen solitude.

From a pragmatic standpoint, most persons who are surveyed are not required to provide data (the decennial census is the main exception). Thus, if statistical agencies are perceived as failing to respect individual autonomy, the supply of data providers may dry up. Even in the case of legally compelled participation, without respect for individual autonomy, evasion and inaccurate reporting are likely to be rampant.[3] Martin (1974:265) stated this well:

> Even when responses to requests for information are required by law, the success of a statistical programme depends in large mea-

sure on the willing cooperation of respondents. Respondents who understand the purposes of the inquiry, who sympathize with the intended uses of the information, and who believe that providing the government with the requested information will not harm them are much more likely to answer truthfully and with a minimum of effort on the part of the data-collection agency.

One element in enlisting such cooperation is the assurance of harmlessness to the respondent, and one of the most common methods of making such assurance in statistical data collection is the provision for keeping the replies confidential.

Agencies must have the trust of data providers.

THE SPECIAL ROLE OF FEDERAL STATISTICAL AGENCIES

Federal statistical agencies have vitally served the government's information function and rightly should serve it in the future. As far back as 1888, for example, the U.S. Bureau of Labor was providing statistical information on the conditions of working women. The bureau reported that 17,500 women averaged $5.24 in weekly earnings, and it drew the policy implication that "the figures tell a sad story, and one is forced to ask how women can live on such earnings" (U.S. Bureau of Labor, 1889:70). Today, the Bureau of Labor Statistics provides such policy-relevant information on earnings and employment without regard to its political consequences.

In this section we examine, first, four reasons why government should be involved with gathering statistical information and then four reasons why federal statistical agencies are more appropriate than federal administrative agencies or private agencies to fulfill this function.

The government collects data because, first, it has an obligation to inform the public on those matters that affect the welfare of the people individually and collectively. This includes facilitating democratic accountability by providing sufficient information on government activities to ensure public knowledge of the government's performance. It further includes providing the empowering information that enables a citizen to have an impact on public policies.

Second, in some cases private financial incentives are insufficient to motivate the collection of data that are essential to a democratic society. Most large, multipurpose national data bases, such as the decennial census and the national income accounts, cost far more to collect than any private firm or group of private organizations could ever recover from the market should they decide to fund such an enterprise. Thus, if the efforts are not publicly funded, such data bases would not exist. The social value of the data far exceeds their private value.[4]

Third, economies of scale are often so large that even though it might be possible to organize multiple sets of private data collectors to do the job, a single public collection would cost significantly less, especially in the case of regularly repeated collections. Further, economies of scale suggest that a large-scale program of data collection has synergies that cannot be obtained by a piecemeal approach. For example, cognitive studies of how respondents interpret various wordings of survey questionnaires can be supported. Such studies may be informative for a range of current and future surveys.

Fourth, private information providers have a natural interest in protecting their investment, which may limit the spread of information.[5] On the other hand, government can disseminate data at cost and ensure that the information is accessible for the public good.

For a variety of reasons, the alternatives to federal statistical agencies, whether private information organizations or federal administrative agencies (which do have an essential role in collecting data for regulatory enforcement), cannot be expected to provide the appropriate data. First, government administrative agencies cannot be expected to fulfill completely the function of providing the information needed for democratic functioning. Administrative agencies have primarily operational tasks, whether militarily defending the country, putting criminals in jail, collecting taxes, or running an air traffic control system. The administrative data such agencies collect can be of general value to society, however.

Second, among most data users, federal statistical agencies have established a reputation for integrity and independence. While certain private sector survey firms and information organizations have fine reputations among knowledgeable statisticians, their reputation does not have the same breadth among the relevant public. Often, private data collection is carried out by interested parties, who are unlikely to be objective, and if they are, the *perception* of possible bias reduces the value of the data.

Third, some data are collected because they have direct value in implementing government policy. This is true, for example, of the decennial census in allocating seats in the House of Representatives among the states, of the Consumer Price Index in determining Social Security benefits, and of the National Center for

Health Statistics infant mortality data in shaping programmatic effort toward prevention. When government policy is directly affected by certain data, the government must assume responsibility for its quality. This suggests that the government must have substantial control over the design and implementation of the data collection and primary analysis.

Finally, federal statistical agencies have historically done the job, and done it well. Because of the way data are produced, much useful and empowering information is not fully provided by the workings of the private market. Data on educational achievements of elementary school students, for example, although often collected through privately developed test instruments, have historically been collected and disseminated through governmental mandate. Federal statistical agencies, such as in this case the National Center for Education Statistics, play a key role in coordinating data gathering, maintaining quality standards, and disseminating information.

DATA ACCESS IN A DEMOCRATIC SOCIETY

Recognized information needs in society are so great and budgets so constraining that government analysts can do only a small fraction of the research that can beneficially be done with federally collected data. Most of the research must be carried out by analysts for various concerned organizations and academic researchers. Moreover, to enhance the integrity of research findings, independent analysts should have access to data, regardless of the organization that collected it. As a critical element of the democratic process, this access can allow reanalysis by groups with different agendas; stimulate new inquiries on important social, economic, and scientific questions; lead to improvements in the quality of data through suggestions for better measurement and data collection methods; and provide information to improve government forecasts and resource allocations (see National Research Council, 1985). As noted, such open access is a necessary condition for a society to function freely and effectively. The ideal result is a robust, resilient society in which individual and collective interests are served through a competition for the truth. In contrast, monopolized access by "a central state planning board" suppresses freedom and hampers efficiency.

The panel maintains that government dissemination of statistical data under appropriate confidentiality constraints is a public good. Failure to provide data may result in substantial lost opportunities. Accountability in a democracy is threatened by restricting the collection of government statistics to only those sought by government policymakers and by restricting access to government statistics to only government policymakers. Wallman (1988:11) makes this point and notes a remark attributed to Christopher DeMuth, the Office of Management and Budget (OMB) administrator for information and regulatory affairs, by Ann Crittenden (*New York Times*, July 11, 1982, Business section:4):

> In the past, agencies collected much greater detail than was needed for national policy-making purposes. It is understood now that agencies justify their data collecting programs to OMB in terms of the needs of the federal agencies alone, not of states, local governments, or private firms.

Wallman further notes,

> In 1985 OMB distributed for comments a draft circular (A-130) that provided that "executive branch agencies are to collect only that information necessary for the proper performance of agency functions and that has practical utility."

After some unfavorable comment, the proposed circular was withdrawn; it was only reissued in July 1993 with the publication of a revised OMB Circular A-130 in the *Federal Register* (58(126):36068-36086). This revised circular is based on quite different principles than the 1985 draft circular. Leading the 1993 circular's Section 7, "Basic Considerations and Assumptions," are the following points:

> a. The Federal Government is the largest single producer, collector, consumer, and disseminator of information in the United States. Because of the extent of the government's information activities, and the dependence of those activities upon public cooperation, the management of Federal information resources is an issue of continuing importance to all Federal agencies, State and local governments, and the public.

> b. Government information is a valuable national resource. It provides the public with knowledge of the government, society, and economy—past, present, and future. It is a means to ensure the accountability of government, to manage the government's operations, to maintain the healthy performance of the economy, and is itself a commodity in the marketplace.

> c. The free flow of information between the government and the public is essential to a democratic society. It is also essential that the government minimize the Federal paperwork burden on the public, minimize the cost of its information activities, and maximize the usefulness of government information (p. 36071)....

The panel agrees with the thrust of these points in the 1993 OMB circular.

Unquestionably, there can be no lively democratic policymaking—and so there can be no constitutional empowerment—unless many individuals and interest groups have access to information. According to Dahl (1982:11), one of the most important characteristics distinguishing modern democracies is that "citizens have a right to seek out alternative sources of information. Moreover, alternative sources of information exist and are protected by law." Smith (1991:7) also notes that "limited public access to data not only gives intramural researchers a monopoly on the data, it also provides federal agencies an effective mechanism to control areas of sensitivity."

The panel, however, should not be misunderstood to be advocating unrestricted access to personal data. To the contrary, we affirm the ethical imperative of individual autonomy, which requires appropriate guarantees on privacy and confidentiality. Also, we recognize that useful data are more likely to be provided by individuals and establishments under suitable guarantees of confidentiality.

PROBLEMS IN ENSURING
CONFIDENTIALITY AND DATA ACCESS

Federal statistical agencies confront a challenging environment—apprehensive respondents, exasperated researchers, skeptical funders, and pressures for administrative uses of confidential statistical records. Not surprisingly in a decentralized statistical system, some of these problems are specific to particular agencies and thus are outside the scope of this report. Nonetheless, a number of problems cut across agencies. Below, we identify a number of general problems and point to chapters of the report where they are considered in depth.

DO STATISTICAL AGENCIES HAVE ADEQUATE AUTHORITY
TO PROTECT DATA?

At times, statistical agencies and respondents to statistical surveys have been under pressure to disclose data in identifiable form. For example, a 1961 court order required the St. Regis Paper Company to deliver to the Federal Trade Commission its file copy of a completed Census Bureau form. "In a swift reaction, Congress amended the Census law to protect copies of Census documents retained in respondent's files from compulsory legal process" (Office of Federal Statistical Policy and Standards, 1978:256). As another example, the statistical arm of the Department of Energy, the Energy Information Administration, collects proprietary information on pricing and production from petroleum companies. In 1990, the Department of Justice's Antitrust Division requested individually identifiable data from the agency to investigate alleged price gouging by oil companies in the aftermath of the Iraqi invasion of Kuwait. The agency refused, citing its policy and pledge to keep the data, which had been collected for statistical purposes, confidential. In the ensuing disputations between the agency and the Department of Justice, it became evident that the agency lacked unambiguous legal authority to sustain its confidentiality pledge. We explore this case in detail in Chapter 7.

In discussing data protection, we emphasize the fundamental distinction between administrative data and statistical data. Important differences exist among the types of data collected by the government, especially data collected for statistical and research purposes versus data collected for the administration of government programs. Administrative data often have inherent research value, and statistical uses are appropriate, provided confidentiality safeguards can be maintained. Data from Medicare and Medicaid records, for example, are properly used in studying the pattern of medical procedures, such as coronary angioplasty, as they vary by region of the country, race, and gender. Although in certain situations access to statistical data may seem administratively convenient, most administrative uses would violate pledges of confidentiality. The simple statement "Your answers are confidential" on the cover of a census form ought to mean, for example, that information provided on household composition will not be used to check eligibility for Aid to Families with Dependent Children. As we have noted, federal statistical agencies have experienced pressure to provide data for administrative purposes. Withstanding such pressure can be especially difficult for federal statistical agencies (or programs with statistical functions) that are housed in units with important regulatory functions. (This point was emphasized by the Office of Federal Statistical Policy and Standards, 1978:258.)

The central concept of providing legislative and procedural protection to ensure that personal data collected about a data subject for a research or statistical purpose are not used for an administrative or other decision about that data subject is generally called *functional separation*. It is not a new concept, having been recommended, for example, in a 1973 study by the Secretary's Advisory Committee on Automated Personal Data Systems (U.S. Department of Health, Education and Welfare). The concept was enunciated by the Privacy Protection Study Commission (1977a:574). Stating the concept as a recommendation for legislation by the U.S. Congress, the commission proposed

> that the Congress provide by statute that no record or information contained therein collected or maintained for a research or statistical purpose under Federal authority or with Federal funds may be used in individually identifiable form to make any decision or take any action directly affecting the individual to whom the record pertains, except within the context of the research plan or protocol, or with the specific authorization of such individual.

We examine this concept throughout the report.

CAN COMMUNICATION WITH THE PUBLIC BE IMPROVED?

For federal statistical agencies to achieve full democratic accountability, they must be continuously cognizant of public perceptions regarding the central issues of data protection and data access. This may require systematic studies of public opinion, as has been done with various surveys of the public's general perception of the Census Bureau.[6] Such studies could examine, for example, the extent to which the public continues to have a general distrust of centralized government records, a distrust of the kind that led to the Privacy Act of 1974. They could also assess the public's concern about the data collection and dissemination powers of the private sector information industry. And they could examine the extent to which various groups of the public distinguish between statistical agencies and administrative agencies regarding issues of data protection and data access.

Interpreting general survey results, however, is not easy; any general political alienation will drive down confidence and be reflected in responses about a specific area of government activity. More easily interpretable are systematic studies of the data provider and data user communities that interact with statistical agencies. A diversified portfolio of study techniques, including targeted surveys, data user and data provider conferences, reinterviews, focus groups, and small-scale experiments may be most effective. In the interests of accountability and openness, the results of such studies should be made publicly available.

How can federal statistical agencies best communicate to the general public, the data provider communities, and the data user communities the importance of the statistical information they can provide? How can they best instill confidence in these diverse groups regarding the three key aspects of their data protection policies: (1) their intention to minimize intrusions on privacy, (2) their intention to minimize the time and efforts of data providers, and (3) their ability to maintain confidentiality?

Given the principle of democratic accountability, how are the interests of the public best served? Institutionally, Congress addresses legislation that, for the most part, sets fairly general guidelines for agency policy and practice. At the more specific level of the development and implementation of agency policy regarding confidentiality and data access, mechanisms are beginning to emerge for ensuring input from representatives of the key affected groups. A variety of such mechanisms are possible, including data user conferences, meetings with privacy advocates regarding the conduct of key surveys, agency review boards with outside representation, and a government-wide Data and Access Protection Board.

The topic of public perceptions and interests is addressed further in Chapters 2, 3, and 4. Alternative mechanisms for ensuring input from the affected groups are discussed in Chapter 8.

ARE DATA PROVIDERS PROPERLY NOTIFIED OR INFORMED?

Most often, for data collected for administrative purposes, the data provider either is legally required to provide the data—as with tax return filings—or must provide the data in order to receive some benefit—as with driver's license applications. In broad terms, the ethics of what the agency should tell the data provider about the use of such administrative data are not controversial. The data provider should be notified about the need for such data and how providing the data might affect him or her—and that one potential use is for statistical purposes. A more complicated ethical question is what options data providers should have in denying various uses of the administrative data they provide.

On the other hand, with the notable exception of the decennial census, response to most statistical surveys of persons and households is voluntary. Law and ethics require that consent for participation in voluntary statistical surveys be informed. Potential respondents should be told how their data will be used and what the consequences will be to them of participating or not participating in the survey. They should be given the opportunity to make a conscious decision whether to provide the data requested.

There are many open questions about the nature of informed consent procedures for voluntary surveys. Do the current practices of the statistical agencies conform fully with legal and ethical requirements? Is appropriate information being given to respondents in language that they can readily understand? Should the same amount of detail be given to all potential respondents? What are suitable procedures for use in telephone and mail surveys? Are the statistical agencies always able to honor the promise of confidentiality protection they give to respondents? To what extent should respondents be allowed to waive standard protections in order to permit data sharing for statistical purposes? We develop these issues in Chapter 3.

Are Current Confidentiality and Data Access Laws Adequate and Appropriate?

We discussed above the issue of whether statistical agencies have adequate authority to protect the data they collect. Here we introduce some other issues of legislation. The laws that govern confidentiality of and access to federal statistical data include some with general reach, like the Freedom of Information Act and the Privacy Act, but others vary widely from agency to agency. At one end of the spectrum, Title 13 of the U.S. Code provides extremely tight confidentiality provisions for the Census Bureau. At the other end, many agencies operate without any specific confidentiality legislation. Critics charge that certain provisions of current legislation not only fail to provide sufficient protection of confidential statistical data but create excessive barriers to data access. For example, the Office of Federal Statistical Policy and Standards (1978:262) noted obstacles to interagency data sharing and, in particular, the inability of agencies to gain access to the Census Bureau's Standard Statistical Establishment List for statistical sampling purposes. There are also obstacles to access by nongovernment data users. Comprehensive revision of the relevant laws risks a final product worse than the status quo. Further, legislation requires support if it is to be effective. Congress and the President must be committed to confidentiality protection and the public must understand its importance. On the other hand, the current approach of ad hoc legislative initiatives is not working very well either. Thus, in Chapter 5, we pose and address questions of variation among statistical agencies in the protection offered identifiable statistical records, possible amendments of the 1974 Privacy Act, legislative language about "zero disclosure risk," and greater opportunities for data sharing among federal statistical agencies for statistical purposes.

How Can Nongovernment Users Be Given Access to Data While Preserving Confidentiality?

Despite efforts by several agencies to improve access to data by researchers and policy analysts outside the government, nongovernment users' need for detailed data is far from being fulfilled. Often, such data contain information on individual respondents over time, as it would for any study of how firms respond to environmental regulations, for example. Specifically, consider assessing the likely impact of a tax, levied in response to the threat of global warming, on the amount of carbon emitted from a plant. Combined information from EIA's Manufacturing Energy Consumption Survey and the Census Bureau's Longitudinal Research Database (see McGuckin and Pascoe, 1988) would show how plants would react to the implied change in the relative price of energy. There are many aspects to such a policy question and to answer it well researchers would have to address it from various perspectives. Weighed against this clear benefit, access poses serious data protection problems, and so the researchers most likely to answer the question may not get access to the data they need.

Statistical agencies have developed some procedures for providing greater access to data to selected researchers under conditions that subject the researchers to enforceable penalties for violations of confidentiality standards. For example, the designation of researchers as special sworn employees has been standard practice at the Census Bureau. This practice has clearly protected confidentiality in that special sworn employees have the same responsibilities as regular employees, but it has also limited the type and amount of research that can be done with the data. The access provided is of a temporary nature and must be carried out on site, under supervision, and only for purposes of the Census Bureau that are designated under Title 13 legislation. Further, it puts at a disadvantage researchers who are not currently in the Washington, D.C., area or cannot easily relocate.

Recently, the National Center for Education Statistics and the National Science Foundation have developed, and are evaluating, approaches for licensing researchers to have access to data for statistical purposes, with penalties for improper use. Further, the Census Bureau has been examining for some time the possibility of establishing facilities for data access outside the Washington, D.C., area, perhaps at its regional offices or at a university under a data protection agreement. Most concretely, the Bureau of Justice Statistics has provided data to form the National Justice Data Archive at the Inter-University Consortium for Political and Social Research, which is located at the University of Michigan. This archive functions under the legal authority and confidentiality protection of the Code of Federal Regulations (§ 28, Pt. 22). The Bureau of Justice Statistics provides a project monitor to the archive.

These topics of data access are further developed in Chapters 6 and 7.

CAN INDIVIDUAL-LEVEL DATA BE PROVIDED FOR PUBLIC USE?

Fritz Scheuren (1989:20), as director of the Statistics of Income Division of the Internal Revenue Service, described this predicament of the data collector:

> Statistical Disclosure Avoidance is an enormous problem. On the one hand, we want to make all the microdata [sets of individual records with identifiers removed] we produce publicly available so researchers can benefit fully; on the other hand, we have to protect respondents (or taxpayers, in my case) from having identifiable information inadvertently disclosed.

While some progress has been made since Scheuren's writing, the complexity of the task and the fundamental nature of the problem leave substantial work remaining. Statistical agencies make difficult decisions on how best to disseminate their products so that maximum value is obtained from them while protecting confidentiality. What kinds of data should be released with no restrictions? What kinds of statistical disclosure limitation techniques should be applied to data before releasing them for unrestricted public use? Will researchers be led to incorrect inferences because of such techniques? What is a reasonably small risk of disclosure of individually identifiable data? How should such decisions be made, and by whom? We develop this topic in Chapter 6.

CAN LEGITIMATE NEEDS FOR DATA SHARING
WITHIN GOVERNMENT BE MET?

Are young Americans entering the labor market prepared for the competitive challenge? Government statistics can help answer only part of this critical question. The National Center for Education Statistics, in its National Educational Longitudinal Study of 1988, started with 25,000 eighth graders and gathered periodic measurements on their academic performance, school and social environments, and family background. The Bureau of Labor Statistics surveys youth employment. The Bureau of Justice Statistics has some information on those in prison. As Hauser (1991:2) succinctly observes, however, "the overall effect of fragmented responsibility and piecemeal coverage is that, once youths leave high school, our statistical system treats them almost as if they had dropped off the face of the earth." Actually, some surveys by the National Center for Education Statistics do track students after high school. For example, the National Longitudinal Study of the Class of 1972 tracked students as they made the transition to their twenties. In general, however, there is a need for suitable interagency coordination in meeting data needs and, possibly, for some interagency data sharing.

Sharing of identifiable data for statistical purposes can have many potential benefits, including the enrichment of cross-sectional and longitudinal data sets, evaluation and improvement of the quality of census and survey data, improvement of the timeliness and consistency of statistical reporting, development of more complete sampling frames, and improvement of comparability between data developed by different statistical agencies. A significant amount of data sharing has occurred without incident, both between statistical agencies and from administrative agencies to statistical agencies. For many years, for example, the Census Bureau has used tax records on individuals and businesses to enhance its demographic censuses and surveys and to evaluate the quality of census and survey data. (Additional detail on this point is provided in Chapter 6.) Similarly, identifiable patient records are routinely used under controlled conditions in medical and epidemiologic research.

Decisions on whether to link records require careful examination of several factors. Will the linking be done under conditions that conform with all statutory confidentiality standards of the agencies involved and with pledges to data providers concerning the use of their information? Is record linkage the only feasible way to develop the desired statistical products? Are the intended uses of these products sufficiently important to justify introducing additional risks of disclosure? Should agencies take into account potential reductions of (1) the time and effort of data providers and (2) the costs of obtaining the desired data by other means? If they should, how would they do it? Who will have access to the linked data sets? Who should decide?

The statutes, regulations, and policies that affect decisions to share data and participate in record linking projects vary widely among agencies. Statistical agencies, like the Census Bureau, and custodians of administrative records, like the Internal Revenue Service, operate under strict statutory controls on disclosure of identifiable data. Other agencies, like the National Agricultural Statistics Service, have the authority to deny access for nonstatistical purposes but also have more flexibility to share data for statistical purposes. Still other agencies operate primarily under general information statutes, like the Privacy Act of 1974, and have little difficulty in finding ways to participate in record linkages for statistical and research purposes, if they choose to do so.

The value of a survey data base can sometimes be substantially enhanced by adding data from administrative records for the persons in the data base (Juster, 1991). In carrying out a health and retirement survey, for example, researchers might like to use earnings records from Social Security files. Other valuable administrative records include case files from public assistance programs, health care claims, and tax returns. Such linkages are valuable for a number of reasons:

• Existing administrative records may be more accurate than survey data obtained from respondents, especially for detailed information that must be recalled for earlier years, like income data.

• Surveys are made less burdensome and intrusive because certain questions need not be asked.

• Administrative records can provide a check on the quality of survey results, and vice versa.

While record linkage may facilitate the basic tasks of a statistical agency, it also raises serious confidentiality concerns. Ivan P. Fellegi, chief statistician of Canada, noted in a May 2, 1991, communication to the panel,

> The issue of "moral outrage" as a possibility is real, but I believe [it] applies particularly to record linkage (matching). For this reason we are particularly careful about it.

The topic of record linkage is developed further in Chapters 4-7.

STRUCTURE OF THE REPORT

In Chapter 2 we briefly review the evolution of the federal statistical system, the findings of earlier studies of confidentiality and data access, and the changes that warrant a reexamination of the issues. To complete the contextual framework of our study, we also provide an overview of our assessment of the responsibilities federal statistical agencies must be able to fulfill in their dealings with the public, data providers and data subjects, data users, other statistical agencies, and custodians of administrative records.

In Chapter 3 we address fair treatment of data providers, in particular the use of informed consent as an instrument for ethical communication by data collectors. Drawing on survey experiments, cognitive studies, and public opinion surveys, we also examine certain research findings related to confidentiality and data access.

We examine in Chapter 4 the legitimate expectations of data users, within and outside government, for access to federal statistical data. We also explore the ethical responsibilities of data users and advocate establishing their legal responsibilities in agency or systemwide statutes.

In Chapter 5 we review legislation governing confidentiality and data access, especially the Privacy Act of 1974, Title 13 of the U.S. Code, the Hawkins-Stafford amendments of 1988 for the National Center for Education Statistics, and the Public Health Services Act as it affects the National Center for Health Statistics. While recognizing a basis for diversity according to agency mission, we emphasize the value of all statistical agencies having a certain minimal standard of statutory authority to protect their data. The experience of the Energy Information Administration and the Bureau of Labor Statistics suggests that some agencies would benefit from having more comprehensive statutory protection of their statistical records.

Extensive dissemination of detailed information is necessary to ensure that ample value can be obtained from federal censuses and surveys. At the same time, statistical agencies must fulfill pledges of confidentiality to data providers. Thus, we examine in Chapter 6 technical and administrative procedures for providing information while ensuring that the risk of disclosure is at most minimal.

In Chapter 7 we address confidentiality issues associated with statistical data on organizations. Using four case studies, we develop a conceptual basis for similarities and differences in the treatment of data on organizations compared with data on individuals and households.

We address the management of confidentiality and data access functions in Chapter 8, with particular attention to interagency coordination and the cross-national experience. We also explore issues of agency staffing and data protection legislation.

Our findings and recommendations are presented in Chapters 3 through 8.

A complete list of recommendations are the last chapter, and our study procedure is described in Appendix A.[7] Biographical sketches of the panel members are provided in Appendix B.

Throughout our deliberations we have been mindful that regardless of the efforts put forth, the tension between data protection and data access will not go away. At best one can hope for a temporary consensus each time the community of interested parties revisits this issue. Ideally, as with isometric exercise, achieving correct dynamic tension in one round builds greater strength for the next round.

NOTES

1. The Environmental Protection Agency, for example, in collecting data on compliance with air pollution regulations for the purpose of flagging offenders is *not* functioning as a statistical agency.
2. See Marx (1988:219-229, 1990) for general arguments about the value of privacy and anonymity.
3. This concern is as valid for data on organizations as it is for data on individuals or households.
4. To illustrate the lack of private financial incentives, studies on the health risks of smoking draw some private support from the insurance industry, but that industry's financial incentives to develop data may pale compared with those of the tobacco industry. With a primary mandate to serve the public interest, the National Center for Health Statistics, along with the National Institutes of Health, can generate the vital data that help inform the debate. As Lave (1990:33-34) notes,

    Strongly held opinions are rarely sufficient to improve public health. For every public health professional who favored anti-smoking and AIDS communication campaigns, there were several people opposed to these campaigns. The strength of belief of the surgeon-general, and the mustering of support of public health professionals were necessary, but not sufficient, conditions for being able to conduct a campaign. The campaigns could not have been mounted without mustering the data to show that the problems were important, and that the proposed actions were likely to improve public health.

5. For example, Allison and Cooper (1991) note a case in which Institutional Brokers Estimate System (IBES) filed suit against a researcher who criticized their data and imposed conditions on academic researchers that (1) require them to clear all potential publications with IBES so the latter can have the opportunity "to identify factual errors or misunderstandings" and (2) require researchers using IBES data to refrain from providing access to others (including research assistants) without prior clearance.

6. See, for example, Bureau of the Census (1982), Louis Harris and Associates, Inc. (1981, 1983), National Research Council (1979), the Roper Organization, Inc. (1980).

7. To facilitate its work, the panel commissioned several background papers on issues bearing on confidentiality and data issues. The papers appear in a special issue of the *Journal of Official Statistics*, 1993(2). See Appendix A for a list of the papers.

2

The Framework of Study

> *You can't have a democratic society*
> *without having a good data base.*
> Janet Norwood, former commissioner,
> Bureau of Labor Statistics, 1991

In Chapter 1, we laid out ethical principles for statistical agencies as they struggle to broker society's insistence that citizens be allowed to lead private lives and that public policies be based on the dissemination of relevant personal information. In this chapter, we first put this struggle in historical context by tracing the evolution of the federal statistical system's response to issues of confidentiality and data access. Because of their importance, these issues have been the subject of examination by various commissions, panels, and committees. Thus, we next briefly review this earlier work and the recommendations made by some of the key groups. We then argue that recent changes in the composition of society and in computer and communications technology make reexamination of these issues a pressing concern. Finally, we identify and describe the responsibilities that federal statistical agencies have to their various constituencies.

EVOLUTION OF THE FEDERAL STATISTICAL SYSTEM

The federal statistical system has evolved apace with the country, and at each step it has had to address confidentiality and data access issues. The Constitutional Convention of 1787 called for a count of Americans every 10 years beginning in 1790. By the second decennial census, Vice-President Thomas Jefferson had successfully urged more detailed collection of data on people's ages so policies could be designed to raise longevity. The seventh federal census (1850) was greatly enlarged to report by individuals rather than families. In addition, the practice of having local marshals collect and tabulate the results was stopped. Instead, local census takers filled out the forms, which were then sent to the census office in Washington, D.C., for uniform classification and tabulation. Some 640,000 pages of census schedules were bound in 800 volumes to provide, for the first time, a comprehensive statistical picture of the social and economic life of the nation. To organize the 1850 census, the new superintendent of the census, Professor of Political Economy James D.B. De Bow, teamed with Lemuel Shattuck, a founder in 1839 of the American Statistical Association.

The first permanent census office was founded following adoption of the Permanent Census Act of March 1902. According to Boorstin (1973:172), Dr. S.N.D. North, the first head of the permanent census office, was ready to divide all modern history "into two periods, the non-statistical and the statistical; one the period of superstition, the other the period of ascertained facts expressed in numerical terms." Further, North continued, "the science of statistics is the chief instrumentality through which the progress of civilization is now measured, and by which its development hereafter will be controlled." The census office of S.N.D. North evolved into the modern U.S. Bureau of the Census, whose responsibilities go well beyond the decennial census.

As the need for information has grown in such areas as labor, education, and health, the nation has created specialized statistical agencies to collect and disseminate data. In other cases, states have assumed data collection responsibilities, especially in the area of vital statistics, such as birth, marriage, and death records. Unlike its northern neighbor, with its Statistics Canada, the United States has a decentralized statistical system, in which there are numerous federal statistical agencies, each with separate enabling legislation and distinct data provider and data user constituencies. Because of this, substantial variations exist in the way agencies and programs seek to protect confidentiality and provide data access. Some variations are justifiable given the agencies' differing mandates; however, some appear more an accident of history and reflect a lack of coordination and systemwide thinking. In either case, the existing decentralized system provides a natural experiment for examining what works and what does not work for data protection and data access.

Over the past two centuries, federal statistical agencies have responded commendably to growing public concerns about protecting individual autonomy. Courtland (1985) reviews this historical progression for the Census Bureau. Through the first six decennial censuses (1790-1840), for the limited data to be collected on each household, each census taker was "to cause a correct copy, signed by himself, of the schedule containing the number of inhabitants within his division to be set up at two of the most public places within the same, there to remain for the inspection of all concerned." By the 1850 census, this practice of public posting had been abandoned and census takers were making assurances of confidentiality. Still, copies of the census returns were filed with state officials and county courts, a practice about which Francis Amasa Walker, the superintendent of the 1870 census, expressed concerns (quoted in Courtlands, 1985:409):

> The whole expenditure has been worse than useless. It has been positively mischievous. The knowledge on the part of the people that the original sheets of the census were to be deposited among the records of the counties to which they relate, has added almost incalculably to the resistance which the inquiries of the census have encountered. It is useless to attempt to maintain the confidential character of a census under such circumstances. The deposit of the returns at the county seat of every county constitutes a direct invitation to impertinent or malicious examination. . . . At every step the work of the assistant marshal has been made more difficult by the fear that the information would be . . . divulged for impertinent and malicious criticism. No one feature of the present method of enumeration has done so much to excite and justify this fear as the provision of the law which requires that the original returns for each county shall be deposited in the office of the county clerk.

By 1890, census legislation required census workers to swear under oath not to disclose census data except to their superiors and eliminated the requirement to file copies with the county court.

During the nineteenth century there was steady growth in the collection of labor, health, agriculture, and education statistics (see, e.g., Duncan and Shelton, 1978). In the early twentieth century, a wealth of federal administrative data began to be assembled with the passage of the Sixteenth Amendment to the Constitution in 1912, which enabled a federal income tax, and the Income Tax Act of 1913, which implemented the income tax.[1] Statistics based on the data were first published pursuant to the Revenue Act of 1916. By 1924 legislation had loosened access to tax data to include public listing of taxpayers and their incomes and access to tax returns by two congressional revenue committees. A reaction to this openness led to the Revenue Act of 1926, which rescinded public access to income data.

Major growth in the federal statistical system began in the 1930s with the implementation of an array of government programs to bring the country out of the Great Depression.[2] Growth in personnel, budget, and responsibilities accelerated in the postwar period with the passage of the Employment Act of 1946 and the accompanying establishment of the Council of Economic Advisers and the Joint Economic Committee of the Congress. The need for social, as well as economic, data was further highlighted by the civil rights movement and Great Society programs of the 1960s.

Paralleling the growth in the scope of its responsibilities, the Census Bureau has paid increasing attention to protecting confidentiality. Starting in 1940, it ceased the release of certain aggregate data—such as tables displaying counts of the number of data subjects in various categories—from its demographic census publications. Data tables were not released that had small cell counts. In the 1960s, the Census Bureau began to release some computer files of records about individuals (i.e., public-use microdata files), but under the oversight of the Census Bureau Microdata Review Panel, it deletes or modifies potentially identifying information in the files.

Confidentiality concerns have arisen not only in regard to the Census Bureau, but, peaking some 20 years ago, more generally in regard to the federal government. During the Watergate period of the early 1970s, for example, the public and Congress were alarmed by the disclosure to the White House of tax information on a number of political opponents. Legislative remedies were then developed. The Privacy Act of 1974 was enacted to provide greater control over the government's use of personal records, and the Tax Reform Act of 1976 curtailed presidential authority to access tax records and to make them available to other agencies and organizations for nontax uses.

Concern about the confidentiality of personal records hampered ordinary statistical uses of federal data, for example, when the Department of Agriculture was blocked in 1973 from using tax return information to construct a directory of names for use in its surveys of farmers. During the 1970s many ambitious proposals, like the President's Reorganization Project for the Federal Statistical System, were developed to coordinate the federal statistical effort, and they generally gave careful attention to confidentiality. As Statistical Policy Working Paper 2, *Report on Statistical Disclosure and Disclosure-Avoidance Techniques*, indicated,

Most agencies that release statistical information are becoming increasingly sensitive to the disclosure issue, and . . . have adopted or are in the process of adopting policies and procedures designed to avoid unacceptable disclosure (Federal Committee on Statistical Methodology, 1978:41).

The decade of the 1980s is widely viewed as a period of retrenchment for the federal statistical system; most of the agencies were on the defensive in an effort to preserve programs and maintain budgets. The 1990s have begun with renewed recognition of the importance of federal statistics and a commitment to improve the quality of the system. For example, in 1991 the Economic Policy Council Working Group of the Council of Economic Advisers (1991), under chair Michael Boskin, proposed several initiatives to improve the quality of economic statistics. *Quality improvement* embraces renewed attention to confidentiality and data access concerns. Robert M. Groves, while at the Bureau of the Census, identified "analysis of risk of disclosure of confidential data" (quoted in National Research Council, 1992a:23) as a key interdisciplinary need closely connected to quality improvement. The Clinton administration now has an opportunity for further changes to improve the federal statistical system.

EARLIER STUDIES OF PRIVACY, CONFIDENTIALITY, AND DATA ACCESS

History suggests that privacy, confidentiality, and data access are ongoing concerns. For the federal government, these issues have been addressed by several groups and organizations, especially during a period of intensive activity in the 1970s.[3] The reports prepared by the various groups chronicle their ideas, many of which remain valid today. The scope of each study was different from that of this study, however. For example, the Privacy Protection Study Commission (1977a, b, c) was concerned with all uses of personal records, not just statistical records, and the Office of Federal Statistical Policy and Standards (1978) examined all aspects of federal statistical programs, going far beyond confidentiality and data access issues. Below, we briefly review three of the studies, which were chosen because they relate most closely to the our mission, and we recommend their reports to all who want to probe these subjects. Additionally, we refer the reader to the discussions in Boruch and Cecil (1979) and Flaherty (1979, 1989).

AMERICAN STATISTICAL ASSOCIATION
AD HOC COMMITTEE ON PRIVACY AND CONFIDENTIALITY

In 1975, Lester R. Frankel, then president of the American Statistical Association, appointed the Ad Hoc Committee on Privacy and Confidentiality to deal with information reporting, privacy, and confidentiality issues. After two years of work, the committee, chaired by Joseph L. Gastwirth, produced a final report, which made the following key recommendations regarding confidentiality:

> • Confidentiality statutes providing full and overriding protection against compulsory disclosure of identifiable records from statistical data systems derived either from surveys or from administrative records should be enacted to cover each federal statistical agency and designated units of other agencies.
> • Disclosure for nonstatistical purposes of data about identifiable individuals collected or derived from administrative records by federal agencies solely for statistical purposes should be prohibited by statute. . . .
> • The Committee urges the Congress to avoid the passage of legislation which has the effect of revoking proper guarantees of confidentiality already given by agencies collecting data to be used solely for statistical and research purposes. Statutes which have already had this effect should be amended to exempt data collected or compiled solely for statistical and research purposes (American Statistical Association, 1977:75-76).

PRIVACY PROTECTION STUDY COMMISSION

Commissioned by the Privacy Act of 1974, the Privacy Protection Study Commission (1977a), chaired by David F. Linowes, prepared a report on *Personal Privacy in an Information Society.* Although the scope of its report is much broader than just research and statistical uses of data, the commission emphasized that such activities (1) benefit society as a whole and (2) depend on voluntary cooperation for accurate information. Voluntary cooperation requires assurances of confidentiality. It also emphasized that the rich lode of administrative data built up by the federal government had barely been tapped for research and statistical purposes. From our standpoint, a key recommendation of the commission in the area of confidentiality and data access was to establish a clear functional separation between the use of information for research and statistical purposes and its use for administrative purposes. It further recommended the establishment of an independent entity within the federal government to monitor and research privacy-related issues and to issue interpretative rulings regarding implementation of the Privacy Act of 1974.

OFFICE OF FEDERAL STATISTICAL POLICY AND STANDARDS

In 1978 the Office of Federal Statistical Policy and Standards (the equivalent at that time of OMB's Statistical Policy Office) issued a report called *A Framework for Planning U.S. Federal Statistics for the 1980's*. Some basic recommendations made in the report regarding confidentiality and data access were as follows:

- All agencies involved in the collection of statistical or research data should have mandated legislative protection for the confidentiality of information collected or otherwise obtained to be used solely for statistical or research purposes. This should apply to both commercial and personal data.
- The uses of statistical data must be restricted to prevent their use in identifiable form for making determinations which would affect the rights, benefits or privileges of the individuals.
- Exchange of data among the "protected enclaves" [see below] should be feasible under controlled conditions.
- Administrative data sets should be accessible to statisticians and researchers in "protected enclaves" for some statistical uses unrelated to the purposes of the original data collection (pp. 280-281).

The report also argued for

enactment of a clear legal status as "protected enclaves" for selected statistical and research agencies in the major departments, and for other clearly identified statistical and research units within other agencies. The enclave must be insulated from intervention and from unauthorized access to data. Employees must be subject to strict ethical standards established with respect to data handling and to penalties for voluntarily releasing identifiable data contrary to law (p. 281).

Such "protected enclaves" have not been established.

WHAT HAS CHANGED TO WARRANT A NEW STUDY?

Since 1980 many changes in the social and technical environment have affected the federal statistical system. Those changes have caused increased concern about the confidentiality of and access to statistical data and led to our reexamination of these

issues. Pertinent developments in the past decade include the
following:

- advances in computer and communications technology,
- an expanding role for outside researchers in the use of
federal data bases for policy analysis,
- expanded use of matching (record linkage) for statistical
and nonstatistical purposes,
- increases in the variety, number, and influence of organizations that have a stake in confidentiality and data access issues,
- increasing difficulties in persuading data providers to participate in censuses and surveys,
- initiation of cognitive research aimed at the improvement
of informed consent and notification procedures for surveys, and
- new developments in research on statistical disclosure limitation.

Below, we briefly describe each of these developments and indicate areas of concern for the federal statistical system.

ADVANCES IN COMPUTER AND COMMUNICATIONS TECHNOLOGY

Rapid advances in computer and communications technology
have resulted in increased demands by data users for microdata
(i.e., data on individual subjects). In 1978, Statistical Policy Working
Paper 2 (Federal Committee on Statistical Methodology, 1978:41)
noted the increased use of microdata files since 1960 and affirmed,
"This development has significantly increased the utility of statistical data bases created by Federal agencies from censuses, surveys and administrative records and promises to do so even more."
Beginning with the introduction of personal computers in about
1981, the rapid proliferation of computing power has radically
altered the mainframe environment of the 1970s.

The increase in computational capability, the rapid decline in
the cost of computer data storage, the development of more sophisticated data base software, the improvement of data transmission capabilities, and the development of computerized data en-
try—all have made it possible to develop and access with ease
large data bases of personal records and thus made confidentiality
issues more salient. And although sophisticated techniques for
disclosure limitation can now be applied, analytic tools also exist
that make it easier for a potential data snooper to identify individual records.

OUTSIDE RESEARCHERS

The role of outside researchers in the use of federal data bases for policy analysis has been expanding. These outside researchers include those who work for other agencies, Congress, academic institutions, businesses, labor organizations, and various other organizations. This expanded role is appropriate. The task of analyzing the collected data in order to obtain maximum information from them is enormous, and yet the statistical agencies necessarily face fiscal and institutional constraints that limit the amount of analysis they can perform.

Outside researchers possess substantial capability for data analysis because of their subject-matter knowledge, computing capability, and professional motivation to obtain new insights from the data. Further, their independent analysis of federal data can provide not only new research and policy interpretations, but also uses that the various government agencies had not envisioned. At the same time, the demands of outside researchers for access to federal data raise additional confidentiality concerns for federal statistical agencies.

RECORD LINKAGE

In order to enhance their ability to answer complex policy-relevant questions, researchers seek to match records in one statistical data base with records from the same data provider in another data base. By matching records, they can avoid having to ask data providers for information they have already given to another data gatherer. The existence of abundant and available computing capability makes matching a more viable option than in prior decades.

In general, record linkage can be an effective tool for statistical and administrative purposes. In administrative procedures, records of federal student loans, for example, can be linked to federal employment records in order to identify federal employees who are delinquent in repaying their loans. In statistical studies, data on federal student loans can be linked to federal employment records to research the value added in human capital of federal loan programs.

For ethical and pragmatic reasons, as we argue in Chapter 1 and elsewhere in this report, data collection for statistical purposes should be protected from administrative uses. Thus, a survey of college graduates that purports to be examining the value of various sources of college financial aid should not be used to locate those who are delinquent on federal student loans. This concept of functional separation is fundamental to the integrity and effectiveness of a federal statistical agency.

ORGANIZATIONS CONCERNED WITH CONFIDENTIALITY AND DATA ACCESSIBILITY

Responding to the demands of an information-rich age, the variety, number, and influence of organizations claiming a stake in confidentiality and data access issues have mushroomed. As an illustration of the scope of this growth in just one area, the Second Conference on Computers, Freedom, and Privacy was held in March 1992, at George Washington University, one year after the first conference. Sponsored by the Association for Computing Machinery, the 1992 conference had 12 co-sponsors, ranging from the American Civil Liberties Union to the Association of Research Libraries to the Committee on Communications and Information Policy of the Institute for Electrical and Electronics Engineers— USA. In addition it had 10 patrons, including Bell Atlantic and the Computer Security Institute. Given the evident range and depth of concern, federal statistical agencies should be sensitive to the views of different stakeholders, accommodate their conflicting needs to the extent possible, and help to inform the public debate by making the various parties aware of each other's views.

PERSUADING DATA PROVIDERS

Many data collectors face mounting difficulties in persuading data providers to participate in censuses and surveys. There is a consensus that, generally, respondent cooperation with survey activities is declining. Dalenius (1988) describes a willingness to provide "self-disclosure" and a "survey-mindedness" during the 1950s and the early 1960s that have since become weaker. Although no U.S. examples of serious consequence have yet emerged, Dalenius cites a European example that suggests caution. According to Dalenius, a 1986 debate over Stockholm University's Project Metropolitan, a longitudinal study of some 15,000 people born in 1953, may have doubled the nonresponse rate to Statistics Sweden's labor force survey. The key issue was the accumulation and linkage, from several administrative and statistical sources, of highly sensitive data for individuals, without their apparent knowledge. Although there was some notification of parents at the start of the study, the subjects themselves were not contacted when they reached the age at which they could make their own decisions (p. 5).

Cognitive Research

In recognition of the personal, and often sensitive, nature of the information that surveys seek from individuals, federal statistical agencies have for many years conducted a variety of survey experiments. More recently, they have conducted cognitive and public opinion research. In the late 1970s, three major studies of informed consent assurances were conducted with survey respondents. In a paper prepared for the panel, Singer (1993) reviews these and other related studies.

The Bureau of Labor Statistics, Census Bureau, and the National Center for Health Statistics have recently set up small units to conduct cognitive research. Within a larger mandate of improving the design of questionnaires, the units have addressed some issues related to confidentiality and data access. Specifically, research studies have been conducted to gain a better understanding of how survey respondents react to personal questions under differing confidentiality pledges and informed consent and notification procedures. In addition, the Internal Revenue Service has sought to elicit respondents' views on the sharing of personal data among selected agencies.

Several public opinion surveys have also addressed privacy issues. For example, a 1990 Louis Harris survey addressed the information practices of business and government agencies (see Equifax Inc., 1990). The Internal Revenue Service has sponsored a series of surveys on such topics as the use of information from mandatory data sets (like income tax returns) for statistical purposes not related to the purposes for which the data were collected (e.g., Internal Revenue Service, 1984, 1987). We explore the impact of the various research activities in Chapter 3.

New Developments in Research on Statistical Disclosure Limitation

Various researchers in statistical agencies and in universities have developed better theoretical frameworks for the construction of statistical disclosure limitation techniques. New disclosure limitation techniques have been developed for tabular data, public-use files of individual data, and data accessed from computer data bases. These developments, which are explored in Chapter 6, are designed to make it possible for statistical agencies to permit data access under conditions that protect confidentiality and maintain the utility of the data for legitimate users.

RESPONSIBILITIES OF FEDERAL STATISTICAL AGENCIES

In Chapter 1 we explored three guiding principles for federal statistical agencies: democratic accountability, individual autonomy, and constitutional empowerment. Each of these principles strongly relates to the responsibilities agencies have to the public, data subjects and providers, data users, other statistical agencies, and the custodians of administrative records regarding confidentiality and data access.

RESPONSIBILITIES TO THE PUBLIC

The principle of democratic accountability highlights the responsibilities of the federal statistical agencies to the public. On confidentiality and data access issues, agencies should establish and maintain a reputation for trustworthy stewardship of data. As an example, in a free enterprise economic system, trustworthy stewardship ensures common availability of accurate economic information. A statistical agency should have sufficient independence to be insulated from political interference so that it can provide facts to public policy debates, fairly and impartially. It should also respond promptly, efficiently, and effectively to data needs in areas that are priorities on the public agenda. In particular, it should provide data needed to evaluate the results of government activity or lack of activity. Further, it should maintain a sufficiently high public profile that its work is known to the public.

RESPONSIBILITIES TO DATA PROVIDERS AND DATA SUBJECTS

Statistical agencies have responsibilities to data providers and data subjects that are congruous with the principle of individual autonomy. They should observe fair statistical information practices. Those practices include (1) protection of confidentiality, (2) nondisclosure of identifiable information for administrative, regulatory, or enforcement purposes, (3) use of informed consent in voluntary surveys, and (4) notification of the conditions of participation in mandatory surveys. History suggests that statistical agencies should anticipate and be prepared to contend with requests by government, the courts, and citizens for individually identifiable data for nonstatistical purposes. Yet, some federal statistical agencies lack the legislative protection they need to ensure the confidentiality they promise. Additionally, congruous with the principle of constitutional empowerment, statistical agencies should respect the willingness of data providers to contribute to society by fairly representing the information they provide and by making it available for appropriate uses (National Research Council, 1992b:5).

In the United States, beyond the decennial census, an individual's cooperation with federal surveys is largely voluntary. Cooperation involves a willingness to provide data and a good-faith effort to provide accurate data. Cooperation is dependent on data providers sensing the value of providing accurate data, having the time to respond, and believing that cooperation will not harm them. These perceptions may be influenced by the particular assurances they receive from the agency collecting the data (see Boruch and Cecil, 1979; National Research Council, 1979; Singer, 1978, 1979; and Singer et al., 1990).

The panel believes that government has different ethical responsibilities to data providers who are individuals or households versus data providers that are organizations. This view derives from the fundamental role of the individual in society, so that what rights organizations derive come from the individuals they represent and to whom they are accountable. A number of questions about appropriate confidentiality and data access policies for organizations cannot be answered by immediate extrapolation from policies for individuals. What confidentiality protection should organizations enjoy? Should tax-exempt institutions, for example, merit less protection than privately held firms? For establishments, is the basic concern access to proprietary and financial data by competitors and regulatory agencies?

In exercising their responsibilities, federal statistical agencies need to be confident that users of their data will not act irresponsibly toward the data providers. Thus, they should subject users seeking access to mechanisms that ensure their accountability about confidentiality. They might well make users bear the liability for violation of confidentiality requirements. If data providers can demonstrate harm resulting from such violations, they should have accessible legal remedies.

Responsibilities to Data Users

In accord with the principle of constitutional empowerment, statistical agencies have responsibilities to a wide range of data users. They should strive to maximize the delivery of timely, accurate, and complete information, subject to constraints on confidentiality and budget.

Responsibilities to Other Statistical Agencies

Sharing of data with other statistical agencies can enhance efficiency and the quality of information that is available for research and policy purposes. Data sharing is consistent with the principles of democratic accountability and constitutional empowerment. In developing policies for data sharing there is an insistent tension with the principle of individual autonomy, and agencies must be mindful of the expectations that data providers have of the uses to which their data might be put. Additionally, as users of data collected by others, statistical agencies are obligated to use those data responsibly. This issue is difficult because different agencies operate under different legislative authority to protect the confidentiality of their data. Thus, an agency with strong confidentiality protection cannot be expected to be forthcoming with data to an agency that lacks such confidentiality protection.'

Responsibilities to Custodians of Administrative Records

In using administrative records, statistical agencies have an obligation to maintain confidentiality. Further, based on the notion that personal records should be accurate and complete, agencies using such records ought to provide feedback that can improve the quality of administrative data bases.

NOTES

1. This discussion of statistical use of tax records is based on Wilson and Smith (1983).
2. Duncan and Shelton (1978) provide a detailed account of the historical development of the federal statistical system from 1926 to 1976. Duncan and Shelton (1992) provide commentary on some developments in the federal statistical system from 1977 to 1992.
3. These groups include the American Statistical Association Ad Hoc Committee on Privacy and Confidentiality (1977), Commission on

Federal Paperwork (1977a, b), Federal Committee on Statistical Methodology (various Statistical Policy Working Papers, especially number 2, which was prepared by the Subcommittee on Disclosure-Avoidance Techniques, 1978), Office of Federal Statistical Policy and Standards (1978), President's Commission on Federal Statistics (1971), President's Reorganization Project for the Federal Statistical System (1981), and Privacy Protection Study Commission (1977a, b, c).

3

Data Subjects

The principle of informed consent is, in essence, an expression of belief in the need for truthful and respectful exchanges between statisticians and human subjects.
International Statistical Institute, 1986

"Telling the truth," therefore, is not solely a matter of moral character; it is also a matter of correct appreciation of real situations and of serious reflection upon them.
Dietrich Bonhoeffer, 1965

The proposition that confidentiality can be protected by entirely prohibiting interagency transfers of identifiable data unless explicit consent is obtained would eliminate many valuable studies.
Office of Federal Statistical Policy and Standards, 1978

INTRODUCTION

Government statistical programs cannot function without the cooperation of data subjects and data providers. Experience in several Western European countries during the past two decades has shown clearly that even a mandatory census of population is dependent on the willingness of most people to respond and, to the best of their ability, provide accurate information (Butz, 1985a). Even when statistics are produced from administrative records, such as tax returns, an aroused public, through its elected representatives and advocacy groups, may block those statistical uses of the records that they consider objectionable.

Statistical agencies have legal and ethical responsibilities toward the data subjects and data providers who are the sources of data used in their statistical programs. It is sometimes difficult for statistical agencies to decide just what constitutes ethical treatment of data subjects and data providers, however. Legislation, especially the Privacy Act of 1974, sets some minimum requirements. Beyond that, much depends on the circumstances under which data are obtained from providers. When data are collected directly for statistical purposes, appropriate rules or guidelines may differ between mandatory censuses and surveys and those for which response is voluntary. And the method of data collection—telephone, face-to-face interview, or mail questionnaire—influences how the conditions of participation in a census or survey are communicated to respondents.

Secondary uses of administrative records for statistical purposes raise additional questions. How much should data providers, for example filers of tax returns, be told about statistical uses of their data and how much control should they have over such uses? Should they be notified of plans to use administrative records for research not directly related to the program for which the records are maintained and perhaps even given a chance to deny the use of their information for such purposes?

There are some important distinctions between individuals and organizations as data subjects, and their concerns are likely to be quite different, as is the legislation that governs the collection and use of information about them. Within the broad category of organizations, for example, there is great diversity. Reynolds (1993) distinguishes units of government, nonprofit organizations, businesses, and voluntary organizations, such as political parties and religious bodies. This chapter focuses mainly on individuals as data subjects and providers. However, many of the considerations that apply to relationships between statistical agencies and data providers apply equally to individuals and organizations.

This chapter explores the relationships of federal statistical agencies with data subjects and providers. How do the former communicate with the latter? How effective is the communication process? How can it be improved? In the section that follows, we examine direct communication between agencies and individual data subjects or providers through the use of informed consent and notification procedures. We also examine issues related to statistical uses of data sets based on information that individuals are obliged to provide to the government in order to obtain benefits or comply with legal requirements.

Next, we review research relevant to the processes of communication between statistical agencies and their data providers. Some experimental research studies have explored the effects of variations in informed consent procedures. Recently, cognitive research techniques have been used in laboratory settings to study respondent understanding of informed consent statements. In addition, a few public opinion surveys have explored people's attitudes about various uses of the data that are collected from them by the government for statistical and other purposes.

Finally, we examine the public information and educational activities of statistical agencies that focus on privacy and confidentiality issues. Such activities are directed at the general public and at organizations that attempt to represent the interests of data subjects and data providers.

INFORMED CONSENT AND NOTIFICATION

Ethics and law demand that data providers be told about the conditions under which they are asked to supply information that will be used for statistical and research purposes. If participation is voluntary, data collectors must let data providers know this and give them enough information to make an informed decision about whether to provide the information requested.

Throughout this report we make a distinction between *informed consent* and *notification*. The former term is appropriate only when data providers have a clear choice and will not be subject to penalties for failure to participate. The term *notification* is more appropriate for the decennial census of population, for which participation is mandatory, and for statistical and research uses of administrative records, such as tax returns or applications for welfare benefits, where failure to provide information needed for administrative purposes may expose individuals to penalties or lead to denial of benefits to which they would otherwise be entitled.

Historical Development of Informed Consent and Notification Procedures

Clinical experiments with human subjects provided the setting for much of the early development of informed consent procedures. Reynolds (1993) cites four criteria that were found to be necessary for active informed consent: (1) a rational adult is making the decision, (2) full information is provided, (3) the decision is obtained without coercion, and (4) the subject is aware of the consequences. Some of these criteria might be regarded as less critical in statistical surveys. Yet, as Mugge (1993:346) points out in a paper prepared for the panel, "Even in the most innocuous such survey a subject may suffer inconvenience, time loss, embarrassment, or psychological distress in giving an interview, and one may also suffer harm through the disclosure, the misuse, or even the planned use of the data to be provided."

The Privacy Act of 1974

Prior to the passage of the Privacy Act of 1974 (P.L. 93-579), there were no general standards for informed consent and notification procedures in federally sponsored data collection activities. The information given to data providers varied widely from agency to agency. The Privacy Act, under the general heading "Agency Requirements" (Title 5 U.S.C. § 552 (a)(e)(3)), required that each person asked to supply information be informed of the following:

- the authority under which the information is requested,
- whether provision of the information is mandatory or voluntary,
- the principal purposes for which the information is intended to be used,
- the "routine uses" that may be made of the information (routine uses generally involve disclosure of individually identifiable information to other agencies or organizations and must be described in a record systems notice published in the *Federal Register*), and
- the effects on the person, if any, of not providing all or any part of the requested information.

These requirements led to a much greater degree of uniformity in the informed consent and notification procedures used by federal statistical agencies. Legally, the Privacy Act requirements apply only to collection of data from individuals, but statistical agencies have also applied them, for the most part, to the collection of data from organizations. From 1974 on, agencies began to pay closer attention to the content of their statements to data providers and, in many instances, gave them more information than they did prior to the passage of the Privacy Act.

The process of improvement was evolutionary rather than immediate, however. It would not be difficult to find some examples of informed consent and notification statements used since 1974 that were incomplete or possibly misleading or that failed to inform data providers of important potential statistical uses of the data, such as the release of public-use microdata sets (see, e.g., Boruch and Kehr, 1983). However, Mugge's (1993) recent review of selected consent and notification procedures, conducted for the panel, found that federal statistical agencies were doing a good job of complying with the requirements of the Privacy Act (see below).

Professional Association Guidelines

The Privacy Act requirements were written in broad terms and did not answer all possible questions about what information should be included in informed consent and notification statements and how the information should be communicated to data providers in different kinds of data collections. Since the passage of the act, the American Statistical Association (ASA) and the International Statistical Institute (ISI) have examined some of the issues and have developed recommendations and guidelines.

The ASA's Ad Hoc Committee on Privacy and Confidentiality issued a report with numerous recommendations in 1977. The committee did not make a sharp distinction between informed consent and notification, but it did explore the question of what people should be told about planned and potential statistical and research uses of information supplied initially for administrative purposes. A particularly controversial question for the committee was whether data providers in voluntary surveys should be given specific information about planned linkages of their data with data from other sources, such as income tax returns. According to the committee's report (American Statistical Association, 1977:73), a majority of the members believed that was not necessary:

> In informing respondents of the uses of the data, it is sufficient to state that the data will be used for statistical purposes only, if such is the case. It is neither feasible nor necessary to spell out the possibly manifold ways, some of which may not be known in advance, in which the statistics may be employed.

However, three members of the committee, including the chair, disagreed with this finding. They believed that data subjects should be given specific information about all linkages, whether planned at the time of data collection or subsequently.

For surveys from which public-use microdata sets were to be released, the committee suggested a statement of purpose such as the following: "The data will be used only for statistical purposes, in which individual reports will not be identifiable." As

Jabine (1986) subsequently pointed out, however, such absolute statements might not be justified because there are no statistical disclosure limitation techniques that could guarantee zero risk of disclosure.

In 1983, the ASA's Ad Hoc Committee on Professional Ethics published on a trial basis its *Ethical Guidelines for Statistical Practice*, which were formally adopted by the ASA Board in December 1988 (see American Statistical Association, 1983, 1989; see also Ellenberg, 1983). Two of the guidelines are directly relevant to informed consent in "collecting data for a statistical inquiry." The committee said that the data collectors should (American Statistical Association, 1989:24)

> 2.B. inform each potential respondent about the general nature and sponsorship of the inquiry, and the intended uses of the data;
>
> 2.C. establish their intentions, where pertinent, to protect the confidentiality of information collected from respondents; strive to ensure that these intentions realistically reflect their ability to do so; and clearly state pledges of confidentiality and their limitations to the respondents.

The committee's ethical guidelines were aimed at statistical inquiries. The committee did not explore the question of notification about planned or possible statistical and research uses of information collected initially for administrative purposes.

At the international level, a *Declaration on Professional Ethics* was adopted by the International Statistical Institute in August 1985 and published in 1986. Section 4 of the declaration, "Obligations to subjects," is considerably more detailed than the guidelines of the two ASA committees with respect to the content of informed consent statements. Noting that "no universal rules can be framed" (p. 235), the declaration suggests that data providers not be overwhelmed with unwanted and incomprehensible details. On the other hand, it states unequivocally that "information that would be likely to affect a subject's willingness to participate should not be deliberately withheld" (p. 235). The declaration lists 12 topics that might be included in an informed consent statement and says that "in selecting from this list, the statistician should consider not only those items that he or she regards as material, but those which the potential subject is likely to regard as such" (p. 236).

Other aspects of the treatment of informed consent and notification in the ISI declaration are of special interest. First, it recognizes the difference between mandatory and voluntary data collections, saying that "statisticians should attempt to ensure that subjects appreciate the purpose of a statistical inquiry, even when the subject's participation is required by law" (p. 236). Second, the declaration approaches the question of statistical uses of administrative data from an unusual perspective, that of minimizing intrusions on data providers:

> One way of avoiding inconvenience to potential subjects is to make more use of available data instead of embarking on a new inquiry. For instance, by making greater statistical use of administrative records, or by linking records, information about society may be produced that would otherwise have to be collected afresh. Although some subjects may have objections to the data's being used for a different purpose from that intended, they would not be adversely affected by such uses provided that their identities are protected and that the purpose is statistical, not administrative (p. 235).

The declaration also states that the guidelines are not meant to be limited to persons. A footnote to Section 4 (p. 234) says, "This section of the declaration refers to *human* subjects, including individuals, households and corporate entities."

Matching Survey and Administrative Data

The practice of matching survey and administrative records for the same individuals has become increasingly common over the past three decades. Such linkages are performed for statistical purposes, most commonly to enhance a survey data base with additional information for the same persons (for an example, see the description of the 1973 Exact Match Study in Chapter 6). Advances in computer power, combined with widespread use of Social Security numbers as personal identifiers by units of government at all levels, have increased the economic and technical feasibility of matching individual records from different sources.

During this same period, the trend has been toward the inclusion of more explicit information about planned linkages in informed consent or notification statements. If Social Security numbers are requested in survey interviews, it becomes a virtual necessity, regardless of any legal or ethical imperatives, to tell data providers how they will be used. Some survey respondents will surely want to know why the numbers are needed.

Waivers

Sometimes a statistical agency may want to use data gathered for statistical purposes in ways that are not ordinarily permitted under their statutes or policies. Such uses may or may not be contemplated when the data are obtained from data providers. If the uses are known at the time, the permission of data providers can be requested as part of the informed consent procedures. If they are not known when the data are being collected and the informed consent statement does not provide for unanticipated research use of the data, some kind of recontact may be necessary later. We use the term *waiver* for this process because it involves asking data providers to waive confidentiality or data access provisions that would normally apply to their data.

In some instances, confidentiality statutes have been interpreted to deny data providers the right to waive the relevant provisions. We provide one example here that relates to data for persons. This example was provided in one of the case study workshops (see Appendix A) that were organized by the Committee on National Statistics and the Social Science Research Council to provide background information for the panel.

The Longitudinal Retirement History Survey (LRHS) was conducted for the Social Security Administration by the Census Bureau, under the authority of Title 13 of the U.S. Code, using a sampling frame based partly on data from the 1960 decennial census. From 1969 to 1979, interviews were conducted at two-year intervals with a sample of persons who had been close to retirement age at the time the survey started. Social Security earnings data from administrative sources were added to the data base containing the survey information for persons in the sample. In addition to published reports and analyses, a public-use microdata file containing matched survey and administrative record data was released.

In the late 1980s, the National Institute on Aging (NIA) wanted to fund a follow-up study in which surviving members of the LRHS sample would be interviewed one or more times. Additional administrative record data for them, from various sources, would be added to the data set; for those who had died, the year and cause of death would be determined by means of a match to the National Death Index.

The NIA, however, was willing to fund the study only if the resulting linked data files could be released to researchers working under NIA grants. Census Bureau policies for release of microdata, which had been revised subsequent to the initial survey, precluded releases of such linked data sets on the basis of the belief that there was a significant risk of reidentification of individuals by the agency holding the administrative data. A possible alternative was for the Census Bureau to approach the persons in the sample to see if they would waive certain of the protections provided to their data under Title 13. Such waivers would make it possible to conduct the follow-up survey under a different authority (e.g., the authority given the Commerce Department by Title 15 of the U.S. Code) that would allow the resulting linked data set to be released to researchers.

The Census Bureau conducted a test of waiver procedures with a cohort of the National Longitudinal Survey sample (this group of persons had also been surveyed under the authority of Title 13). The test revealed that about two-thirds of the persons approached were willing to sign a waiver. Subsequent to the test, however, Office of Management and Budget (OMB) lawyers ruled that Census Bureau employees could not release such data, even though waivers had been obtained. Consequently, the NIA abandoned its effort to fund follow-up interviews and to add information from administrative record sources (for additional details, see Jabine, 1993a). The agency subsequently funded a new longitudinal study, the Health and Retirement Study, which is being conducted under arrangements that will permit the release of microdata files containing linked survey and administrative record data for persons who have provided written consent. However, an opportunity to enhance the utility of an existing and uniquely valuable data set had to be forgone.

CURRENT POLICIES AND PRACTICES

Mugge (1993) reviewed the informed consent or notification statements for 15 data collection programs of federal statistical agencies, plus the statement included with individual income tax forms. He also reviewed three examples of informed consent procedures used in connection with the collection of Social Security numbers in statistical surveys. He checked each statement for conformance with Privacy Act requirements and the inclusion of a confidentiality pledge. He also reviewed the formats used and other features of interest.

Mugge concluded that the statements for the 15 statistical surveys were scrupulous in their compliance with Privacy Act requirements, when applicable. Most of the requirements were also met for economic surveys in the group, even though not called for by the act. However, he questioned the adequacy of the statement in the tax return package, which tells filers that their information will be disclosed to other federal agencies and to state and local governments "as provided by law." The statement contains little information about the kinds of disclosures that will be made, and it makes no specific mention of statistical uses or linkages with other records.

When a government agency asks individuals to disclose their Social Security number, the Privacy Act requires that the agency "inform that individual whether that disclosure is mandatory or voluntary, by what statutory or other authority such number is solicited, and what uses will be made of it" (P.L. 93-579, Sec. 7(b)). Mugge found that these requirements were followed, in different ways, in each of the three examples he reviewed. However, two of the three questionnaires did not have provisions for distinguishing whether the absence of a Social Security number meant that the respondent refused to provide it, the respondent did not know it, or the data subject did not have one. Lacking this information, an agency that wanted to follow a policy of not linking data when the number was refused (recommended in Jabine, 1986) would be able to attempt linkages only for those cases for which Social Security numbers were reported by respondents.

Finally, Mugge found that notification statements were delivered to survey respondents in several different ways, including a transmittal letter, a separate Privacy Act notice, a question-and-answer sheet, a brochure describing various aspects of the survey, separate instructions for completing the questionnaire, and on the face sheet of the questionnaire itself. In several instances a multitiered approach was used; that is, the information was supplied at more that one stage, and a telephone number, frequently toll free, was provided for use by respondents wanting more information.

Special techniques have been developed for telephone surveys, because it is not always possible to meet the Privacy Act requirement that the notification statement be on the questionnaire form or on a paper to be retained by the data provider. Lawyers at the Department of Health and Human Services have approved the procedure developed by the National Center for Health Statistics of having telephone interviewers sign a statement that they have read the full notification statement to the respondent or, for computer-assisted surveys, enter information to that effect in the computer.

Evaluation studies, especially those in which census or survey responses are matched with administrative records and vice versa, pose special problems for the use of informed consent procedures. For example, what information about linkages should be given to participants in ethnographic studies designed to investigate factors associated with undercoverage in the census of population or to respondents to a postcensal household survey of census response behavior? What about a survey of voting behavior (voting tends to be overreported in household interviews) in which the survey responses are to be matched with voting records or the sample of respondents has been selected from voting records? The dilemma in such instances is that full disclosure of the purposes and procedures of the study may prejudice the accuracy and utility of the results. Social scientists have wrestled with such questions (see, e.g., Beauchamp et al., 1982:Pt. 3), but, insofar as we have been able to determine, federal statistical agencies that undertake or sponsor such studies do not have any generally accepted set of guidelines to refer to in developing their informed consent procedures.

Mandatory Data Sets: Controlling Information About Oneself

We turn our attention now to one of the more difficult questions we faced, as well as some of our predecessors: When individuals are required by law to provide personal information to the government, to what degree should they be allowed to control uses of that information for purposes other than the immediate ones for which they were required to furnish it?

For voluntary surveys, maintaining control over one's own information is fairly straightforward if the agency collecting the data provides accurate, complete, and clear information about the voluntary nature of the survey and the uses that will be made of the data. If appropriate informed consent procedures are used and the agreed conditions of use are followed, data providers have full control over the information they supply. Prospective data providers who do not like the conditions associated with the survey may decline to participate. They may sometimes be asked for their reasons, but they cannot be required to give any.

When provision of information is mandatory, however, data providers no longer have full control over the uses that will be made of their information. For most persons, the consequences of failing to file a tax return or refusing to provide information needed to establish eligibility for Social Security benefits are too unpleasant to consider. Failing to respond to the decennial census may be less likely to have serious repercussions; nevertheless, there is a strong possibility of being subjected to pressure from a census field supervisor and there is a small possibility of being prosecuted.

Even though society, through its legislators, has determined that reporting for a particular purpose shall be mandatory, there is still the question of whether individuals should have any control over uses of the same information about them for other purposes. Our concern here focuses on cases in which those other uses are for statistical or research purposes. The trade-offs we examine are between individuals' interest in controlling use of their own information and the public interest in obtaining information that can be used to improve public policy and advance science and knowledge of the society.

The Privacy Act of 1974 included among its goals the following:

> (b) The purpose of this Act is to provide certain safeguards for an individual against an invasion of personal privacy by requiring Federal agencies, except as otherwise provided by law, to . . .
>
> (2) permit an individual to prevent records pertaining to him obtained by such agencies for a particular purpose from being used or made available for another purpose without his consent;
> . . .
>
> (5) permit exemptions from the requirements with respect to records provided in this Act only in those cases where there is an important public policy need for such exemption as has been determined by specific statutory authority (P.L. 93-579).

These general principles are clearly stated, but, as we explain in Chapter 5, their interpretation in specific instances is seldom obvious. By and large, individuals do not have control over statistical uses of identifiable information about themselves that they or others supply to agencies like the Internal Revenue Service, the Social Security Administration, or the Health Care Financing Administration (the operating agency for Medicare) for administrative purposes. To the extent that statistical uses of administrative data are permitted by statutes and regulations, the data subjects and providers are usually not asked for their consent, and as noted above, in some instances they are not even given any notification of such uses.

The issue of individuals' control over statistical and research uses of data about themselves in administrative record systems was addressed explicitly in a document titled *A Framework for*

Planning U.S. Federal Statistics for the 1980's, issued in 1978 by the Office of Federal Statistical Policy and Standards (OFSPS). The preface to the document stated that it was not a statement of official agency policies; rather, it was "expected to serve as a background for decisions concerning individual programs, so that these decisions can take place in the context of the entire statistical effort of the Federal Government" (p. v).

The OFSPS document specifically rejected the proposition that individual consent should be obtained for any interagency transfers of individually identifiable administrative data for statistical and research purposes. "The price of that approach . . . is great, leading to biased data, increased public expenditure, and the failure or impossibility of some valuable statistical and research studies" (p. 259). The following recommendation, which has not been implemented, was made at the end of the chapter on "Confidentiality of Statistical and Research Data":

> 4. Administrative data sets should be accessible to statisticians and researchers in "protected enclaves" for some statistical uses unrelated to the purposes of the original data collection (p. 281).

The concept of protected enclave used in the OFSPS document is closely related to that of functional separation as we defined the latter in Chapter 1. The goal in either instance is to prohibit nonstatistical uses of data obtained for statistical purposes, regardless of their source.

With respect to notification, OFSPS recommended the use of "a statement at the time of data collection about the *general* character of potential statistical uses" (p. 281). It also recommended that the power to authorize interagency transfers be lodged in a review agency such as OFSPS (the equivalent at that time of the OMB Statistical Policy Office) and that the review agency use a clear set of criteria to determine when such transfers were sufficiently in the public interest to justify them.

As we explained earlier in this section in connection with waivers, lack of informational control can work in both directions. Respondents to the Longitudinal Retirement History Survey were, in the final outcome, not allowed to waive any of the confidentiality protections that were given to their information as required by the Census Bureau's Title 13 authority.

What balance should be struck between the data needs of society and individuals' control over information about themselves that they are required to provide to government agencies? The following factors should be considered in searching for a reasonable answer:

- *The degree to which statistical and research uses are related to the administrative purpose for which the data were obtained*: One would expect that very few people who receive Social Security benefits would have any objection to their covered earnings and benefit data being used to conduct statistical analyses of the characteristics of beneficiaries and the relationships between earnings and benefits for different age cohorts and other population subgroups. Given that society has agreed to have various programs of benefits, taxation, licensing, and regulation, most people would agree that good information is needed to monitor and improve those programs.

- *The potential benefits to society of the proposed statistical and research uses*: It can be argued that individuals' control over uses of their information should extend to those activities that offer little promise of important benefits to society, even if such uses can bring no harm to the data subjects.

- *The effectiveness of the confidentiality protections associated with the statistical and research uses of the data*: Do the intended uses require transfer of individually identifiable records to other agencies, organizations, or individuals? Do they require matching with data for the same persons from other data sets? If so, will the confidentiality of the records be adequately protected?

- *The definition of the population whose data are wanted for statistical and research uses*: Should a distinction be made between records generated for programs with wide general coverage and records for needs-tested entitlement programs and other programs for specially defined groups? What about criminal records?

- *The feasibility and cost of using informed consent procedures to cover some types of statistical and research uses of administrative records*: Some records, like Social Security files containing date of birth, sex, and until recently, race-ethnicity, are being created at the time of the data subject's birth, so that some kind of proxy procedure would be necessary to obtain consent to any uses deemed to require it. Would such consent remain in force during the individual's lifetime or would it be revocable? What would be the additional cost to custodians of such records of labeling each record according to its current availability status for voluntary research and statistical uses?

- *Alternative sources of data*: If the records from mandatory data sets cannot be used, are there other feasible methods for acquiring the data needed for statistical analyses and research? Will it be necessary to ask some of the same individuals for information they have already supplied for other purposes?

Whatever general principles may be developed for statistical and research uses of mandatory data sets, their application in specific instances will require the establishment of an orderly and fair process that takes into account the interests of data subjects, users, and custodians. Judgments will be necessary concerning the importance to society of the proposed uses, whether they are relevant to the program for which the data were collected, the adequacy of confidentiality protections, and whether there are reasonable alternative methods for obtaining the information. In Chapter 8 we discuss alternative mechanisms for making such judgments.

FINDINGS AND RECOMMENDATIONS

Recommendation 3.1 Federal statistical agencies should follow a flexible, multilayered approach to informing data providers of the conditions under which they are being asked to provide information.

Basic information should be given to all data providers. Those who want more information should have the opportunity to obtain it directly from interviewers or by other means, such as supplementary written statements or toll-free telephone inquiries to the agency. The goal should be to give each data provider as much information as is necessary to make his or her consent as informed as he or she wishes it to be.

Recommendation 3.2 Basic information given to all data providers requested to participate in statistical surveys and censuses should include

(a) for data on persons, information needed to meet all Privacy Act requirements. Similar information is recommended for data on organizations, except that the requirement to inform providers about routine uses (as defined by the Privacy Act) is not applicable.

(b) a clear statement of the expected burden on the data providers, including the expected time required to provide the data (a requirement of the Office of Management and Budget) and, if applicable, the nature of sensitive topics included in the survey and plans for possible follow-up interviews of some or all respondents.

(c) no false or misleading statements. For example, a statement that implies zero risk of disclosure is seldom, if ever, appropriate.

(d) information about any planned or potential *non-statistical* uses of the information to be provided. There should be a clear statement of the level of confidentiality protection that can be legally ensured.

(e) information about any planned or anticipated record linkages for statistical or research purposes. For persons, this notification will usually occur in conjunction with a request for the data subject's Social Security number.

(f) a statement to cover the possibility of unanticipated future uses of the data for statistical or research purposes.

(g) information about the length of time for which the information will be retained in identifiable form.

To meet the requirements of item (b), agencies must determine which of the data they plan to collect may be considered sensitive by data providers. As the authors of Statistical Policy Working Paper 2 concluded, there are no general rules for establishing whether data are sensitive. That decision involves community standards and generally must be made on a case-by-case basis. However, financial data—like income and assets—and data on illegal or ethically questionable behavior are typically understood to be sensitive.

In preparing an informed consent or notification statement, a statistical agency should carefully review the purposes and design of the data collection activity, especially when multiple contacts with respondents or linkages with data from other sources are planned or may prove to be desirable. Agencies should seek expert opinions as to what kinds of data are currently or may in the future be relevant to the goals of the statistical or research activity. Even experts, however, cannot foresee all future needs. Item (f) is intended to allow for unanticipated statistical and research uses of the data that are not inconsistent with provisions of the initial statements to data providers.

With regard to item (g), some statistical records, such as those from the decennial censuses of population, may be retained permanently in identifiable form. The subject of archiving of statistical records is covered in Chapter 6.

In general, similar information about statistical uses should be given to persons or organizations that are asked to provide information about themselves for compliance or programmatic (administrative) purposes, whenever there is a possibility that their data will also be used for statistical purposes. In such instances, it is likely that the major concern of data providers will be with the nonstatistical uses of their data, so that the basic notification statement should emphasize that aspect, rather than statistical uses. However, full information on statistical uses should be available to data providers who want it.

As discussed earlier in this section, the panel believes that there have been instances in which unnecessarily strict interpretation of some confidentiality statutes has precluded the use of waiver procedures to enhance the utility of policy-relevant data sets.

> **Recommendation 3.3** In keeping with the objective of giving individuals control over their own information whenever societal needs do not clearly take precedence, data subjects or data providers should be allowed to waive certain aspects of confidentiality protection that would usually be accorded to the information they provide. Agencies should take special care to ensure that any such waivers are based on fully informed consent.

The panel considered a broad set of options with respect to individuals' control over statistical and research uses of data they are *required* to provide for administrative purposes. At one end of the spectrum, individual data subjects would have total control—they would be allowed to opt out of any or all such uses. At the other end, they would have no control—any uses permitted by law and considered appropriate by the custodians of the data would be acceptable. There are many intermediate options under which data subjects would retain control over some uses but not others. Also at issue were the questions of how much information should be given to data subjects about such uses and, if they are to be given the opportunity to opt out in some instances, whether the mechanism should require affirmative informed consent or simply notification of their right to opt out (passive consent).

Not surprisingly in view of past experience, the panel was unable to reach a consensus on this issue. Where individuals came out depended largely on their personal views about how best to resolve the conflicts among the requirements of the three fundamental principles that were presented in Chapter 1. In this instance, the trade-offs are between democratic accountability and constitutional empowerment on one side and individual autonomy on the other.

One proposed solution was supported by most of the panel members, but three members preferred different solutions, two in the direction of greater democratic accountability and constitutional empowerment and one in the direction of greater individual autonomy. We present first the majority position and an explanation of its features, followed by the views of those who did not fully agree with it.

The majority view was that data subjects should be allowed control over research and statistical uses of data they are required to provide for administrative purposes when

1. they are required to provide the data as a condition for participation in needs-tested entitlement programs that provide benefits to special population groups, *and*
2. the proposed uses are not clearly related to the mission and function of the agency or system that collected the data.

This position represents an attempt to reconcile the rights of individuals to control uses of their data with the rights of society to obtain the information it needs for efficient design and management of programs and policies designed to promote the general welfare. The position is deliberately stated in broad terms, and those who supported it did not try to spell out the implications of its provisions in every circumstance. Programs like Food Stamps and Aid to Families with Dependent Children would clearly be covered by provision 1; Medicare and Social Security retirement benefits would not. Provision 2 would not necessarily give data subjects control over all transfers of identifiable information about them to other agencies. It would apply only if the proposed use of the data by the recipient was not clearly related to the purpose for which they were collected.

Whenever provisions 1 and 2 both apply, those who supported this position believe that data subjects should be clearly informed of their option to withhold their data from certain kinds of statistical and research uses and that no pressure should be applied to dissuade them from exercising that option. They believe that a passive consent mechanism, which assumes consent except for data providers who, when given the opportunity, express their desire not to have their information used for such purposes, would be adequate to protect the interests of individuals.

One consideration that led to this proposed solution was the absence of any clear mechanism, independent of the agencies directly involved and representing the interests of data subjects and data users, for reaching decisions on what kinds of statistical and research uses of mandatory data sets are appropriate and under what circumstances data subjects should be allowed to opt out. In Chapter 8, where we discuss the management of confidentiality and data access functions in the federal statistical system, the panel expresses its support (Recommendation 8.5) for the creation of an independent federal advisory body that would be responsible for promoting enhanced protection for all federal data about persons and responsible data dissemination for statistical and research purposes. If such a body is created, it could play a very constructive role in decision making on specific uses of mandatory data sets.

Two panel members preferred a different method of treating proposed statistical and research uses not directly related to the mission and function of the agency or system that collected the mandatory data. They believe that all such uses, regardless of the nature of the population groups affected, should require review and approval by an organization or institution other than the data collecting agency and the agency, organization, or individual desiring to use the data. For approval of a proposed use, three conditions would have to be met:

1. The intended use is to provide evidence pertinent to a general social concern, scientific discovery, or significant public policy issue.

2. The intended analyses cannot be demonstrated to be incapable of providing such evidence.

3. The intended analyses would not compromise the dignity and personal freedom of the data providers.

Notification statements to data providers would include information about any such uses approved prior to the time of data collection. They might also mention the possibility that additional statistical and research uses might be approved and would describe the process that would govern such determinations.

One panel member expressed a preference for more restrictive conditions on statistical and research uses of mandatory data sets than those provided in the majority position. This member believes that persons providing data for administrative purposes should have control over *all* such uses that are not clearly relevant to the program for which the data were collected, without regard to the kind of population covered by the program. In effect, the first condition attached to the majority proposal would be eliminated. A "passive waiver" procedure would be acceptable, that is, the data could be shared if the data provider did not explicitly forbid it after being notified of the proposed uses. This position was taken based on the member's subjective weighing of the value of individual autonomy and control over information about oneself compared with the value of more nearly complete and economically obtained data.

RESEARCH RELATED TO CONFIDENTIALITY AND DATA ACCESS

CONTROLLED SURVEY EXPERIMENTS

Three major U.S. studies have conducted included experiments on informed consent procedures for a statistical survey of the general population. In the late 1970s, the Committee on National Statistics (National Research Council, 1979) conducted a face-to-face survey in which the confidentiality assurances given to respondents were systematically varied. Five separate versions were studied: (1) assurance of confidentiality in perpetuity, (2) assurance of confidentiality for 75 years, (3) assurance of confidentiality for 25 years, (4) no mention of confidentiality, and (5) a statement that replies could be given to other agencies and the public. Participation rates decreased monotonically with decreasing assurances of confidentiality, but the observed spread among the five versions was less than three percentage points. Further, two-thirds of the refusals came from persons who declined to participate before the interviewer had a chance to read the introduction to the survey. For those who did participate, nonresponse and underreporting to the income question, which was the most sensitive one included in the survey, were greater when weaker confidentiality assurances were given.

In an experiment that was also part of a face-to-face survey, Singer (1978) investigated the effects of more versus less information about sensitive subject matter in survey introductions, varying assurances of confidentiality, and requiring or not requiring a signature to document consent. Varying the information given to respondents about the content of the survey had no observable effect on participation rates or the quality of survey response, nor were participation rates affected by varying assurances of confidentiality. However, response rates to sensitive questions were higher for those who had been given absolute assurances of confidentiality. Asking respondents to sign a consent form would have caused a significant drop in participation rates for the survey if it had been required in order to conduct the interview. However, signing the consent form was not required and most of the respondents who refused to sign were still willing to be interviewed.

In a telephone survey, Singer (1979) investigated the effects of variations in information about survey content and the purpose of the study on participation rates and response rates to individual questions. She found no significant differences.

Singer (1993) has prepared a comprehensive review of the above and other related studies, including some conducted in Germany. The review, originally prepared for the panel, includes some studies of passive consent procedures whereby data subjects or providers are notified that some step will be taken (e.g., their children will be enrolled in a school-related research study) unless they notify the researchers of their disapproval. Some of the studies, in addition to varying treatments experimentally, asked participants directly about their attitudes and perceptions on matters related to informed consent, privacy, and confidentiality.

The results of the various studies do not always agree but, taken in all, they provide the basis for some tentative conclusions:

- Behavior does not necessarily mirror expressed concerns. Most persons, when asked directly, thought that assurances of confidentiality would make people more willing to answer questions, but experiments embedded in surveys of the general public showed only small differences in participation rates between those given strong assurances and those given weak assurances or none at all. Moreover, some recent experiments have shown that elaborate assurances of confidentiality can reduce willingness to participate (Singer et al., 1990).

- When potential survey respondents are contacted without prior notice, such as an advance mailing, most refusals to participate occur before the interviewer has had a chance to explain the confidentiality protections that will be given to survey responses.

- Requiring a signature to document consent significantly reduces survey participation rates.

- To a point, verbal assurances of confidentiality appear to result in less nonresponse and more accurate responses to questions on sensitive topics, like income. In some instances, however, especially when the assurances immediately preceded the sensitive question, there were more refusals to answer.

• Studies involving technical means of ensuring confidentiality, such as randomized responses, have sometimes yielded higher estimates of sensitive behavior, but the lack of significant changes in some studies or for some variables indicates that the conditions required for this to occur are not clear.

• There is evidence that many people do not hear, understand, or remember precisely what is said in the introduction to an interview (Singer, 1979).

COGNITIVE RESEARCH

The past decade has seen increasing recognition of the contributions that the cognitive sciences can make to survey research (see, e.g., Tanur, 1992). Three federal statistical agencies, the Bureau of Labor Statistics, the Census Bureau, and the National Center for Health Statistics, have established small units to undertake laboratory and field studies of the cognitive processes of respondents who are asked to comprehend survey questions, retrieve relevant information from memory, and make judgments about how to answer the questions. Most of the research has been aimed at improving questions on specific topics. However, the Behavioral Sciences Research Group at the Bureau of Labor Statistics, with support from the Statistics of Income Division, Internal Revenue Service (IRS), has recently begun a program of research on how providers of personal data understand and interpret words and phrases contained in informed consent and notification statements (van Melis-Wright et al., 1992).

The research at the Bureau of Labor Statistics has two components. An initial investigation will identify and evaluate people's perceptions of the language, terms, and concepts that might be used in assurances of confidentiality. The second phase will investigate the effect of various terms and concepts on participation decisions in order to determine which of them may be effectively and ethically used to promote participation and truthful answers in surveys. The analyses will include terms and concepts related to data providers' willingness to have the information they provide shared in identifiable form with another organization.

PUBLIC OPINION RESEARCH

Several U.S. public opinion surveys have addressed privacy questions, and a few have been devoted entirely to such issues, notably a series of surveys conducted by Louis Harris and Associates in recent years. However, these surveys have focused primarily on privacy and confidentiality issues related to uses of information about individuals by the private sector, and they provide only limited information on public attitudes about government statistical activities. A 1990 survey in the series was sponsored by Equifax Inc. (1990), a provider of consumer and business information services. Most of the questions were about information practices of commercial organizations and government agencies in general. One item asked respondents about how much they trusted several different organizations, including the Census Bureau, to collect information about them and treat it responsibly. The proportion who had high or moderate trust in the Census Bureau (81 percent, with 2 percent not sure) was as large as that for any other organization and considerably larger than most (e.g., 67 percent for the Internal Revenue Service, with 1 percent not sure).

The Internal Revenue Service (1984, 1987) has sponsored several national surveys of taxpayers to study their opinions and attitudes about IRS personnel, programs, and activities. Some of the results are relevant to the questions discussed earlier in this chapter concerning the use of information from mandatory data sets (such as those based on income tax returns) for statistical purposes not directly related to the purposes for which the information was obtained. Most of the taxpayer opinion surveys, for example, included questions about statistical and other nontax uses of information provided on tax returns. The most recent survey, the 1990 Taxpayer Opinion Survey, included questions on knowledge of tax laws and policies governing sharing of tax data, views on what the provisions of those laws and policies *should* be, views on sharing tax data for specified purposes, and the possible use of IRS and Social Security Administration records in future population censuses.

The 1990 survey data (see Table 3.1) indicated that most taxpayers had limited knowledge of the relevant laws and policies and had not read or thought much about the sharing of tax data with other parts of the government. Nevertheless, the majority said they had substantial interest in the subject. When asked in general terms for their views about policies for sharing tax data, the majority of respondents took a fairly restrictive view. For example, 64 percent agreed strongly or agreed that the IRS should never release information about people's income to other government agencies under any circumstances. However, when respondents were subsequently asked about several kinds of releases of

TABLE 3.1 Taxpayer Attitudes on Specific Releases of Tax Data

Agency and Purpose	Favor	Oppose	Not Sure
The Department of Justice—for major criminal investigations (such as drugs and organized crime)	77	21	1
The Veterans Administration—for determining whether veterans are eligible to receive benefits because they are unable to work	70	27	3
The Census Bureau—for identifying where people have moved in order to study population trends (statistical use)	65	33	3
The Department of Agriculture—to maintain an up-to-date list of farms for crop and livestock surveys (statistical use)	59	37	4
State governments—for improving state collection of taxes from businesses	56	42	2
State governments—for improving state collection of taxes from individuals	44	52	4
Members of Congress—for any use they consider appropriate	13	84	3

SOURCE: Tabulations from the 1990 Taxpayer Opinion Survey provided by the Research Division, Internal Revenue Service.

tax data to particular agencies *for specific purposes*, their reactions were quite different, as shown in Table 3.1. For example, when taxpayers were asked what they thought about the use of certain kinds of administrative records in the decennial census in order to reduce the cost of the census and the burden on respondents, 70 percent favored the use of Social Security information on date of birth and sex, and 61 percent favored the use of IRS information on place of residence and income.

Data from the 1990 and earlier taxpayer opinion surveys should be used with caution, for several reasons. First, the wording and format of the questions about sharing tax information differed significantly from one survey to the next. Second, the data reflect only the opinions of the member of each tax-filing family (as defined for individual income tax purposes) considered to be most knowledgeable about that family's tax-filing practices. Third, most respondents to the 1990 survey had little knowledge of laws and policies governing nontax uses of their return information and had not given much thought to such matters. Subject to these caveats, the survey results suggest that the majority of taxpayers support the idea of sharing their tax information with other agencies for statistical purposes. However, minorities of taxpayers, generally in the range of 15 to 20 percent, are strongly opposed to such data sharing.

At the time this report was being prepared, the full IRS report and the public-use data file from the 1990 Taxpayer Opinion Survey had not been released. When these outputs become available, it will be possible to analyze how the demographic and social characteristics of taxpayers are associated with their attitudes toward statistical and other nontax uses of their tax return information.

FINDINGS AND RECOMMENDATIONS

Statistical agencies need to "know their respondents." How do data providers interpret concepts like privacy, confidentiality, disclosure, data sharing, and statistical purposes? How well do they understand informed consent and notification statements, and how are their decisions on survey participation influenced by different formats and modes of presentation? What kinds of information about themselves do they consider to be most sensitive? What do they think about the linkage of their information from two or more sources? How do their reactions vary by race-ethnic group, gender, and socioeconomic status?

The research described in this section has begun to provide useful answers to some of these questions. Such research should continue because it is not complete and because public opinion about statistical data collection activities may vary gradually over time as a result of changes in the technological, social, and political environments in which public surveys are undertaken. Moreover, sudden changes in the environment for conducting public surveys are possible in response to highly publicized incidents involving improper disclosure and uses of confidential personal data in connection with nonstatistical activities, either in the public or private sector.

Recommendation 3.4 Statistical agencies should undertake and support continuing research, using the tools of cognitive and survey research, to monitor the views of data providers and the general public on informed consent, response burden, sensitivity of survey questions, data sharing for statistical purposes, and related issues.

PUBLIC INFORMATION ACTIVITIES OF STATISTICAL AGENCIES AND ORGANIZATIONS

CURRENT PRACTICES

Statistical agencies explain their positions on confidentiality questions and fair information practices to individual data providers through the use of informed consent procedures and notification statements. They also attempt to communicate their positions on such matters to the general public or to particular groups and organizations through various kinds of public information activities. The motivation for some of these activities is to enlist the support of the public and various organizations for specific programs, such as the decennial census. In other instances, public information activities develop as responses to specific allegations or suggestions that data collected for statistical purposes are not being kept confidential.

Following are some examples of constructive public information activities that have come to the attention of the panel:

• The Bureau of the Census (1985) has developed a general-purpose brochure, *How the Census Bureau Keeps Your Information Strictly Confidential,* which succinctly describes the legal and physical security protections that are provided for information collected by the Census Bureau. The brochure cites favorable comments from several newspapers and other sources about the confidentiality provided to Census Bureau data.

• The Census Bureau discussed the application of statistical disclosure limitation techniques (see discussion of these techniques in Chapter 6) to small-area tabulations from the 1990 census with representatives of several organizations, including the American Civil Liberties Union (ACLU), to determine their views, as data users and privacy advocates. In the discussions, the ACLU representatives had to balance their privacy concerns against their interest in ensuring that minority groups receive proper voting representation. In this instance, the latter concern won out. It was agreed that the exact counts of persons aged 18 and over by race or ethnicity should be published and that the planned use of techniques to reduce disclosure risks would be applied only to other variables.

• The American Statistical Association's (1991) Committee on Privacy and Confidentiality has developed a brochure on *Surveys and Privacy* to answer questions about privacy and confidentiality, clarify the responsibilities of survey takers, describe a respondent's reasonable expectations, and encourage survey response. In addition to survey respondents and survey takers, the intended audience for the brochure includes "the public, the media, and Congress." The committee obtained funding from four statistical agencies to print and distribute a large number of the brochures.

An example of unfavorable publicity requiring a response or clarification of the Census Bureau's confidentiality policies is provided by the announcement, early in 1990, by the Lotus Development Corporation and Equifax of plans to market a CD-ROM product called Lotus Marketplace: Households. Prospective purchasers were offered a data base containing information on 80 million U.S. households, including names, address, gender, marital status, income, buying preferences, and even "psychographic categories," such as "cautious young couple" or "inner-city single."

The sales brochure for Lotus Marketplace: Households mentioned the Census Bureau as one of the product's important sources of data. A quick reading of the brochure might have given the impression that household incomes were being obtained directly from individual census returns (some press reports conveyed this impression; see, e.g., Lewis, 1991). They were not. As was made reasonably clear in the technical portion of the brochure, the household income values were model-based estimates obtained by using small-area data from the decennial census plus household size and other variables from other sources. Nevertheless, the Census Bureau received some indignant inquiries as to why individual census information was being made available for a commercial data base.

Because of strong objections about the privacy and confidentiality aspects of this data base by many organizations and individuals, Lotus Marketplace: Households was withdrawn from the market early in 1991. A particular objection to the product was that the CD-ROM format would preclude the possibility of corrections to individual data items. However, similar data bases in other formats are being developed and sold. Small-area data from the decennial census and geocoding systems developed and released by the Census Bureau are likely to be used in many of these systems. Statistical agencies can expect more questions to be raised about their relation to such commercial enterprises, and they must face the possibility that objections to them might have a spill-over effect on public willingness to participate in government surveys.

RECOMMENDATIONS

The panel believes that the risks of major or deliberate violations of privacy or confidentiality are extremely low in the federal statistical system. The risks are somewhat higher for federal administrative records, as illustrated by recent revelations of sales of Social Security records to private investigators (see *Washington Post*, December 28, 1991:A1; *Baltimore Sun*, February 29, 1992:1A), and probably highest of all for private sector record systems, as illustrated by the Lotus Marketplace example. The public, however, does not always distinguish among these different types of records, and there is a danger that violations not involving statistical data bases can create moral outrage and have damaging spill-over effects on federal statistical programs.

Recommendation 3.5 Federal statistical agencies should continue to develop systematic informational activities designed to inform the public of their ability to maintain the confidentiality of individually identifiable information, including use of legal barriers to disclosure and physical security procedures, and their intentions to minimize intrusions on privacy and the time and effort required to respond to statistical inquiries.

Recommendation 3.6 Agencies should be prepared to deal quickly and candidly with instances of "moral outrage" that may be directed at statistical programs from time to time as a result of actual or perceived violations of pledges of confidentiality given to data providers by data collectors. The agencies should be prepared to explain the purpose of specific data collection activities and the procedures used to protect confidentiality. They should accept full responsibility if a violation occurs and should announce measures to prevent future violations.

Recommendation 3.7 As part of the communication process, statistical agencies should work more closely with appropriate advocacy groups, such as those concerned with civil liberties and those that represent the rights of disadvantaged segments of the population, and with specialists on ethical issues and human rights.

Some agencies may want to include members of such groups on their advisory committees.

4

Data Users

Please, sir, I want some more.
Charles Dickens, *Oliver Twist*

Statistical agencies serve as intermediaries and mediators between data providers and data users. In Chapter 3 we asserted that the federal statistical system could not function without the cooperation of data providers. It is equally true that the system would be in serious trouble if it was not able to satisfy, to a reasonable degree, the needs of a broad array of users inside and outside government. Failing this, it would not be fulfilling its purpose and would not deserve to be supported with public funds. Data users would have to place greater reliance on commercial data sources, which could have potentially undesirable consequences for the scope, cost, and quality of data available to them.

In addition, feedback from a wide data user community is essential for maintaining and improving the quality of federal statistics. It is an effective way to find errors and uncover anomalies in the data and to assess data quality.

In this chapter, we examine the relationships between federal statistical agencies and the persons and organizations that use their statistical products. The chapter has three sections. In the first, we set the stage by defining basic concepts associated with data access. Next, we consider the expectations that data users have about access to federal statistics and the extent to which those expectations are being and should be met. Finally, we examine the ethical and legal responsibilities of data users. At present, users' formal responsibilities extend almost entirely to the statistical agencies, but in a broader sense data users also have ethical and pragmatic responsibilities to data subjects and to society at large.

BASIC CONCEPTS RELATED TO DATA ACCESS

The data products of statistical agencies are released to other agencies, organizations, and individuals for statistical and research uses. These uses include *end uses,* such as policy analysis, commercial and academic research, advocacy, and various educational applications in the private and public sectors. They also include *intermediate uses,* such as the development of sampling frames for surveys, the enhancement of existing data sets by adding information from other sources, and the evaluation of data quality by comparing aggregate data or individual records (microdata) from different sources.

Most releases of publicly collected data for intermediate statistical uses are to other government agencies and their contractors or grantees. The spectrum of end users is very broad, however, especially in the private sector. In government, it includes policymakers, policy analysts, program planners and evaluators, researchers, and educators. In the private sector, it includes all of the foregoing, plus advocacy groups, market analysts, and the media.

Depending on users' requirements, the products released to them may consist of aggregate data or individual records, with or without explicit identifiers, such as name, address, and Social Security or Employer Identification number. Media for release may be hard copy or electronic, and the latter may assume various forms, such as tapes, diskettes, CD-ROM, or direct on-line transmission. On-line access may be in the form of transmission of complete data sets or outputs resulting from queries of in-house data sets.

A significant attribute of data access, the term for *release* when seen from the user's side, is whether access is *unrestricted* or *restricted.* We consider data access to be unrestricted if aggregate data or microdata are available to anyone who wants them (and is willing to pay any user fees that may be required), without restrictions or conditions of any kind on the uses to be made of the data. Access is restricted whenever any conditions on use are imposed.

Restricted access is important for two reasons. The first relates to end uses of the data. In preparing data for unrestricted access, agencies may have to limit severely the amount of information included in statistical summaries or individual records in order to comply with requirements to preserve the confidentiality of individually identifiable information. Such limitations may prevent users from performing the analyses best suited to their needs. As a result, returns from the investment of public funds in data collection and processing may not always be as great as they otherwise would be. The use of various forms of restricted access can overcome some of the limitations by allowing access to more detailed data, under controlled conditions, for selected users outside the producing agency.

It is also important that there be data sharing for intermediate statistical uses. In the decentralized federal statistical system, in order to improve the quality and consistency of information collected by different agencies and to avoid costly duplication of effort, data are sometimes shared among statistical agencies. Such data sharing cannot be unrestricted, however, because it usually requires access to individually identifiable information.

EXPECTATIONS OF DATA USERS

BACKGROUND

Increasing Demands for Access

Demand for access to federal statistical data increased at an extraordinary rate in the 1980s and will surely continue to do so in the 1990s. This demand has been fueled by the development of powerful, widely accessible computers and sophisticated analytic software, improved data transmission capability, the creation of large-scale administrative data sets with numerical identifiers, and favorable user experience with public-use microdata sets based on statistical and administrative data collections.

Some of the demand for access is being satisfied. Data users have access to federal data that they could scarcely have imagined 50 years ago. Nevertheless, potential users inside and outside government continue to assert that they have important needs that are not being met. Are they like spoiled children, never satisfied with what they receive, always wanting more, or is there some legitimacy to their complaints? Are statistical agencies being sufficiently receptive to user needs, or could they do more? Below we summarize the evidence that we have obtained and draw some conclusions on these complicated questions.

Meeting User Needs: Successes and Failures

The picture over the past two decades is mixed. Overall, there can be little doubt that user access to data has increased, but so has demand. Some new restrictions have also been imposed. To convey the flavor of developments during this period and a sense of the current situation, we present examples of movement in both directions. (These examples apply only to data on persons. User access to data on businesses and other organizations is discussed in Chapter 7.)

Following are some developments that signify a potential for greater user access:

- substantial growth in the use of public-use microdata sets issued by federal statistical agencies;
- increased in-house access to more detailed microdata files for researchers participating in the American Statistical Association/National Science Foundation (ASA/NSF) fellows program and other similar arrangements; in addition, some statistical units, like the National Agricultural Statistics Service and the Statistics of Income Division of the Internal Revenue Service, have made arrangements for researchers to use such data under controlled conditions in the unit's state or regional offices;
- increased use of formal user licensing agreements by government agencies and nongovernment organizations that have developed important research data bases with federal funding—these agreements provide for access, at the user's work site, to detailed microdata sets under controlled conditions;
- initiation of the release, by the National Center for Education Statistics (NCES), of encrypted microdata files in CD-ROM format with built-in software for analysis—this mode of release may permit more widespread dissemination of microdata sets that link survey and administrative data on persons;
- the undertaking of research to explore the possibility of releasing microdata sets that do not contain data for any specific individual but would allow users to draw valid inferences from the data (see Chapter 6 and Rubin, 1993, for details); and
- increased use of formal agreements for interagency sharing of identifiable data about persons for statistical and research purposes. Until recently, for example, the Bureau of Labor Statistics (BLS), the primary funding agency for the Census Bureau's Current Population Survey, had access only to tabulations and public-use microdata files from the survey. However, the Census Bureau and BLS have recently concluded an interagency agreement that allows the latter to have access, for use in special analyses and methodological research, to nonpublic microdata from the Current Population Survey. (Chapter 6 provides details on this and other examples.)

On the other side of the ledger, the following are instances in which attempts to arrange for interagency sharing of data or access by nongovernment users for legitimate and often potentially important statistical uses have not succeeded:

• Gates (1988) provides several examples of user requests for Census Bureau demographic microdata that were denied because of confidentiality concerns. The topics that the users had hoped to study included a disparity in Social Security benefits between adjacent cohorts of retirees, the economic well-being of persons living outside metropolitan areas, racial segregation in the United States, and the outcomes of the Selective Service draft lotteries held in the 1970s.

• The Tax Reform Act of 1976 ended presidential authority to allow access to tax return information through executive orders (Wilson and Smith, 1983). The act specified which organizations could have access to tax return data and for what purposes. It created new barriers to access, for statistical and research purposes, to employee earnings data and other tax return information, such as taxpayers' current addresses. Among the consequences of this legislation have been (1) almost complete denial of external access to the Social Security Administration's (SSA's) Continuous Work History Sample, (2) increased difficulty in tracing study populations in epidemiologic follow-up studies, (3) increased difficulty in developing arrangements for the sharing of lists of businesses among federal statistical agencies, and (4) barriers to the linkage of survey and tax return data for studies of the income distribution of the general population or selected subgroups.

• For many years, the National Center for Health Statistics (NCHS) used a sampling frame based on address lists from the decennial census for its National Health Interview Survey (NHIS), a continuing national sample survey on health topics, for which the sample selection and field work are done by the Census Bureau. However, the confidentiality provisions required of the Census Bureau (Title 13 U.S.C.) prevented NCHS from using the sample of households derived from census addresses for other surveys in which data were to be collected for NCHS by private contractors. In the early 1980s, NCHS abandoned the use of decennial census address lists and, at a very substantial cost, switched to a sampling procedure that required independent listing of addresses in sample areas by field workers. The Census Bureau continues to select the sample and, using the new frame, collect the NHIS data for NCHS; because the survey is now conducted under the provisions of Title 15 U.S.C., the Census Bureau is able to share identifiable information with NCHS for the latter's statistical uses in other surveys and analyses. Release of data to other users is governed by NCHS confidentiality requirements, as stated in Title 42 U.S.C.

•   As a result of recent arrangements between SSA and state vital statistics offices for joint issuance of birth certificates and Social Security numbers, SSA no longer receives race-ethnic information for most births. Information on the race-ethnic status of the parents is recorded on birth certificates, but it is not being made available to SSA. While the immediate consequences are limited, in the longer run this practice will make it difficult or impossible for SSA to analyze the effects of its programs on different racial-ethnic groups and for the Census Bureau to provide reliable intercensal population estimates by race. It will also be a negative factor in considering a possible shift to greater reliance on administrative records in conducting the decennial censuses of population.

•   Although some researchers are gaining restricted access to microdata sets at agency sites through fellowship programs and similar arrangements, many other potential users of such data sets cannot be accommodated or could work more effectively at their home sites because of the reduced cost and better access to computing facilities. As noted, a few agencies (e.g., NCES) are offering off-site access under licensing agreements, but others either lack the legal authority (especially the Census Bureau) or do not choose to offer such arrangements.

•   As discussed in Chapter 3, the Office of Management and Budget recently issued a legal opinion that the Census Bureau's data subjects and providers cannot waive their entitlement to confidentiality under Title 13. The ruling caused the National Institute on Aging to abandon efforts to conduct a potentially valuable follow-up study of surviving panel members from the Longitudinal Retirement History Survey, which had been conducted in the 1970s for the SSA by the Census Bureau under the authority of Title 13.

Because of legal restrictions or other concerns about the confidentiality of the data requested, most federal statistical agencies, unlike the Census Bureau, do not systematically document cases in which they have denied data user requests or provided only part of the data requested. If they did, and the panel believes they should, we probably could have presented similar examples from several other agencies.

Factors That Affect Agency Decisions on Access

In deciding what kinds of releases of personal data can and cannot be made, federal statistical agencies must first ensure that they comply with all relevant statutory requirements and honor all pledges made to data subjects and providers. Failure in either respect could seriously compromise their ability to carry out their mission. Many agency officials believe that in addition to adhering to legal requirements and honoring commitments to respondents, they must be *perceived* by the public as doing so (see, e.g., Butz, 1985b). On the other hand, to survive, statistical agencies must be perceived by the public and especially by the executive and legislative branches of government as fulfilling their basic mission by providing information that is relevant to important social and economic policy questions and that can be used in ways that benefit society.

Federal statistical agencies must also consider the costs associated with various forms of dissemination. All forms of dissemination have some costs, but restricted access procedures tend to be more resource intensive. Even if users are willing to pay some of the costs, agencies with employment ceilings must give priority to their primary data collection, processing, and dissemination activities, as opposed to, say, undertaking special tabulations on a reimbursable basis, providing staff support and computer services for an ASA/NSF fellow, or making a site visit to a licensed user to ensure that all access conditions are being observed.

User Influence on Agency Decisions

To what extent and by what means are users able to influence agency decisions on access? Few mechanisms are available specifically for this purpose. The panels that have been established at the Census Bureau and the National Center for Education Statistics to determine how much information can be included in microdata files that are released to nonagency users do not include any representatives of nongovernment data users. The Census Bureau, we understand, has been considering an arrangement whereby outside advisors representing data subjects and data users would review decisions of its Microdata Review Panel twice a year and recommend whatever changes in release policies they consider appropriate.

Users have opportunities—at meetings of the American Statistical Association, the Association for Public Data Users, the Council of Professional Associations on Federal Statistics, and other professional organizations—to discuss dissemination procedures with other users and with agency representatives. Discussions of this kind influenced the Census Bureau's choice of statistical disclosure limitation procedures for summary tape files from the 1990 decennial census. The bureau switched from the cell-suppression procedures used in previous censuses, which had caused many problems for users, to a new procedure that did not require any cell suppression.

Another topic that is often discussed in such settings is the population size cutoff for the smallest geographic areas that can be identified for individual records in public-use microdata sets. The Census Bureau lowered its general cutoff from 250,000 to 100,000 in 1981, but some users would like to see it lowered further.

A few users who have been denied data they want have requested access to the data under the Freedom of Information Act. However, most regular users of federal data for research and statistical purposes are reluctant to take such a step because of concerns, whether justified or not, that their ongoing dealings with the statistical agencies might be prejudiced.

Another option might be to seek changes in the statutes that restrict access to data. Given the complexity of existing confidentiality statutes and the legislative process in general, it is hard to predict the outcome of attempts to change the rules for data access through changes in legislation. (The confidentiality legislation now in force and the pros and cons of seeking changes are discussed in Chapter 5.)

FINDINGS AND RECOMMENDATIONS

Data Sharing Within Government

A substantial amount of data sharing occurs between agencies for statistical and research purposes. Nevertheless, some of the laws that govern the confidentiality of statistical data prohibit or severely limit interagency sharing of data collected by some agencies. Laws that control access to administrative records, such as tax returns and earnings records, restrict their use for important statistical applications. As noted by the Council of Economic Advisers (1991), barriers to data sharing for statistical purposes have led to costly duplication of effort, inconsistencies among related data sets, and excessive burden on individuals and organizations who are asked to supply information. They have also made it difficult or impossible to develop data sets needed for policy analysis on important topics, such as trends in income distribution and the long-range consequences of occupational and other environmental exposures to suspected carcinogens.

Recommendation 4.1 Greater opportunities should be available for sharing of explicitly or potentially identifiable personal data among federal agencies for statistical and research purposes, provided the confidentiality of the records can be properly protected and the data cannot be used to make determinations about individual data subjects. Greater access should be permitted to key statistical and administrative data sets for the development of sampling frames and other statistical uses. Additional data sharing should only be undertaken in those instances in which the procedures for collecting the data comply with the panel's recommendations for informed consent or notification (see Recommendations 3.2 and 3.3).

The panel supports the proposal of the Council of Economic Advisers (1991:6) that legislation be developed that would permit "limited sharing of confidential statistical information solely for statistical purposes between statistical agencies under stringent safeguards."

Access to Data by Nongovernment Users

Because of legitimate concerns about the possibility of disclosure of individual information, statistical agencies have limited the amount of detailed data provided to nongovernment users in tabulations and public-use microdata files. This lack of detail limits the ability of users to do research that could contribute to the understanding and resolution of significant economic and social problems. Some agencies have developed mechanisms for providing access to more detailed information on a restricted basis, but existing arrangements are far from meeting all legitimate needs.

Recommendation 4.2 Federal statistical agencies should seek to improve the access of external users to statistical data, through both legislation and the development and greater use, under carefully controlled conditions, of tested administrative procedures.

We believe that this can be done without sacrificing confidentiality protection for data subjects and providers. As discussed further in Chapter 5, legislation should not pose unnecessary barriers to interagency data sharing for statistical and research purposes. It should extend legal sanctions for violations of confidentiality to include data users who are not employed by the agency that produced the data. Among the administrative procedures, the panel believes that licensing agreements that allow users to analyze data sets at their own work sites are a particularly promising solution.

It is difficult to evaluate the trade-offs between confidentiality of and access to data without better information on the numbers and types of user requests for data that are being denied for confidentiality reasons. Without such information it is hard to define the problems that inhibit data access.

Recommendation 4.3 All federal statistical agencies should establish systematic procedures for capturing information on a continuing basis about user requests for data that have been denied or only partially fulfilled. Such information should be used for periodic reviews of agency confidentiality and data access policies.

Better information on denied requests, however, will not fully reveal the extent to which important uses of data are not made because the data are not accessible. Users who already know that certain data sets are not available are unlikely to make much effort to develop plans for analyses that would require access to such data.

LEGAL AND ETHICAL RESPONSIBILITIES OF DATA USERS

BACKGROUND

Legal Responsibilities of Users

Users given restricted access to personal data are asked and sometimes required by law or written contracts to comply with various conditions relating to their use and disposition of the data. Such conditions may include the following:

- use of the data solely for purposes specified in an access agreement,
- use of the data only at specified physical locations,
- allowing access only to specified individuals,
- observing limitations on further releases of the initial data set or the products produced from it,
- observing provisions for eventual disposition of the data and outputs,
- application of statistical disclosure limitation techniques and physical security measures to protect the data from unintended disclosure, and
- execution of a written agreement between the releasing agency and the recipient and formal extension of the agreement to all individuals who will have access to the data.

In some instances users who violate conditions associated with their access to the data are subject to criminal or civil penalties.

The features of arrangements for providing restricted data access vary according to the uses that will be made of the data. Intermediate statistical uses generally involve transfer of data with identifiers from one agency to another, based on formal interagency agreements covering all or most of the conditions of use listed above. A basic principle of such agreements is that there must be full compliance with the legal confidentiality requirements of both agencies at all times. For releases of Census Bureau data, this is accomplished by having persons in the receiving agency who will have access to identifiable data take oaths as special sworn employees of the Census Bureau, which makes them subject to the same penalties as regular Census Bureau employees for any improper release or disclosure of identifiable information.

The conditions associated with restricted access for end uses and the penalties for violations are much more varied, especially when the recipients of the data are not other federal agencies. Among the more restrictive conditions are those associated with access obtained by individual researchers under a ASA/NSF fellows program that has been in operation since 1978. For research requiring access to potentially identifiable records, fellows must usually work on-site at one of the federal agencies that participate in the program, and they are subject to the same penalties as regular agency employees for violation of confidentiality requirements. In addition, ASA/NSF fellows usually have access to the data only for the term of their appointment.

Less restrictive procedures are used by the National Center

for Health Statistics (NCHS) in its release of microdata files based on the National Health Interview Survey and other surveys. Prior to release of the file, which can be used at the recipient's work site, NCHS applies standard statistical disclosure limitation techniques to the files, but it recognizes the impossibility of reducing the risk of disclosure of individually identifiable information to zero. Thus, each recipient is required to sign a document (see Figure 4.1) indicating acceptance of restrictions on how the data will be used and on re-release of the file to other organizations. Recipients must agree not to attempt to identify individual units in the file and, if a unit should be inadvertently identified, notify the NCHS and refrain from disclosing the discovered identity to others. If NCHS learns that the agreement has been violated in any way, the user responsible would probably be denied further access to NCHS microdata files.

The NCHS has recently begun to release some of its microdata files on CD-ROMs, without requiring a signed data release agreement. Whenever the CD-ROM is used, the user is presented with an on-screen notification of the data restrictions, which are essentially the same as those shown in Figure 4.1. This screen cannot be bypassed and the striking of a specific key is taken as the indication that the user has read and agreed to the restrictions and recognizes the penalties (National Center for Health Statistics, 1992a).

The National Center for Education Statistics is experimenting with a form of restricted access that occupies an intermediate position with respect to conditions of use. Under a licensing agreement, researchers in organizations and agencies are allowed to use confidential NCES data at their own sites for statistical purposes. The agreement incorporates several provisions designed to maintain the confidentiality and physical security of the data, including agreement by the users to be subject to unannounced inspections of their work site. All persons who will have access to the data must sign affidavits of nondisclosure and are subject to severe penalties for violation of their oath.

Licensing agreements are also being used by university-based research organizations to allow restricted access to detailed microdata sets based on federally funded surveys. Jabine (1993a) provides two examples, one relating to the Panel Study of Income Dynamics and the other to the National Longitudinal Survey of Youth. The conditions are similar to but somewhat less rigorous than those of the NCES licensing agreement just described. One of the organizations involved includes a hidden unique identifier in each

DATA USE AGREEMENT—The Public Health Service Act (42 U.S.C. 242m(d)) provides that the data collected by the National Center for Health Statistics (NCHS) may be used only for the purpose for which they were obtained; any effort to determine the identity of any reported cases, or to use the information for any purpose other than for health statistical reporting and analysis, would violate this statutory restriction and the conditions of the data use agreement. NCHS does all it can to assure that the identity of data subjects cannot be disclosed; all direct identifiers, as well as characteristics that might lead to identifications, are omitted from the data set. Nevertheless, it may be possible in rare instances, through complex analysis and with outside information, to ascertain from the data sets the identity of particular persons or establishments. Considerable harm could ensue if this were done.

Therefore, the undersigned gives the following assurances with respect to all NCHS data sets:
- I will not use nor permit others to use the data in these sets in any way except for statistical reporting and analysis;
- I will not release nor permit others to release the data sets or any part of them to any person who is not a member of this organization, except with the approval of NCHS;
- I will not attempt to link nor permit others to attempt to link the data set with individually identifiable records from any other NCHS or non-NCHS data set.
- If the identity of any person or establishment should be discovered inadvertently, then (a) no use will be made of this knowledge, (b) the Director of NCHS will be advised of the incident, (c) the information that would identify an individual or establishment will be safeguarded or destroyed as requested by NCHS, and (d) no one else will be informed of the discovered identity.

My signature indicates my agreement to comply with the above-stated statutorily-based requirements with the knowledge that deliberately making a false statement in any matter within the jurisdiction of any department or agency of the Federal Government violates 18 U.S.C. 1001 and is punishable by a fine of up to $10,000 or up to 5 years in prison.

Signed:_____   Date: _____

Print or Type
Name: _____
Title: _____
Organization: _____
Address:_____
City: _____   State _____   Zip: _____

Phone
Number: _____

FIGURE 4.1   Data use agreement by the National Center for Health Statistics.

of the data sets it releases so that it would be able to determine the origin of any copy found in unauthorized hands. Both of the agreements carry financial penalties for violations.

This brief account portrays some of the steps that have been taken in recent years to accommodate the needs of users for data sets that are too detailed to release without any conditions of use attached to them. The sentiment is growing among government statisticians that producers and users of statistical data should share responsibility for adherence to the confidentiality pledges given to data subjects and providers and that violations of that understanding by users, like violations by agency staff, should be subject to penalties. At present, the nature of the penalties and the legal authority for assessment of penalties on users varies, and there does not appear to be a consensus on what would be most effective.

The idea that data users should be held legally responsible for the confidentiality of the data to which they have access is not new; it was advanced by the ASA's Ad Hoc Committee on Privacy and Confidentiality in its 1977 report. The committee encouraged the dissemination of microdata sets by statistical agencies and said that they should be released without restrictions or conditions, provided all explicit identifiers had been removed and "it is virtually certain that no recipients can identify specific individuals in the file" (American Statistical Association, 1977:75). The committee recommended that data sets *not* meeting the second requirement be made accessible for research and statistical uses only if a specific set of conditions on use were agreed to in advance, in writing, by the recipient. They recommended further that the releasing agency assume responsibility for ensuring that users are observing these conditions and that "both the recipient and the agency staff are subject to enforceable penalties for failure to observe the agreed conditions of use" (p. 75).

A less detailed recommendation about release of microdata files was included in the Bellagio principles, which were developed at a 1977 international conference on Privacy, Confidentiality, and the Use of Government Microdata for Research and Statistical Purposes (see Flaherty, 1978). The Bellagio principles support widespread dissemination of data, including microdata, for research and statistical purposes, subject to confidentiality controls. A specific recommendation was that users of microdata should be required to agree in writing to protect the confidentiality of the files. No reference was made, however, to sanctions for users who violate confidentiality requirements.

Ethical Responsibilities of Users

In a search for material related to the obligations and responsibilities of external users of data, that is, users not directly associated with the agencies or organizations that developed the data sets, the panel reviewed guidelines and standards established by several professional associations and other groups. As described in Chapter 3, the American Statistical Association and the International Statistical Institute have developed detailed guidelines covering the responsibilities of agencies and organizations that collect data and, in some instances, use their own data for analyses. However, we found that those and other guidelines of professional societies had relatively little to say about the ethical obligations of those who use data provided by other organizations.

One exception comes from the Bellagio principles. Principle 14 (Flaherty, 1978:277) reads as follows:

> Professional or national organizations should have codes of ethics for their disciplines concerning the utilization of individual data for research and statistical purposes. Such ethical codes should furnish mutually agreeable standards of behavior governing relations between providers and users of governmental data.

The report of the ASA's Ad Hoc Committee on Privacy and Confidentiality recommended that "training in ethical standards and in privacy safeguards should be incorporated into the statistics and survey research curricula at colleges and universities" (American Statistical Association, 1977:76). This would be a useful step, but to reach a larger part of the ever-growing population of external users one would need to ensure the inclusion of similar training in curriculums for sociology, economics, and other disciplines whose members are likely to be secondary users of federal and other data sets.

What appears to be an unnecessarily rigorous requirement for data access is included in the ASA's *Ethical Guidelines for Statistical Practice*. A recommendation to data collectors was to

> ensure that, whenever data are transferred to other persons or organizations, this transfer conforms with the established confidentiality pledges; and require written assurance from the recipients of the data that the measures employed to protect confidentiality will be at least equal to those originally pledged (American Statistical Association, 1989:24).

Since the term "data" was not defined, this recommendation seems to suggest that *no* data, whether in aggregate or microdata form, with or without identifiers, should be transferred for any purpose without obtaining written assurance from recipients that they will protect confidentiality. We suspect this was not really the intent of the recommendation. Perhaps the committee meant the recommendation to apply only to data in explicitly or potentially identifiable form. If this supposition is correct, the committee's position and the panel's recommendations below would be consistent.

FINDINGS AND RECOMMENDATIONS

Secondary data users tend to be impatient with restrictions that inhibit access to data they want for their research, and they may occasionally attempt to circumvent such restrictions. The panel strongly urges all data users to recognize that the continued ability of federal statistical agencies to meet user needs depends on scrupulous observance of confidentiality pledges given to data subjects and data providers. Users must be willing to accept responsibility for appropriate use of data entrusted to them. They must abide by agency-imposed confidentiality requirements that include features such as licensing agreements, bonding, access only at authorized sites, and legal sanctions for failure to abide by agreed conditions of use. If they believe that restrictions on access to some kinds of data are unnecessarily stringent, the ethical course is to work through existing institutions to change the rules, not to seek ways to circumvent the rules.

Recommendation 4.4 *All* users of federal data, regardless of the formal conditions of access, should subscribe to the following principles for responsible data use:

(a) Conscientiously observe all conditions agreed to in order to obtain access to the data. Allow access to the original data set only by those permitted access under the agreed conditions of recipiency and ensure that all such persons are aware of the required conditions of use.

(b) Make no attempt to identify particular individuals or other units whose data are considered to be confidential.

(c) In the event that one or more individuals or other units are identified in the course of research, notify the organization that provided the data set, and do not inform anyone else of the discovered identities.

Recommendation 4.5 To promote knowledge of and adherence to the principles of responsible data use,

(a) Federal statistical agencies should ask all recipients of federal microdata sets to submit to the releasing agency, in writing, their agreement to observe the above principles, plus any other conditions deemed necessary for specific data sets.

(b) Professional societies and associations that have ethical codes, standards, or guidelines should incorporate these principles in them.

(c) The principles and the justifications for them should be included in academic and other training for disciplines whose members are likely to be users of federal statistical data.

Other potentially relevant types of controls are in place in universities and in some government settings, such as the National Institutes of Health. For example, investigators planning research involving human subjects must have their research proposals approved by the local institutional review board. A more recent development is the establishment of procedures for promoting scientific integrity and investigating allegations of fraud and misconduct in university-based research. Such oversight mechanisms, with suitable definition of their scope to cover research uses of federal data sets, could serve to reassure custodians of federal data that adequate controls are in place to monitor compliance with data protection rules and regulations by users in the research community. The panel applauds the development of local institutional mechanisms to promote ethical behavior in the research community and hopes that they will include fair statistical information practices and compliance with the data protection requirements of statistical agencies among their concerns.

5

Legislation

Information maintained and used solely for statistical or research purposes is not treated uniformly under existing law.

Commission on Federal Paperwork, 1977

The Commission believes that existing law and practice do not adequately protect the interests of the individual data subject.

Privacy Protection Study Commission, 1977

. . . to change or make a law involves a long, cumbersome process, while technologies and social conditions sometimes change very fast.

Edmund Rapaport, 1988

Legislation in large part determines and constrains federal policies and practices affecting data subjects and data users. For federal statistical agencies, pertinent statutes determine when response to surveys is mandatory, who can have access to individually identifiable information collected for statistical and research purposes, the conditions of access, and the penalties for unlawful uses and disclosures of the information. Statutes also determine who can have access to administrative records for statistical and research purposes.

Two kinds of legislation provide the framework for federal policies and practices with respect to confidentiality and data access: government-wide and agency-specific legislation. In the former category, the Privacy Act of 1974 (P.L. 93-579) is the most important, and the Freedom of Information Act of 1966 (P.L. 89-487) and the Paperwork Reduction Act of 1980 (P.L. 96-511) are also relevant. In the latter category, several federal statistical agencies, for example, the Bureau of the Census, the National Agricultural Statistics Service (NASS), the National Center for Education Statistics (NCES), and the National Center for Health Statistics (NCHS), are subject to laws that go beyond the government-wide statutes in specifying the confidentiality and data access policies they must follow. Among legislation that affects the statistical and research uses of administrative records, the Tax Reform Act of 1976 (P.L. 94-455) is of special significance.

In its consideration of the legislation that regulates statistical and research uses of federal records, the panel benefited greatly from the endeavors of earlier commissions and other groups and individuals who have explored these issues, including Cecil (1993), the Commission on Federal Paperwork (1977a, b), Flaherty (1979, 1989), Newton and Pullin (1990, 1991), the Office of Federal Statistical Policy and Standards (1978), and the Privacy Protection Study Commission (1977a, b, c). The problems we identified were well documented by our predecessors, and they proposed reasonable solutions to them. Most of the problems persist, however, and their significance has only increased because of the changes since the late 1970s in the environment in which federal statistical agencies operate.

The regulatory structure provided by the government-wide and agency-specific statutes mentioned above is exceedingly complex. There is little uniformity in the treatment of confidentiality and data access questions, and the ability of federal statistical agencies to protect the confidentiality of individually identifiable records is not always backed by suitable statutory provisions. Conversely, in some instances excessive restrictions on access needlessly limit opportunities to share records across agencies for statistical purposes and to make detailed microdata sets available to potential users.

This chapter has three sections. We describe the main features of the relevant government-wide information statutes in the first section and agency-specific statutes for some of the major statistical agencies in the second. In the third section we present findings and recommendations.

The general plan of this report has been to deal primarily with issues relating to data for individuals in Chapters 1 through 6 and to address issues relating to data for organizations in Chapter 7. However, this chapter constitutes an exception to the general plan because many provisions of agency-specific legislation apply equally to both kinds of data.

GENERAL REGULATION OF
FEDERAL STATISTICAL AND RESEARCH RECORDS

The Privacy Act of 1974 is the most prominent feature of a general system of regulation that also includes the conflicting demands of the Freedom of Information Act of 1966, the Paperwork Reduction Act of 1980, and the Computer Matching and Privacy Protection Act of 1988 (P.L. 100-503). The Freedom of Information Act specifies the conditions under which the disclosure of federal agency records, including statistical records, may be compelled. The Paperwork Reduction Act is intended to reduce unnecessary requirements for paperwork by federal agencies, and it permits review of data collection requests by the Office of Management and Budget (OMB). The Computer Matching and Privacy Protection Act regulates the use of computer matching of federal records subject to the Privacy Act. Matches performed for statistical purposes are specifically excluded from the coverage of the act, however.

Below we summarize two components of this general system of regulation, the Privacy Act and the Freedom of Information Act. Our focus is the impact of each act on federal data used for research and statistical purposes. The Privacy Act applies only to data on identifiable individuals; the Freedom of Information Act applies to data on individuals and organizations.

THE PRIVACY ACT

The administrative abuses of data held by the federal government that occurred in the early 1970s eroded public trust and confidence and led to the passage of the Privacy Act of 1974 and the Tax Reform Act of 1976. The Privacy Act was the first attempt by Congress to provide comprehensive protection of an individual's right to privacy by regulating the collection, management, and disclosure of personal information maintained by government agencies (Title 5 U.S.C. § 552a).[1] It specifies a general system of regulation for individually identifiable federal records.

Before the Privacy Act was passed, federal policy on data management practices encouraged data sharing among agencies in order to reduce the burden and expense of reporting. This open-access policy was restricted only when statutes provided for the confidentiality of specific sensitive record systems. In 1974, the Privacy Act reversed this general policy by recognizing the right of individuals to control dissemination of information they provided about themselves to federal agencies. The Privacy Act sought to strike a balance—to preserve individuals' interests in controlling identifiable information while recognizing the legitimate uses of that information.[2]

Briefly, the general provisions of the Privacy Act require that federal agencies (1) grant individuals access to their identifiable records maintained by the agency, (2) ensure that existing information is accurate and timely and limit the collection of unnecessary information, and (3) limit the disclosure of identifiable information to third parties. This third provision of the Privacy Act, which forbids the disclosure of any identifiable record without the prior written consent of the individual (Title 5 U.S.C. § 552a(b)), is the crux of the right of privacy provided by the act.[3] An enforceable informed consent requirement in the act could thwart the disclosure of identifiable information for purposes that the individual never considered and would not approve. As described below, however, numerous exceptions are possible.

The Privacy Act seeks to enforce its standards through civil and criminal penalties. Employees of agencies and their contractors who knowingly and willfully disclose personal information contrary to the requirements of the act may be fined up to $5,000 and the agency may be sued for "actual damages" (Title 5 U.S.C. § 552a(g)(1)(D),(i)(1)). Because of the need to show that the agency acted in a willful and intentional manner and the need to demonstrate actual damages, there have been few successful lawsuits (Flaherty, 1989:342-343; Lodge, 1984). Consequently, the effectiveness of these penalties has been questioned (see, e.g., Coles, 1991).

Twelve categories of exceptions to the consent requirement of the Privacy Act are intended to accommodate legitimate needs for individually identifiable information. For instance, an agency may, at its discretion, disclose identifiable records without prior written consent to officers and employees of the agency who have a need for the record in the performance of their duties. While such an exemption is certainly necessary, several federal organizations have interpreted the term *agency* quite broadly, thereby restricting the protections of the Privacy Act. For example, the Department of Health and Human Services has defined the entire department as a single "agency" under the terms of the Privacy Act, thereby permitting exchange of identifiable information throughout the department as long as there is a job-related need for such information (National Center for Health Statistics, 1984). Other exceptions include disclosures that are required by the Freedom of Information Act (see below); exceptions granted to the Bureau of the Census (for planning or carrying out a census, survey, or related activity under Title 13 of the U.S. Code), the General Accounting Office (to permit auditing of federal programs), and the National Archives; and disclosure in emergency circumstances involving the health and safety of an individual. The Privacy Act also permits disclosure of identifiable information without written consent to other federal agencies for authorized civil or criminal law enforcement activities and disclosure pursuant to a court order—disclosures to which individuals would most likely decline to consent.

Of special interest to data users is an exception that permits access to records that are not individually identifiable upon "written assurance that the record will be used solely as a statistical research or reporting record" (Title 5 U.S.C. § 552a(b)(5)). The Privacy Act poses no barrier to the dissemination of anonymous information; if the research objectives can be accomplished with nonidentifiable data, rendering the data anonymous satisfies the standards of the Privacy Act and the information can be disseminated. In fact, as Cecil (1993) notes in a paper prepared for the panel, this exemption offers very little, because a record that is not individually identifiable is not a "record" within the definition of the Privacy Act (see note 3) and therefore is not subject to the restrictions on disclosure imposed by the act.

Obtaining data from individually identifiable federal records for statistical purposes can be difficult for data users, even those in other federal statistical agencies. The restrictions of the Privacy Act can bar the disclosure of identifiable records unless the disclosure is brought within one of the exemptions. In an ideal situation, data collectors would be able to anticipate such disclosure needs and obtain the informed consent of data subjects at the time the information is gathered. When the need for statistical or research access to agency records was not anticipated or when the initial consent becomes invalid, a data collector may have to recontact the data subjects to obtain proper consent. Recontacting data subjects who participated in an earlier statistical or research study imposes special difficulties, however. For example, some target populations are highly mobile, and thus addresses and telephone numbers that were obtained at the time the individuals were originally contacted may be outdated. Recontacting such data subjects is also likely to be expensive and subject to self-selection biases.

One of the Privacy Act exemptions permits disclosure of an

identifiable record for a "routine use," that is, "for a purpose that is compatible with the purpose for which it was collected" (Title 5 U.S.C. § 552a(a)(7)). An agency may choose to designate statistical analysis as a routine use of all or a selected portion of its record systems (see note 3). This enables the agency to give outside data users access to data from identifiable records for statistical purposes without first gaining the consent of the data subjects to whom the records pertain. Instead of obtaining data subjects' consent prior to disclosure for such a "routine use," the agency must only publish a notice of the anticipated routine uses of the record in the *Federal Register* and accept comments from the public for a period of 30 days (Title 5 U.S.C. § 552a(e)(4)(D),(e)(11)). Such routine uses must also be explained to data subjects when similar information is gathered in the future.

A great many agency notices in the *Federal Register* allow disclosure for statistical and research purposes as a routine use. For instance, the Department of Health and Human Services has been particularly thorough in identifying record systems that have research potential and publishing notices permitting research as a routine use (O'Neill and Fanning, 1976:171-188). One version of the department's routine-use notice requires an assessment of the risks and potential benefits of the research and requires the data user to sign an agreement to protect the records from subsequent disclosure. This is one instance in which the discretion delegated to agencies by the Privacy Act has been used to fashion a specific set of standards to permit data users from outside the agency to analyze data contained in individually identifiable records for statistical purposes while maintaining safeguards appropriate to the information. However, the need to rely on the routine-use exemption to overcome the failure of the statute to provide for statistical and research access to identifiable records is an awkward solution to the problem. Without a statutory policy concerning access to federal records for statistical and research purposes, individual agencies are free to develop regulations that may either be too restrictive or fail to offer adequate protection to the identifiable information provided by data subjects.

It is important to note that the Privacy Act, which applies indiscriminately to statistical and administrative records, offers little protection from improper disclosure of statistical records for nonresearch purposes. An agency could conceivably use the routine-use exemption to the act to diminish the protection for such records by designating audit and enforcement as routine uses after the data are gathered. Also, the Privacy Act places no obligation on outside data users to maintain the confidentiality of the records or limit subsequent disclosure; once the records are released to a data user who is not under the jurisdiction of the act there is no assurance that the data subject's rights will be protected. The restrictions of the Privacy Act extend to contractors only when "an agency provides by a contract for the operation by or on behalf of the agency of a system of records to accomplish an agency function" (Title 5 U.S.C. § 552a(m)).

In summary, the Privacy Act's failure to distinguish statistical and research purposes from administrative purposes in restricting access to individually identifiable records can pose a major obstacle for data users who want to analyze such information for statistical or research purposes. Regulation of administrative records is based on the awareness that the records may be used to make decisions regarding individuals, such as the award or termination of benefits. Such a system of regulation does not recognize dissimilar analytic uses of data for statistical or research purposes in which the information is not used to make decisions regarding individual data subjects. Data users have become adept at framing their statistical or research needs, and the associated data protections, within the standards developed for administrative records. In some instances, it may be possible to anticipate the statistical or research purposes and obtain consent for disclosure of identifiable data at the time they are collected. Otherwise, the data user must structure a request for statistical or research use of individually identifiable data to fit within one of the exceptions to the consent requirement of the Privacy Act, such as the routine-use exception.

FREEDOM OF INFORMATION ACT

The Freedom of Information Act of 1966 (Title 5 U.S.C. § 552) also regulates the disclosure of research and statistical records. The act permits public access to records maintained by federal agencies unless the request for access falls within one of nine specific exemptions. Statistical records maintained by federal agencies, even those developed by private parties, are subject to disclosure under the act if not otherwise exempt. For example, records concerning differences in breast-fed and formula-fed infants that were collected by a group of nonprofit, church-related organizations and deposited with a federal agency for statistical analysis were ordered disclosed when producers of infant formula requested copies of the data from the agency under the act (see *St. Paul's*

Benevolent Educational and Missionary Institute v. U.S., 506 F. Supp. 822 (N. D. Ga. 1980)). If the research records are not maintained by the federal agency, the act does not compel disclosure, even if the agency funded the research and relies on the results in setting public policy. For example, the Supreme Court declined to order the disclosure of research records developed under an extended research grant awarded to a group of private physicians and scientists studying the effectiveness of treatments of diabetes. Even though the Food and Drug Administration relied on the controversial findings of the study to restrict the labeling and use of certain drug treatments and refused to make the data available for independent reanalysis, the Court determined that the act does not reach records maintained by grantees (see *Forsham v. Harris*, 445 U.S. 169 (1980)).

Two exemptions to the general disclosure mandate of the Freedom of Information Act are of concern to researchers. First, an exemption under the act may be appropriate for identifiable records if such records will yield sensitive information about individual research participants. Exemption 6 of the act restricts disclosure of "personnel and medical and similar files the disclosure of which would constitute a clearly unwarranted invasion of personal privacy" (Title 5 U.S.C. § 552(b)(6)). This exemption is intended to protect sensitive information identifiable to an individual, including research and statistical information, from unwarranted disclosure. If the court determines that disclosure of identifiable agency records "can reasonably be expected to invade [a] citizen's privacy," disclosure will not be ordered (see *D.O.J. v. Reporters Committee for Freedom of the Press*, 489 U.S. 749 (1989); *New York Times Co. v. N.A.S.A.*, 920 F.2d 1002 (D.C. Cir. 1990) (en banc)). Although there have been a few cases in which identifiable research records have been the object of a request, evolving standards of protection and different standards of protection across federal circuits result in considerable uncertainty regarding the degree of protection under this exemption.[4] Nonetheless, the pro-privacy provisions appear to be a strong protection.

Second, research information with commercial or financial value may be withheld under exemption 4 of the Freedom of Information Act, which extends protection to "trade secrets and to information which is commercial or financial, obtained from a person, and privileged or confidential" (Title 5 U.S.C. § 552(b)(4)). Such records need not be individually identifiable and may include records of organizations. This exemption, however, has been narrowly construed, which has made it difficult for most research and statistical records to qualify. To qualify for the exemption, the research records must be of commercial or financial value that will be diminished by disclosure. Further, the research records must qualify as "privileged or confidential." A promise of confidentiality when the research data were collected will be given some weight in determining if this standard is met, but such a promise alone will not be sufficient to protect the data. Exemption 4 has been granted only when there has been a further demonstration that disclosure of information would result in competitive harm to a commercial enterprise (see *Public Citizen Health Research Group v. Food and Drug Administration*, 539 F. Supp. 1320 (D. D. C. 1982)) or that release of such information is likely to "impair the government's ability to obtain necessary information in the future" (see *National Parks Conservation Association v. Morton*, 498 F.2d 765, 770 (D.C. Cir. 1974)). These standards were recently interpreted to recognize a greater interest in maintaining the confidentiality of information that is provided the government on a voluntary basis if it is of a kind that the provider would not customarily release to the public (*Critical Mass Energy Project v. N.R.C.*, 1992 U.S. App. Lexis 19336 (D.C. Cir., 1992), (en banc)). This categorical exemption for information supplied to the government on a voluntary basis is intended to ensure its continued availability.

AGENCY-SPECIFIC LEGISLATION

As with the government-wide statutes, agency-specific legislation is not uniform in specifying the conditions of access to individually identifiable data for statistical and research purposes and the requirements for maintaining the confidentiality of such data. To implement agency-specific legislative provisions, federal statistical agencies have developed administrative policies, practices, and procedures, some of which we cover in this section. We provide a more thorough discussion of the administrative mechanisms used by the federal statistical agencies in Chapter 6.

In this section, we first summarize the agency-specific legislation that governs three major federal statistical agencies (Bureau of the Census, National Center for Education Statistics, and National Center for Health Statistics). We also discuss the impact on federal statistical activities of the Tax Reform Act of 1976, the legislation that governs access to the data collected by the Internal Revenue Service (IRS). Our presentation is not meant to be an exhaustive discussion of agency-specific legislation; other federal statistical agencies, such as the Bureau of Justice Statistics (BJS) and the National Agricultural Statistics Service, have statutes that protect the confidentiality of their data, and we refer to selected provisions of those statutes in presenting our findings and recommendations.

Next, we address issues raised by the fact that federal statistical agencies without adequate statutory protection for the confidentiality of their data must rely on administrative policies that have no statutory basis. We use the Bureau of Labor Statistics (BLS) and the Energy Information Administration (EIA) to illustrate the difficulties that agencies have encountered and the strategies they have employed when protection of data in their custody is not addressed by statute. We conclude this section with a discussion of the legislation for two new statistical agencies, one established by statute in the Department of Transportation in 1991 and another that has been proposed for environmental statistics.

Most of the background material for this section was provided by the agencies discussed in response to the panel's request for information about their current statutory requirements, policies, and practices. We appreciate the agencies' willingness to help by providing this material.

BUREAU OF THE CENSUS

In contrast to the lax protection of statistical records under the Privacy Act of 1974, the statutory protection of statistical information collected by the Census Bureau under Title 13 of the U.S. Code is extremely rigorous. It allows few opportunities for those outside the agency to use individually identifiable records for statistical purposes. In recent years the Census Bureau has made some effort to develop standards and procedures that would permit greater access to information that it maintains (Gates, 1988). But the statutory standards, and interpretation of those standards by the Supreme Court, still pose a formidable barrier to the release of data outside the Census Bureau in a form that permits the range of statistical analyses desired by sophisticated data users.

The Census Bureau is governed by legislation that permits the bureau to (1) use census information only for statistical purposes (with one limited exception, an agreement with the National Archives, which is discussed in Chapter 6), (2) publish data only in a way that prevents the identification of individuals, and (3) prohibit anyone from examining information that identifies an individual unless they are Census Bureau employees sworn to uphold the confidentiality provisions of Title 13 (U.S.C. § 9(a)). In addition, this statute allows the Census Bureau to employ temporary staff to do work authorized by Title 13 provided they are sworn to uphold the confidentiality provisions specified in the legislation (see Title 13 U.S.C. § 23). Such "special sworn employees" may be employed in another government agency. Violation of Title 13 standards by employees or special sworn employees carries a penalty of a fine of $5,000 or five years in prison, or both (Title 13 U.S.C. § 214). The statute also permits the Census Bureau to furnish "tabulations and other statistical materials which do not disclose the information reported by, or on behalf of, any particular respondent" and to "make special statistical compilations and surveys, for . . . [parties outside the Census Bureau] upon the payment of the actual or estimated cost of such work" (Title 13 U.S.C. § 8(b)).

The statutory standards governing the Census Bureau are among the few that have the benefit of an interpretation by the Supreme Court. In *Baldrige v. Shapiro* (455 U.S. 345 (1982)) the Court considered the extent to which master address lists, compiled as part of the decennial census, can be made available outside the Census Bureau. Several cities challenged the 1980 census count of their populations, contending that the census had erroneously counted occupied dwellings as vacant, and they sought to compel disclosure of a portion of the address lists used by the Census Bureau in conducting its count in their respective jurisdictions. Although the case involved access to this information for purposes other than research, in ruling on the case the Court also offered an interpretation of Title 13 that clarifies the limits of the discretion of the Census Bureau to release statistical information that is individually identifiable.

The district court had ordered the Census Bureau to make the address register available, reasoning that the confidentiality limitation is "solely to require that census material be used in furtherance of the Bureau's statistical mission and to ensure against disclosure of any particular individual's response." The Supreme Court reversed this decision, interpreting the standards of Title 13 to suggest that the release of *any* microdata, even microdata not identifiable to an individual, is inconsistent with the standards of Title 13. The Court cited the constitutional purpose of the census in apportioning representation among the states and the importance of public cooperation in obtaining an accurate census. According to the Court, the confidentiality protections of

Title 13 are intended to encourage public cooperation by explicitly providing for the nondisclosure of certain census data, and "[n]o discretion is provided to the Census Bureau on whether or not to disclose the information referred to in §§ 8(b) and 9(a)" [of Title 13] (*Baldrige v. Shapiro*, 455 U.S. 355 (1982)).

The cities that sought the master address lists had argued that the confidentiality protections were intended to prohibit disclosure of the identities of individuals who provided census data. The Court, however, rejected the contention that the confidentiality provisions protect raw data only if the individual respondent can be identified, thereby raising questions regarding the authority of the Census Bureau to release individual census data even when the identification of individuals is not possible:

> [Various parties] vigorously argue that Sections 8(b) and 9(a) of the Census Act are designed to prohibit disclosure of the identities of individuals who provide raw census data; for this reason, they argue, the confidentiality provisions protect raw data only if the individual respondent can be identified. The unambiguous language of the confidentiality provisions, as well as the legislative history of the Act, however, indicates that Congress plainly contemplated that raw data reported by or on behalf of individuals was to be held confidential and not available for disclosure (*Baldrige v. Shapiro*, 455 U.S. 355 (1982)).

The Census Bureau has not interpreted the Title 13 standards as broadly as this language would permit and has continued to release unidentifiable microdata for statistical purposes. The Court's opinion, while speaking of "data" and "statistical uses," is in fact about the authority of states and municipalities to audit the findings of the Census Bureau, a purpose that was specifically precluded when the statute was passed. Further, access to address lists would imply access to any individuals living at the addresses, so characterization of the research data as "unidentified" seems misplaced. Nevertheless, the language of the Supreme Court suggests that the Census Bureau is limited in its discretion to release data to persons who are not sworn to uphold the confidentiality provisions of Title 13.

The restrictions discussed above extend to all data collections undertaken under the authority of Title 13. The Census Bureau also may undertake survey research under alternative authority, such as Title 15, that allows it to conduct specific studies for other organizations, thereby avoiding the restrictions of Title 13 on release of identifiable information. Growing demand for identifiable information that can be used in conducting follow-up surveys or linked with administrative data has resulted in the Census Bureau's conducting under Title 15 authority an increasing number of reimbursable surveys sponsored by other agencies. There are two primary differences in the way the Census Bureau conducts such surveys. First, the bureau cannot use the decennial census as a sampling frame if identifiable microdata from the survey are to be shared with the sponsoring agency. Second, when seeking the consent of respondents to participate in a Title 15 survey, the bureau makes clear that it is collecting the information as an agent of the sponsoring agency and that the sponsor, not the Census Bureau, will be responsible for maintaining the confidentiality of the information.

NATIONAL CENTER FOR EDUCATION STATISTICS

Statistical data collected by the National Center for Education Statistics is governed by legislation that follows closely the pattern of protection for data gathered by the Census Bureau. In April 1988, Public Law 100-297, the Augustus F. Hawkins-Robert T. Stafford Elementary and Secondary School Improvement Amendments of the General Education Provisions Act (GEPA), was passed. The Hawkins-Stafford amendments (U.S.C. § 1221e-1) established a rigorous system of protection of educational statistical data collected and maintained by NCES. The system (1) prohibits the use of "individually identifiable information" for purposes other than the statistical purposes for which it was supplied, (2) prohibits the publication of information that will permit the identification of an individual, (3) permits examination of individually identifiable reports only by persons authorized by the NCES commissioner, and (4) limits access to individually identifiable data to those who take an oath not to disclose such data. The amendments allow NCES to use temporary employees to analyze individually identifiable data for statistical purposes if such persons are sworn to observe the limitations described above.

Information collected as part of the National Assessment of Educational Progress (NAEP), one of the ongoing studies of NCES, is subject to a separate confidentiality requirement under the Hawkins-Stafford amendments. To maintain the confidentiality of NAEP records, the amendments state that

> the Commissioner shall ensure that all personally identifiable information about students, their educational performance, and their families and that *information with respect to individual schools* remain confidential, in accordance with section 552a of

title 5, United States Code (emphasis added) (P.L. 100-297,
§ 3403(a)(i)(4)(B)(i)).

This section of the amendments cites the Privacy Act of 1974 as
the standard for maintaining confidentiality of the information,
even though the Privacy Act applies only to individuals, not to
institutions and organizations such as schools (see Newton and
Pullin, 1990). The provision requiring that school information
remain confidential poses particular difficulty for those who wish
to use NAEP data to study the effects of programs in schools with
certain characteristics.

In 1990 the statutory framework governing NCES records was
further confused by the passage of amendments to GEPA that
specifically exempted from the protections of the Hawkins-Stafford
amendments data gathered as part of several longitudinal studies
of individuals at the postsecondary level and financial aid surveys
(see § 252 of the Excellence in Mathematics, Science and Engineering Act of 1990, P.L. 101-589). It appears that these data are
governed now by the comparatively lax protections of the Privacy
Act. The resulting exceptions to the general provisions of the
Hawkins-Stafford amendments provide a fragmented pattern of
regulation that is likely to leave data subjects and providers uncertain of the extent to which their information will remain confidential.

Inadvertent disclosure is an especially difficult problem. The
educational research community has developed a number of data
sets with identifiable information that are beyond the reach of
this legislation, some of which include information gathered by
NCES prior to the Hawkins-Stafford amendments. The possibility of matching survey data to existing records, thereby inadvertently disclosing information that can be associated with specific
data subjects, is much greater for educational records than for
individual Census Bureau records. Thus, when the individual is
the unit of analysis and similar surveys exist that would permit
the linking of information, an NCES policy statement (National
Center for Education Statistics, 1989) directs NCES staff to examine common variables and distributions of responses to minimize
the risk of disclosure. Staff of NCES also review nonfederal data
files to ensure that such files will not present an opportunity for a
match with NCES data that would yield individually identifiable
information. Other information that NCES staff must take into
consideration before releasing a public-use data file is set forth in

"Standard for Maintaining Confidentiality" (see Standard IV-01-92 in National Center for Education Statistics, 1992:39-41).

Files in which data on individuals are nested within assessments of institutions and organizations (e.g., school, district, state) require additional scrutiny. Many educational research programs rely on such nested research designs to assess the effectiveness of classroom- and school-based programs. If data on individual students or teachers are associated with specific schools, the released data cannot include schools that can be uniquely identified. According to the policy statement,

> the assumption is made that school and school district administrators will know which students or teachers were interviewed in the survey, regardless of any procedures used to disguise the identity of these individuals or attempts to keep this information from the administrators. Therefore, if a school or district can be identified in a file, that file cannot be linked to student or teacher records (National Center for Education Statistics, 1989:5).

While the legislation governing release of NCES statistical information is similar to the restrictive legislation governing the Census Bureau, NCES has developed policies that permit greater access to statistical data. For example, the center has disseminated microdata in encrypted CD-ROM format and developed licensing agreements that allow researchers to use data at their own work sites (see Chapter 6 for a discussion of such techniques). The center has more freedom to develop such policies because it is free of the restrictive statutory regulations governing the Census Bureau. But, in other ways its task is even more difficult. Its system of nested surveys of individuals and organizations complicates the protection of schools, teachers, and students. Publicly available information on individual schools and districts, in addition to a network of sophisticated educational researchers who are familiar with existing data sets, increases the opportunity for inadvertent disclosure beyond that faced by the Census Bureau. These differences result in considerable tension when legislative protection patterned after the Census Bureau is extended to NCES.

NATIONAL CENTER FOR HEALTH STATISTICS

Statutes protecting health records collected, maintained, and disseminated by the National Center for Health Statistics offer another example of how the inadequate protection provided by the Privacy Act can be supplemented through specific statutory authority. Section 308(d) of the Public Health Service Act (P.L. 85-58) restricts use of data obtained by NCHS to the purposes for which they were originally obtained (42 U.S.C. § 242m(d)). When NCHS requests information, it informs the person or organization supplying the data of the general anticipated uses, which are usually limited to statistical research and reporting, and subsequent uses of the information are then so limited. Section 308(d) further indicates that such information may not be disclosed outside the agency in identifiable form without the advance, explicit consent of the person or establishment to which they relate.

A number of manuals, policy statements, and publications expand on these requirements (see Mugge, 1984; National Center for Health Statistics, 1978, 1984). For instance, the *NCHS Staff Manual on Confidentiality* (National Center for Health Statistics, 1984) provides a thorough discussion of how the requirements are to be interpreted.[5] The most noteworthy aspect of NCHS's policy is the explicit recognition that there is some risk of disclosure of individually identifiable information with the release of published tables and public-use data files and that such risks must be balanced against the importance of sharing statistical information. This is one of the very few instances in which explicit recognition of this fact appears in an official agency policy statement.

Showing the center's awareness of the difficulty in ensuring confidentiality of data when publishing tables with small cell sizes, the manual presents guidance for avoiding inadvertent disclosure. It states that "mitigating circumstances in a given situation which may make it acceptable to publish data that, strictly speaking, could result in 'disclosures'" would justify a "special exception" to the guidelines (p. 17). For example, if data are based on a sample that is a small fraction of the universe, it might be assumed that disclosure will not occur through published tables. Errors in the data or incomplete reporting may also reduce the likelihood of disclosures taking place to a point that would justify permitting publication of otherwise revealing tables. Similarly, in discussing the standards for the development of public-use microdata files, the manual recognizes that

> the only absolutely sure way to avoid disclosure through microdata tapes is to refrain completely from releasing any microdata tapes, but this would deprive the Nation of a great deal of very important health research. Therefore, the Center must make a determination as to when the public's need is sufficiently great to justify the risk of disclosure. It is the Center's policy to release

microdata tapes for purposes of statistical research only when the risk of disclosure is judged to be extremely low (p. 18).

In assessing the acceptability of the risk, NCHS considers the extent to which the data involve a sample of the universe of relevant individuals or establishments, the extent and availability of outside information necessary to identify an individual or establishment, the expense of undertaking such an effort, and the sensitivity of the information provided.

According to the NCHS manual, one exception to the above standards that did not require a "special exception" involved the publication of vital statistics. For example, a table could be published that indicated that within a specific county during a specific period there was one infant death or two deaths from rabies. Such exceptions were permitted because of "a longstanding tradition in the field of vital statistics not to suppress small frequency cells in the tabulation and presentation of data" and because such publication "rarely, if ever, reveals any information about individuals that is not known socially" (p. 17). However, in 1989 NCHS began to reexamine its policy on the release of vital statistics data because the publication of statistical tables by county or the release of detailed public-use microdata files might inadvertently reveal a cause of death, such as acquired immune deficiency syndrome (AIDS), that was not "socially known" in the community. The center and the states were concerned about controlling inadvertent disclosure in the public-use microdata files because the center had been releasing county-level data in its vital statistics.

The center obtains its vital statistics data from state health departments under a contractual arrangement that assures that no information will be released that could permit the identification of a specific individual or institution. However, two court cases (a 1987 case involving the *Atlanta Constitutional Journal* and the State Health Department of Georgia, and another in 1991 involving the American Civil Liberties Union and the State of Illinois) raised the concern of the states, as well as NCHS, that the center was releasing data in public-use microdata files that might result in the inadvertent disclosure of individuals.[6] As part of its policy reexamination, NCHS held a special session at the July 1991 Public Health Conference on Records and Statistics to discuss the issues and a variety of alternative solutions with its data users.

As a result of its reexamination, NCHS changed its policy beginning with the release of the 1989 natality and mortality public-use microdata files, which were released in the fall of 1992 (see National Center for Health Statistics, 1992b). According to this new policy, NCHS will release public-use microdata files in three versions:

1. *Single-year format*: This format will be for a single calendar year and include data for cities, counties, and metropolitan areas with a population of 100,000 or more. Certain dates (date of the event and date of birth of mother, father, and/or decedent) will be excluded from the file. This file will be distributed by the National Technical Information Service (NTIS).

2. *Multiyear format*: This second format will contain data for a three-year period (e.g., 1987-1989) for all counties and metropolitan areas and for cities with a population of 50,000 or more. Again, certain dates (date and year of the event as well as date of birth of mother, father, and/or decedent) will be excluded from the file. This file will also be distributed by NTIS.

3. *Special formats*: NCHS will consider releasing vital statistics microdata files to data users whose needs cannot be met by either the single-year or multiyear format. Such users must contact NCHS and explain their additional data needs. Users who obtain specially formatted data files from NCHS will be required to sign a more extensive agreement on data use than the one that NCHS typically requires, an agreement that provides additional guidelines on avoiding inadvertent disclosure (see Figure 4.1 and the discussion of NCHS's data use agreement in Chapter 4).

NCHS will reevaluate its new policy on the release of vital statistics data after it has been in effect for one year.

The NCHS standards address in a straightforward manner the difficult issue of deductive disclosure of information. Any disclosure is viewed as entailing some degree of risk, and NCHS is frank in acknowledging this in balancing the degree of risk against the benefit to the public that is likely to arise from the research. The NCHS has a number of advantages that may permit it the latitude to develop such policies. First, it is an agency that recognizes its primary role as being research, thereby avoiding the difficulties that arise when trying to design a system for handling records that are used for administrative purposes as well. Further, it collects much of its own information and does not require the cooperation of agencies that may follow more restrictive practices. (The NCHS vital statistics program is an exception to this point; this program must rely on statistical information reported by state registrars and is subject to varying state restrictions. Since

NCHS began relying on information the Census Bureau collects for it under the authority of Title 15, rather than Title 13, it has avoided the more onerous restrictions regarding disclosure of information by the Census Bureau.) Finally, NCHS maintains a staff of skilled researchers, which enables it to conduct some of the more sensitive analyses within the agency. Nevertheless, its data collection and dissemination activities provide an opportunity to examine the consequences of having policies that recognize the possibility of an inadvertent disclosure of identifiable information and attempt to minimize that risk while releasing information that permits statistical research and reporting goals to be accomplished.

INTERNAL REVENUE SERVICE

Income information is perceived by many as among the most sensitive and most useful information collected by the federal government. Studies based on levels and changes in levels of reported income address a wide range of economic issues. The staff of the Statistics of Income Division, IRS, uses data from income tax returns and other sources to prepare publications and studies on a wide range of topics (see Wilson and Smith, 1983). When the success of such studies requires the use of individually identifiable information from other agencies, such data can sometimes be made available within the standards of the Privacy Act. However, the policy of the Census Bureau is that identifiable census records cannot be transferred to the IRS for statistical purposes even if the IRS employees who will have access to the records are special sworn employees of the Census Bureau.[7]

Difficulties also arise when outside agencies require income information for the conduct of studies. Although no abuses of income information released for statistical purposes are known to have occurred, the Tax Reform Act of 1976 sharply limited outside access to IRS income information for statistical purposes. The passage of this act and the subsequent restrictions on existing research practices illustrate how reforms directed at abuses of administrative records may inadvertently hamper statistical and research uses of such records.

Prior to 1976 a number of executive orders permitted outside agencies to use IRS income information if they followed certain standards in maintaining the confidentiality of the information. However, in 1976 the Congress, partly in response to the publicized disclosure of income tax information to the White House, passed the Tax Reform Act of 1976 (see Wilson and Smith, 1983; U.S. Code Congressional and Administrative News, 1976:2897-4284, P.L. 94-455). This act denied tax return information to the President and other executive agencies (§ 6103(j) of the Internal Revenue Code) and expanded the definition of tax return information to include a broader range of Social Security earnings reports. As a consequence, access to income information for statistical and research purposes was sharply restricted.

The Internal Revenue Code, as amended by the Tax Reform Act of 1976, provides that tax returns and "return information" are confidential and not to be disclosed except as authorized by law (§ 6103(a)). "Return information" is extensively defined to include virtually every aspect of information filed with the IRS, including a taxpayer's identity and address and the fact that a return was filed (§ 6103(b)(2)). As a result, most releases of filing information to other federal agencies for purposes of statistical research must be in anonymous form. Exceptions are made for specified statistical and research uses by other units of the Treasury Department, the Census Bureau, the Bureau of Economic Analysis, and by a subsequent amendment (P.L. 95-210), the National Institute for Occupational Safety and Health (§ 6103(j) and § 6103(m)(3)). The IRS may undertake special statistical studies at the request of another agency, even merging IRS records with records from the other agencies (§ 6108). Such opportunities, however, may be limited by the resources and interests of the IRS, as well as the need of the requesting agencies for access to detailed and potentially identifiable data used in such studies.

A serious loss of important statistical products, as well as significant increased costs, was imposed on the federal statistical system as a consequence of the Tax Reform Act. For example, external uses of the Social Security Administration's Continuous Work History Sample were substantially curtailed, as was access to IRS name and address information for medical follow-up and epidemiologic studies (see Chapter 6 for details). And, as a result of the act, federal statistical agencies faced a new obstacle in their efforts to promote sharing of business lists (see Chapter 7).

Agencies Lacking Explicit Statutory Protection of Establishment Data

With few exceptions, the statutory protection of information on establishments and other organizations that is collected for statistical purposes is far weaker than the statutory protection of personal data. Although we address the uses of statistical data on organizations in Chapter 7, we mention them here to provide a contrast with the regulatory schemes for personal records. Several agencies that collect statistical information primarily from establishments and organizations do not have statutes that explicitly protect the confidentiality of such information.

The experience of the Energy Information Administration in attempting to maintain the confidentiality of statistical information collected from oil companies illustrates the problem. At the time the data were gathered, the EIA assured the companies involved that the information would be used only for statistical reporting purposes. The EIA relied on its statutory authority to administer this statistical program to develop regulations that were intended to guard against administrative uses of such information (see the Department of Energy policy statement contained in the *Federal Register*, 45(177):59812-59816). However, conflicting statutory authority requires the disclosure of such information to other federal agencies for official use upon request. Specifically, Title 15 U.S.C. § 771(f) states that "information [referred to in section 1905 of Title 18] shall be disclosed by . . . the [secretary of energy], in a manner designed to preserve its confidentiality — (1) to other Federal Government departments, agencies, and officials for official use upon request. . . ."

When the Antitrust Division of the Department of Justice sought identifiable information to aid in two investigations of price gouging, the EIA resisted and the matter was referred to the Office of Legal Counsel in the Department of Justice, which ruled that EIA must produce the information requested by the Antitrust Division. Protracted negotiations regarding the precise nature of the data to be released ensued; the Justice Department eventually closed the cases without having received any proprietary data. The Justice Department, however, continues to hold that it is legally entitled to such data (U.S. General Accounting Office, 1993; see Chapter 7 for additional detail).

The Bureau of Labor Statistics also collects extensive statistical information on establishments and other organizations, much of which is reported voluntarily, without specific statutory protection to preserve the confidentiality of identifiable information. However, BLS has been more successful than EIA in fashioning a protective shield for such information. Based on a combination of regulations and lower court decisions, BLS has developed policies that enable it to honor the pledges of confidentiality that are given when it collects establishment data.

The basic philosophy of BLS is to protect the confidentiality of the data that it collects. This fundamental position is articulated in a series of policy directives that set forth procedures for safeguarding sensitive BLS information. The secretary of labor has authorized the commissioner of BLS to develop policies to govern the disclosure of all data collected by BLS (U.S. Department of Labor, 1972). These policies are intended to ensure that "data collected or maintained by, or under the auspices of, the Bureau under a pledge of confidentiality shall be treated in a manner that will assure that individually identifiable data will be accessible only to authorized persons and will be used only for statistical purposes or for other purposes made known in advance to the respondent" (Bureau of Labor Statistics, 1980:6).

This pattern of regulation was upheld by a federal district court when employment data from unemployment insurance (UI) reports that would identify individual establishments were sought under the Freedom of Information Act (see *Hufstead v. Norwood*, 529 F. Supp. 323 (S. D. Fla. 1981)). The reports had been voluntarily supplied to BLS by a state employment security agency, which was required by state law to keep such reports confidential, and BLS had pledged to keep the reports confidential. The court refused to order disclosure, finding the information to be exempt from the disclosure provisions of the Freedom of Information Act because such disclosure "would impair the Bureau of Labor Statistics' ability to collect that data in the future." More specifically, the court found that BLS met the test for an exemption from disclosure under exemption 4 of the Freedom of Information Act (Title 5 U.S.C. § 552(b)(4)), established in *National Parks and Conservation Ass'n v. Morton*, 498 F.2d 765, 767 (D. C. Cir. 1974), 529 F. Supp. at 326. In addition, because each state has laws and regulations protecting the confidentiality of its UI data, BLS is given extra protection. That is, if UI data are requested, BLS cannot release the data without conforming to the states' laws and regulations.

While BLS has been successful in honoring pledges of confidentiality without formal statutory protection, it has had relatively few legal tests of its pledge. Will promises of confidentiality be honored if the secretary of labor should revoke the delegation of authority to BLS's commissioner and begin to use this information in enforcement proceedings, or share some of it with the Department of Justice for investigatory purposes? Without clear statutory protection, the adequacy of the protection for confidential information on business establishments may be constrained by the policies of successive administrative officials and varying interpretations of courts of different jurisdiction.

The Bureau of Labor Statistics has, on occasion, sought statutory protection for the confidential statistical information that it collects. For instance, a letter from Secretary of Labor Elizabeth Dole to the Hon. Thomas Foley, Speaker of the House of Representatives, dated June 21, 1990, describes a proposed Labor Statistics Confidentiality Act. As of early 1993, however, no action had been taken on such legislation.

NEW STATISTICAL AGENCIES

Legislation passed late in 1991 established a new statistical agency, the Bureau of Transportation Statistics, in the Department of Transportation. Also in 1991, legislation was considered, but not passed, that would have created a Department of the Environment, with a Bureau of Environmental Statistics as one of its components. The roles of the two agencies, one already authorized and the other being considered, differ somewhat from the common conception of what a federal statistical agency does. Instead of their collecting data on relevant topics directly from persons or organizations, it is apparently intended that each of the two agencies will accomplish its mission primarily by compiling, analyzing, and publishing data collected by other components of its parent department.

The Bureau of Transportation Statistics was created by Section 6006 of the Intermodal Surface Transportation Efficiency Act of 1991 (P.L. 102-240). The only provision of the act that relates to confidentiality and data access is the following short paragraph:

> (e) PROHIBITION ON CERTAIN DISCLOSURES.—Information compiled by the Bureau shall not be disclosed publicly in a manner that would reveal the personal identity of any individual, consistent with the Privacy Act of 1974 (5 U.S.C. 552a), or to reveal trade secrets or allow commercial or financial information provided by any person to be identified with such person (§ 111).

The above provision mentions only public disclosure. It does not establish a clear basis for full functional separation of data that might be received by the Bureau of Transportation Statistics from other statistical agencies or from administrative sources and used by it for statistical and research purposes. The Conference Report on the legislation goes somewhat further in this direction, stating that the conferees intend that the Director establish such procedures as necessary to ensure that all Bureau data are collected and stored in such a way that they cannot be used to prosecute individuals or reveal business information that could harm persons or corporations (102nd Cong. lst session, Conference Report 102-404:461-462).

At this time, it is difficult to predict what kinds of problems the Bureau of Transportation Statistics is likely to have in managing its confidentiality and data access functions given this less-than-comprehensive statutory basis.[8]

The key portion of the confidentiality provision drafted for the proposed Bureau of Environmental Statistics is a statement almost identical to the one cited above from the transportation legislation. One is left with the overall impression that in drafting confidentiality legislation for new statistical agencies the drafters have given relatively little attention to what can be learned from experience. What statutory provisions are needed to maintain the principle of functional separation of administrative and statistical or research data and to maximize the dissemination of useful data while protecting confidentiality? How can demands for access to individually identifiable statistical data for nonstatistical purposes be successfully resisted? How does the statutory language affect the agency's ability to share identifiable data with other federal agencies for statistical and research uses? A look at the experiences of the statistical agencies whose legislation we have described in this chapter (and the experiences of the Energy Information Administration described in Chapter 7) would have provided valuable insights into what has worked well and what has not.

FINDINGS AND RECOMMENDATIONS

Current legislation impedes the constructive exchange of data for statistical and research purposes while failing to provide adequate protection of the confidentiality of statistical and research records. The panel notes two major inadequacies of the current situation.

First, many agencies not covered by specific confidentiality legislation have to rely on the Privacy Act to protect identifiable data on individuals. There are serious limitations to the protections provided by the Privacy Act for data from individuals, however. The panel notes three related limitations to the Privacy Act:

1. Although the Privacy Act does provide for separate treatment and disclosure of anonymous statistical data, it does not distinguish between administrative uses of data and statistical uses. Thus, it does not provide for the separate treatment of identifiable statistical data and identifiable data from administrative record systems. Distinctions between statistical and administrative data correspond to the purpose for which the data were collected and the assurances offered to the respondent. (The panel strongly supports the principle of functional separation of statistical and administrative data; see discussion in Chapter 1.)

2. The Privacy Act does not prohibit administrative and regulatory uses of individually identifiable data obtained for statistical purposes. Exceptions to the informed consent requirement may permit statistical data to be used for administrative and regulatory purposes, in violation of assurances given the individual at the time the information was collected that the information would be used for the exclusive purpose of conducting research or statistical analysis.

3. The Privacy Act requires agencies to inform individuals of the anticipated routine uses that will be made of their data at the time the data are collected. However, the routine-use exemption permits exchange of identifiable information for an unanticipated purpose if that purpose is "consistent" with the original purposes mentioned when the information was collected. Loose standards for defining a consistent use may diminish the protection afforded statistical records by permitting the release of identifiable research records for administrative, enforcement, and other nonresearch purposes that may jeopardize the interests of data subjects (see Coles, 1991).

Second, there is wide variation among statistical agencies in the degree of confidentiality protection that is afforded by legislation. Among the agencies reviewed in this chapter, protection varies greatly, from the rigorous protection provided for data collected under Title 13 by the Census Bureau, to the currently uncertain protection of data collected by the Energy Information Administration, to the absence of specific statutory protection for the Bureau of Labor Statistics. The panel notes three major effects of this variation:

1. The degree of data protection often is determined by the statutes governing the specific agency maintaining the information. As a result, the same kind of information may receive greater

or lesser protection depending on the agency that maintains it, and without regard to the sensitivity of the information.

2. Variation in protection among agencies may thwart the exchange of information across agencies. Those agencies that are required by law to maintain an especially high degree of confidentiality are not able to transfer data to agencies that do not have the same level of protection. For example, the National Agricultural Statistics Service (NASS) transfers lists of farms to the Census Bureau for the latter's use in developing a mailing list for the Census of Agriculture. However, NASS cannot obtain the complete mailing list for the Census of Agriculture for use in developing a sampling frame for its own surveys. Instead, it must develop its own sampling frame at considerable additional cost, even though both agencies collect data from essentially the same universe.

3. Differing levels of statutory protection across agencies may cause confusion for data subjects and providers who do not pay close attention to subtle differences in the assurances of confidentiality that accompany agency requests for information. These assurances often are carefully drafted to correspond with the unique level of protection provided by each agency. But the distinctions may become blurred or lost when data providers respond to requests for information from several agencies. As a result, data providers may place too much trust in agencies with limited means of protecting data used for statistical and research purposes, and they may not know which agencies have a sound legal basis for offering more rigorous protection.

> **Recommendation 5.1** Statistical records across all federal agencies should be governed by a consistent set of statutes and regulations meeting standards for the maintenance of such records, including the following features of fair statistical information practices:
>
> (a) a definition of statistical data that incorporates the principle of functional separation as defined by the Privacy Protection Study Commission,
> (b) a guarantee of confidentiality for data,
> (c) a requirement of informed consent or informed choice when participation in a survey is voluntary,
> (d) a requirement of strict control on data dissemination,
> (e) a requirement to follow careful rules on disclosure limitation,

(f)   a provision that permits data sharing for statistical purposes under controlled conditions, and

(g)   legal sanctions for those who violate confidentiality requirements (see Recommendation 5.3 for further discussion of this requirement).

The panel believes that such legislation should be crafted so that it does not require renewal in short intervals. The confidentiality legislation for the National Agricultural Statistics Service, for example, is contained in the Food Security Act of 1985 (P.L. 99-198, § 1770), which must be renewed every five years. We believe that all statistical agencies should have permanent confidentiality legislation so as to meet the legitimate expectations of respondents for confidentiality.

The seven features listed above are intended to be an integrated package, not a shopping list of possible options. While the list contains the minimum standards, the panel does not wish to discourage the high standards on confidentiality that are already in place for some agencies. Existing and proposed legislation should balance such competing values as data protection and data dissemination.[9]

To attain the proposed standard for the maintenance of statistical records, the panel sees two complementary approaches:

1.   The standards might take the form of new government-wide legislation, a "Federal Statistical Records Act," that would protect the confidentiality of records used for statistical purposes across the entire federal government. Such an act would (1) distinguish between administrative and statistical records on the basis of use, (2) establish and mandate functional separation between administrative and statistical records, (3) encourage disclosure of statistical records for statistical uses, and (4) restrict disclosure of statistical records for nonstatistical uses. The legislation would complement the Privacy Act and perhaps be incorporated in it. However, amending the Privacy Act, which extends protection only to individuals, will not be a suitable means of addressing concerns regarding statistical data maintained by federal agencies on establishments and organizations. (See Chapter 7 for the panel's recommendations concerning statistical data on organizations.)

2.   A second approach would be to incorporate the standards in agency-specific confidentiality legislation, adapting them to the specific mission and programs of each statistical agency. For this approach, the panel suggests that specialized legislative provisions be developed that apply the standards outlined above to the spe-

cific tasks of each statistical agency. Thus, there would be two levels of protection: first, the Federal Statistics Records Act and, then, specific legislation governing each agency.

These approaches are not mutually exclusive, and some combination of strategies may be appropriate. For instance, the Privacy Act could be amended while model legislative provisions were being developed.

Statutory standards that prohibit disclosure of statistical data if there exists *any* possibility of association with a specific individual or organization place an unnecessarily strict limitation on exchange of data for research. Although statutory requirements for nondisclosure (other than those in government-wide statutes such as the Privacy Act of 1974) vary considerably from one agency to another, most are stated in absolute terms to the effect that no information can be released if it can be associated with a specific individual or organization. For example, the Census Bureau's Title 13 prohibits the publication of any data from establishments or individuals collected under this statute if the data can be identified. Similarly, legislation governing the National Center for Education Statistics prohibits the publication of data that would permit the identification of an individual.

If taken literally, requirements of "zero disclosure risk" would virtually eliminate the dissemination of statistical data, especially in the form of public-use microdata. Removal of explicit identifiers (such as name, address, and Social Security number) and careful application of statistical techniques to protect confidentiality (see Chapter 6) are not enough to protect individually identifiable data from ever becoming known. There is almost always some residual risk, which cannot be easily quantified, that a diligent "snooper" who wanted to do so might identify one or more data subjects included in a tabulation or microdata file.

In practice, many of the statutory requirements that are expressed in absolute terms have been interpreted to mean that unrestricted access to a particular data set requires that a reasonable effort be made to keep the risk of disclosing individually identifiable information at an acceptably low level. Agency officials exercise judgments to decide what statistical disclosure limitation procedures must be applied in order to keep disclosure risk acceptably low. Judgments are required because no one can have full knowledge of the externally available data sets and other factors that might lead to disclosure and because the concept of what constitutes an acceptably low risk of disclosure is inherently subjective. Also, the incentive for "snooping" will vary greatly across different data sets, thus affecting risk.

The implementing regulations for the Privacy Act allow federally supported researchers to disseminate project findings that do not contain information that could reasonably be expected to be identifiable. A criterion of a "reasonably low disclosure risk" has been used by OMB in its interpretation of the Privacy Act. In providing executive branch agencies with guidelines for implementing the Privacy Act, OMB defines the phrase "not individually identifiable" to mean that "the identity of the individual can not reasonably be deduced by anyone from tabulations or other presentations of the information" (*Federal Register*, 40(132):28954).

> **Recommendation 5.2** Zero-risk requirements for disclosure of statistical records are, in practice, impossibly high standards. Regulations and policies under existing statutes should establish standards of reasonable care. New statutes should recognize that almost all uses of information entail some risk of disclosure and should allow release of information for legitimate statistical purposes that entail a reasonably low risk of disclosure of individually identifiable data.

Few sanctions for improper dissemination of research records are designed to extend beyond federal agencies to contractors, grantees, and nonagency researchers. In most of the statistical agencies the panel reviewed, employees take an oath or sign an affidavit to indicate that they are aware of the statutory confidentiality provisions associated with the data and the penalties for violating those provisions.

Among the federal statistical agencies included in our review, only the National Center for Education Statistics and the Bureau of Justice Statistics have legislation that includes penalties for violation of confidentiality provisions by nonemployees. For NCES, such penalties are for data users who have access to data from a subset of surveys that were listed in the 1990 amendment to the Hawkins-Stafford amendments (see § 252 of the Excellence in Mathematics, Science and Engineering Act of 1990, P.L. 101-589). The statute for BJS is much broader—contractors and grantees are subject to a maximum fine of $10,000 for violating the confidentiality provisions of BJS's legislation (42 U.S.C. § 3789g(a)).

Legislative sanctions for violating confidentiality provisions are desirable for all data users, within and outside a federal agency.

Currently, some penalties for violating confidentiality have the force of law, but others do not. Informal penalties, such as declining to provide additional data to users who fail to observe agency confidentiality standards, are among the few options currently available to agencies that do not have statutory provisions for penalizing such users. Such practices could be effective for users whose statistical activities require frequent use of federal data sets. However, they would be unlikely to deter those who want to identify individual units in a data set merely to satisfy their curiosity or to embarrass the agency that released the data.

Legislative sanctions and informal penalties for violating confidentiality have not been widely applied. This could be due to the fact that there have been few violations, that violations have occurred without agencies' knowledge, or that agencies have been reluctant to impose sanctions for violations due to the adverse publicity that might result. Nevertheless, it is clear that sanctions authorized by legislation can play an important role in protecting the confidentiality of statistical data by raising the consciousness of data custodians and data users.

As noted in Chapter 4, data users are pressing agencies to provide greater access to statistical data. Currently, federal agencies are the ones who "suffer" the consequences when confidentiality violations occur. They fear such negative outcomes as lower response rates or decreased cooperation from respondents and are understandably cautious about broadening access to confidential statistical data since it merely increases the risk for them. Nonemployees who are data users must also share responsibility for maintaining the confidentiality of data. Data users must recognize their responsibilities and data providers need the assurance that sanctions bring to users' responsibilities.

> **Recommendation 5.3** There should be legal sanctions for all users, both external users and agency employees, who violate requirements to maintain the confidentiality of data.

This recommendation is tied to the panel's position discussed in Chapter 4, that is, that users must be prepared to accept legal and contractual sanctions for violations.

Contractual sanctions for violating confidentiality might also be broadened to include the data user's organization. One enforcement device that has been used in federally supported survey research is the requirement that the user's organization deposit a specified sum of money before the data user can obtain the microdata.

The money is forfeited if the data user fails to live up to the specified provisions of the agreement on data release. This approach has been used by the University of Michigan's Survey Research Center in releasing detailed microdata files from longitudinal surveys conducted with grant support from the National Science Foundation (see Jabine, 1993a).

NOTES

1. This discussion of the Privacy Act is taken, in part, from Cecil (1989).
2. For a more detailed discussion of the origins of the Privacy Act, as well as a discussion of the way in which it is inappropriate to contemporary recordkeeping practices, see Flaherty, 1989:306-314, 366-370.
3. The Privacy Act defines a *record* as "any item, collection, or grouping of information about an individual that is maintained by an agency, including, but not limited to, his education, financial transactions, medical history, and criminal or employment history and that contains his name, or the identifying number, symbol, or other identifying particular assigned to the individual, such as a finger or voice print or a photograph" (Title 5 U.S.C. § 552a(a)(4)).

    The term *statistical record* is defined in the Privacy Act as "a record in a system of records maintained for statistical research or reporting purposes only and not used in whole or in part in making any determination about an identified individual, except as provided by § 8 of Title 13 (which governs the Census Bureau)" (Title 5 U.S.C. § 552a(a)(6)).

    The Privacy Act defines a *system of records* as "a group of any records under the control of any agency from which information is retrieved by the name of the individual or by some identifying number, symbol, or other identifying particular assigned to the individual" (Title 5 U.S.C. § 552a(a)(5)).
4. For an example of the differing standards that have been adopted under this exemption for disclosure of names and addresses contained in files held by federal agencies, see Rubin (1990). For a discussion of the evolving nature of this exemption, see Andrussier (1991).
5. See "Requirements Relating to Confidentiality and Privacy in Data Collection Contracts" and "Requirements Relating to Confidentiality and Privacy in Data Processing Contracts," Appendixes A and B, respectively, in National Center for Health Statistics (1984).
6. The cases are *The Atlanta Journal et al. v. Ledbetter et al.*, Superior Court of Fulton County, State of Georgia, Civil Action File No. D-40588 (1987) and *Jane Doe II et al. v. Lumpkin*, United States District Court, Central District of Illinois, Case No. 89-1224 (1991).
7. One of the requirements of Title 13 is that the Census Bureau not

publish results from data collected under this authority that could be used to identify respondents. In its effort to reduce the risk that a respondent to a Title 13 survey could be identified, the Census Bureau has adopted a microdata protection criterion that precludes release of information that is obtained from or matchable to administrative records systems. (For more information, see Gates, 1988.)

8. Late in 1992, toward the end of the Bush administration, Secretary of Transportation Andrew H. Card, Jr., announced the formation of the Bureau of Transportation Statistics and appointed Robert Knisely as deputy director (U.S. Department of Transportation, 1992). As of early 1993, the first director of the Bureau of Transportation Statistics had not been appointed.

9. The panel is not the first group to find statutory inadequacies and to recommend the passage of government-wide legislation that would protect the confidentiality of federal statistical records. Among those recommending the passage of such legislation were the Privacy Protection Study Commission (PPSC), which was created by the Privacy Act of 1974, and the 1978-1979 President's Reorganization Project for the Federal Statistical System. One of the PPSC's key recommendations for statistical records was that government-wide legislation be passed that established the principle of functional separation (Privacy Protection Study Commission, 1977a). The President's Reorganization Project for the Federal Statistical System (1981:203) concluded that "existing legislation did not provide a consistent framework for the protection of statistical confidentiality" and similarly recommended the passage of government-wide confidentiality legislation for statistical records.

6

Technical and Administrative Procedures

The federal government has led the way in the development of statistical methodology . . . to protect the confidentiality of respondents, usually called disclosure avoidance techniques.

Barbara Bailar, 1990

The disclosure control to be applied to the release should ideally be based on information about . . . i. the degree of protection provided by a specific scheme; and ii. the amount of loss of information introduced by that scheme.

Tore Dalenius, 1991

VA officials acknowledged their Income Verification Match project had gone awry. A computer malfunction in Chicago caused more than 650 veterans to receive another veteran's income tax information.

Washington Post, May 27, 1992

INTRODUCTION

The general and agency-specific information statutes discussed in Chapter 5 provide the framework for the confidentiality and data access policies and practices of federal statistical agencies. Within this broad and complex framework, the agencies have substantial latitude to develop and apply specific technical and administrative techniques in order to achieve wide dissemination and use of publicly collected data while protecting the confidentiality of individual information.

Statistical agencies have two main options for protecting the confidentiality of released data—providing *restricted data* and providing *restricted access*. The first option entails restricting the content of data sets or files to be released. Before releasing a microdata

file, for example, an agency would usually remove explicit identifiers (e.g., name, address, and Social Security number) and might
further curtail the information in the file (e.g., by giving people's
ages in five-year intervals rather than by exact date of birth). The
second option entails imposing conditions on who may have access to agency data, for what purpose, at what locations, and so
forth. (A similar distinction was made by Marsh et al. (1991b) in
a paper about data dissemination practices in the United Kingdom. Instead of *restricted data* and *restricted access*, they used
the terms *safe data* and *safe setting*.) Microdata sets that are
released with no restrictions on access (but typically with many
restrictions on content) are commonly referred to as *public-use*
data sets.

There is an inverse relationship between restrictions on data
and restrictions on access: as data restrictions increase, fewer
restrictions on access are needed and vice versa. Some user needs
cannot be met with restricted data, however, because the data
transformation required to ensure data confidentiality is so ex-
treme that the restricted data are useless for inference purposes.
In response, an agency may allow more restricted access to less
restricted data. Conversely, to ensure confidentiality, access may
have to be so restricted that a legitimate user cannot, as a practical matter, obtain the data. Again in response, an agency may
allow less restricted access to more restricted data. Neither restricted data nor restricted access alone is a panacea. To make
effective use of data while protecting confidentiality, both options are needed, often in combination. On the other hand, without assurances of adequate confidentiality shields, data collection
may be stymied. A study of draft evaders who fled to a neutral
country, for example, was never conducted because researchers
were unable to convince the potential respondents that their anonymity could be ensured (Sagarin, 1973). Thus, the comment by
Dalenius quoted at the beginning of this chapter is to the point.
Confidentiality protection shields must be both effective and faithful
to the original data. The goal of technical and administrative
shields is to protect confidentiality adequately while leaving the
statistical agency sufficiently unencumbered that it can furnish
faithful data. The criterion for faithful data is simple and compelling: "The user expects to be the peer of the data collector in
answering a research question" (David, 1991:94).

This chapter has two main sections. In the first section we
discuss statistical techniques for protecting the confidentiality of
data on persons and other data subjects included in released data
sets. It is widely accepted that it is virtually impossible to re-

lease data for statistical use without incurring some risk that one or more persons can be identified and information about them disclosed, especially if substantial resources are used in a deliberate attempt to do so. The goal of using statistical disclosure limitation techniques (mathematical methods that depend on statistical characteristics of the data) prior to releasing data is to reduce the magnitude of that risk.[1]

In the second section of the chapter, we discuss agency policies and procedures for providing restricted access to data on persons. We also present examples of several kinds of restricted access, including data sharing between agencies for statistical purposes and access by end users outside the government. One of the examples includes the release of microdata in encrypted form. Encryption is a technical procedure, but it is not generally thought of in the context of statistical disclosure limitation techniques, and so we include it in our discussion of restricted access procedures.

RESTRICTED DATA: STATISTICAL TECHNIQUES FOR PROTECTING CONFIDENTIALITY

In this section we focus on the search for statistical techniques that restrict statistical data so as to protect the confidentiality of the data while maintaining utility to the legitimate data user. Although the topic is technical, our treatment is not. Nor do we provide a primer on available techniques. That would only duplicate concurrent work of the Federal Committee on Statistical Methodology (1993), Subcommittee on Disclosure Limitation Methodology, which is chaired by Nancy Kirkendall. We do describe the key concepts of the approach, evaluate its value for confidentiality protection and data access, and present our recommendations. In so doing, we address four topics: the nature of disclosure risk and statistical procedures for disclosure limitation; current statistical disclosure limitation practices of federal statistical agencies; the impact of increased computer and communications capability on disclosure risk; and current statistical disclosure limitation research.

Disclosure Risk and Statistical Disclosure Limitation Techniques

As defined in Chapter 1, a *disclosure* occurs when a data subject is identified from a released file (*identity disclosure*), sensitive information about a data subject is revealed through the released file (*attribute disclosure*), or released data make it possible to infer the value of an attribute of a data subject more accurately than otherwise would have been possible (*inferential disclosure*). Inferential disclosure may involve either identity disclosure or attribute disclosure.[2] The most general of these concepts is inferential disclosure, which was defined by Dalenius (1977), supported by the Federal Committee on Statistical Methodology (1978), and summed up by Jabine et al. (1977:6) in the following statement: "If the release of the statistic S makes it possible to determine the (microdata) value more closely than is possible without access to S, a[n inferential] disclosure has taken place." As discussed in Chapter 5, the only way to have zero risk of inferential disclosure is not to release any data. In practice, the extent of disclosure can only be limited to below some acceptable level. Indeed, in Recommendation 5-2 the panel suggested that new legislation should recognize this fact and allow for release of information for legitimate statistical purposes when it entails a reasonably low risk of disclosure.

Fellegi's (1972) view that disclosure requires identity disclosure *and* attribute disclosure is closest to what is commonly understood by *disclosure* and provides a reasonable basis for legislative language. On the other hand, the concept of inferential disclosure is useful to statistical agencies developing and analyzing statistical disclosure limitation techniques. Also, inferential disclosure encompasses a broader range of confidentiality risks that an agency should examine.

Statistical disclosure limitation techniques involve transformations of data to limit the risk of disclosure. Use of such a technique is often called *masking* the data, because it is intended to hide characteristics of data subjects. Some statistical disclosure limitation techniques are designed for data accessed as tables (tabular data), some are designed for data accessed as records of individual data subjects (microdata), and some are designed for data accessed as computer data bases. Common methods of masking tabular data are deleting table entries (cell suppression) and altering table entries (random error, or noise introduction). Common methods of masking microdata are deleting identifiers, dropping sensitive variables, releasing only a small fraction of the data records,[3] and grouping data values into categories (as in topcoding, whereby data values exceeding a certain level are assigned to the top category). As discussed below, direct access of computer data bases, a recent phenomenon, may involve either tabular data or microdata, but it raises new statistical disclosure limitation issues.

Prior to releasing statistical data, a statistical agency removes from the data records any explicit identifiers (such as name, address, Social Security number, telephone number) of data subjects that are not needed for statistical purposes. In many situations, however, this obvious step of deidentification or anonymization is not adequate to make the risk of disclosure reasonably low.[4] To go beyond ad hoc measures to reduce the risk of disclosure, it is necessary to have ways of measuring the nature and extent of disclosure possible in specified circumstances. In the context of inferential disclosure, Duncan and Lambert (1986) measure the extent of disclosure in terms of the change in uncertainty about a shielded value prior to data release and after data release. Common disclosure limitation policies, such as requiring the relative frequencies of released cells to be bounded away from both one and zero, are equivalent to disclosure rules that allow data release only if specific uncertainty functions at particular predictive distributions exceed a limit. This effort generalizes work of Cassel (1976) and Frank (1976, 1979) and demonstrates the analytic power of the inferential disclosure formulation.

A seemingly different approach was taken by Bethlehem et al. (1990), who focus on the number of unique individuals in a population, and so use identity disclosure limitation. To illustrate how surprisingly often individuals prove to be unique based on just a few common variables, they noted that a certain region of the Netherlands contained 83,799 households. Of those households, 23,485 were composed of a father, mother, and two children. Looking only at ages of the father and mother and ages and sexes of the two children (all ages in years), 16,008 of the 23,485 households (68 percent) were unique. If a microdata file was released containing this key information on ages and gender plus other sensitive information, confidentiality could easily be compromised in most cases by any individual having only basic background information about a household. At least that would be the case if confidentiality was attacked broadly, for example, by an individual who simply sought to identify any one household among all households rather than some specific household. Such "fishing expeditions," although presumably rare in practice are a concern to agencies worried that someone might seek to discredit their confidentiality policies.

A disclosure-risk analysis based on the number of unique entities can be one element of the Duncan and Lambert (1986) framework.   Release of a microdata file in which key variables are generally widely available in the external world could permit linking data for all of the unique households. This would raise the disclosure risk drastically for the shielded sensitive information.[5]

When disclosure risk is too high, data can be masked prior to release. As noted above, different statistical masking techniques are used for public-use microdata files and tables. In the case of a public-use microdata file, statistical disclosure limitation techniques can be classified into five broad categories (Duncan and Pearson, 1991):

1. *Collecting or releasing only a sample of the data*:   For example, the Bureau of the Census first released a public-use microdata file with a 1-in-1,000 sample from the 1960 Census of Population and Housing; microdata products from the 1980 census included one based on a 1 percent sample and another based on a 5 percent sample.

2. *Including simulated data*:   This technique has not been implemented, but it is conceptually akin to including several identical limousines in a motorcade under threat of terrorist attack.

3. *"Blurring" of the data by grouping or adding random error to individual values*:   Presenting subjects' ages in 10-year intervals is an example of grouping. For an example of addition of random error, the Census Bureau prepared a microdata file for researchers at the National Opinion Research Center from the 1980 census that contained census tract characteristics (e.g., percentage of blacks and Hispanics, unemployment rate, median house value). Because the tract characteristics had unique combinations and those characteristics could readily be learned from Census Bureau publications, the records could be linked to the actual tract of residence. That would have violated the Census Bureau policy of not identifying a geographic area with fewer than 100,000 residents. To reduce this risk, tract characteristics were masked by adding random error, or noise (see Kim, 1990).

4. *Excluding certain attributes*:   An agency might provide a subject's year of birth but not the month and day, or quarterly employment data could be replaced with yearly summaries.

5. *Swapping of data by exchanging the values of just certain variables between data subjects*:   For example, the value for some sensitive variable in a record could be exchanged for that in an adjacent record.

For data released as tables, the blurring and swapping techniques described above have been used. Three other statistical disclosure limitation techniques are unique to tables (see Cox, 1980, 1987; Sande, 1984):

1. Requiring each marginal total of the table to have a minimum count of data subjects.

2. Using a "concentration" rule, also known as the (N,K)-rule, where N entities do not dominate K percent of a cell; for example, requiring that the reported aspects of the two dominant businesses in a cell comprise no more than a certain percentage of a cell.

3. Using controlled rounding of table entries to perturb entries while maintaining various marginal totals.

The more sophisticated the masking technique, the less accessible the data and their analysis will be to many social scientists and policymakers. The statistical disclosure limitation approach that creates the least problems for analysts is masking through sampling because (at least with simple random sampling) standard statistical inference tools readily apply. However, for public-use microdata files, other statistical disclosure limitation techniques, such as the addition of noise, present measurement error or errors-in-variables problems for the user of the masked data (see, e.g., Sullivan and Fuller, 1989).[6] This can introduce bias in the inferences that are drawn.[7] In general, the choice of an appropriate statistical disclosure limitation method depends on the statistical procedure to be used to analyze the data.

SELECTED STATISTICAL DISCLOSURE LIMITATION
PRACTICES OF FEDERAL STATISTICAL AGENCIES

Some federal statistical agencies—notably the Census Bureau—have devoted considerable attention to the development and implementation of statistical disclosure limitation techniques.[8] In an enduring contribution, the Federal Committee on Statistical Methodology (1978) issued Statistical Policy Working Paper 2, *Report on Statistical Disclosure and Disclosure-Avoidance Techniques*. The report summarized the practices of seven federal agencies,[9] presented recommendations regarding statistical disclosure limitation techniques, and discussed the effects of disclosure on data subjects and users and the need for research and development in this area. Because of their continued relevance, the panel endorses certain key recommendations from Statistical Policy Working Paper 2 in presenting its own recommendations below. Attention to this area is perhaps even more justifiable today because most statistical disclosure limitation methods that are employed in practice lack theoretical roots (see Duncan and Lambert, 1986; Greenberg and Zayatz, 1992). Their ad hoc nature leads to criticism by potential users that they are excessively conservative. For decades, for example, the Census Bureau used an area size cutoff of 250,000 residents to limit the disclosure risk based on geographic specification, a cutoff that was lowered to 100,000 residents for most surveys and censuses after systematic studies were conducted (see Greenberg and Voshell, 1990a,b).

Procedures Used for Tables

Several statistical agencies have applied disclosure limitation to tabular data. In practice, most agency guidelines provide for suppressing the values in the cells of a table based on minimum cell sizes and an (N, K) concentration rule. Minimum cell sizes of three are almost invariably used, because each member of a cell of size two could derive a specific value from the other member. A typical concentration rule specifies that no more than $K = 70$ percent of a cell value is attributable to $N = 1$ entity. Often, the particular choice of N and K is not revealed to data users. Cell suppression in tables always results in a loss to the data user of some detailed information. Because cell sizes are typically small in geographic areas with small populations, geographic detail is often lost (see below).

Procedures for Microdata Files

Only about half of the federal statistical agencies that replied to the panel's request for information included materials that documented their statistical disclosure limitation techniques for microdata. Some that did merely indicated that the statistical disclosure limitation techniques for surveys they sponsored were set by the Census Bureau's Microdata Review Panel because the surveys had been conducted for them by the Census Bureau.

Major releasers of public-use microdata (that is, the Census Bureau, the National Center for Health Statistics (NCHS), and more recently the National Center for Education Statistics, or NCES) have all established formal procedures for review and approval of new microdata sets. In general those procedures do not rely on parameter-driven rules like those used for tabulations. Instead, they require judgments by reviewers that take into account such factors as the availability of external files with comparable data, the resources that might be needed by a "snooper" to identify individual units, the sensitivity of individual data items, the expected number of unique records in the file, the proportion of the study population included in the sample, and the expected amount of error in the data.

Since locating a data subject geographically increases disclosure risk, a common disclosure limitation method is to coarsen geographic detail. The Census Bureau and NCHS specify that no geographic codes for areas with a population of less than 100,000 can be included in public-use microdata files. If a file contains a large number of variables, a higher cutoff may be used. The inclusion of local-area characteristics, such as the mean income, population density, and percentage of minority population of a census tract, is also limited by this requirement because if enough variables of this type are included, the local area can be uniquely identified. For example, in the Energy Information Administration's Residential Energy Consumption Surveys, local weather information has had to be masked to prevent disclosure of the geographic location of surveyed households. Lack of geographical coding may have limited effect on certain analyses of national programs, like Food Stamps. Yet expunging state of residence of a sampled household, as is done in the public-use microdata files of the Survey of Income and Program Participation (SIPP), precludes many useful analyses of programs (e.g., Aid for Families with Dependent Children) for which eligibility criteria vary by state.[10]

THE IMPACT OF IMPROVED COMPUTER AND
COMMUNICATIONS TECHNOLOGY

The President's Commission on Federal Statistics reported in 1971 that

> the development of new methods of storing and recalling information by computer has generated considerable confusion in the public mind about the government's need for personal information about individuals, and apprehension about the use of such information (pp. 198-199).

This comment remains emphatically legitimate today, over 20 years after the publication of the report of the presidential commission. The public fears that the government's amassing of large data bases will reach into the private lives of citizens (see, e.g., Burnham, 1983; Flaherty, 1989).

The computer revolution that caused concern in 1971 is still ongoing. In the 1960s and 1970s mainframe computers were available to comparatively few individuals. Beginning with the mass introduction of personal computers by International Business Machines (IBM) in 1981, significant computing power became available on the desks of most researchers. Because of improvements in computer and communications technology, the prevailing mode for data storage today is a computer data base, and a frequent mode of access is through remote telecommunications. The latter permits large data bases to be developed and maintained according to strict quality control standards while allowing easy access by a widely dispersed group of data users. In the commercial field the growth of airline reservation systems is a prototypical example of this phenomenon. In the area of research and policy analysis, this technology allows rich data bases to be assembled, provides access without a special trip to the site where the data are stored, and in some cases enables researchers to use their own software in analyzing the data. An often-cited example of such an arrangement is the Luxembourg Income Study (Rainwater and Smeeding, 1988), which maintains microdata sets containing measures of economic well-being for many developed countries. The key consideration for custodians of remotely accessed data bases is to provide the benefits of this easy access while ensuring confidentiality. Only statistical aggregates, such as tabulations, should be obtainable. The ability to download individual records should be precluded. Further, and this is more difficult, the data user should not be able to infer the information contained in individual records from permitted queries about aggregates.

Data base security has both administrative and technical aspects. Administratively and at a systemwide level, the institution maintaining the data base must create an environment in which passwords are not shared and the use that individuals can make of secure data is subject to periodic audit and review. Technically and at the data base level, reliance on access control procedures, such as the use of passwords, is not fully adequate. All modern data bases are designed to provide security against direct query of certain attributes. In this way, any user can be allowed to access only a restricted part of a data base. Such a multilevel data base basically stores data according to different security classifications and allows users access to data only if their security level is greater than or equal to the security classification of the data. Unfortunately, this simple device does not preclude the existence of what is called an *inference channel* (see Denning and

Lunt, 1988). An inference channel is said to exist in a multilevel data base when a user can infer information classified at a high level (to which the user does not have access) based on information classified at a lower level to which the user does have access. Such a channel may be hard to detect because it may involve a lengthy chain of inference and combine information that is explicitly stored in the data base and other, external information.

Further, a data user may have legitimate access to statistical aggregates, such as averages and regression coefficients for such sensitive attributes as medical or salary information, while not being permitted access to information that is identifiable to a specified individual. In such situations, inferential disclosure control is usually implemented through query restriction (Fellegi, 1972) or response modification (Denning, 1980). In query restriction, certain queries, such as those pertaining to a few entities in the data base, are not answered. In response modification, the answers to certain queries are modified, for example, by adding random error or rounding. In either instance, a problem stems from the fact that the data base can be repeatedly queried. Each individual query may be innocuous, but the sequential queries may be sufficient to compromise the data base. This particular problem is an area of ongoing research (see Adam and Wortman, 1989; Duncan and Mukherjee, 1991, 1992; Keller-McNulty and Unger, 1993; Matloff, 1986; Tendick, 1991; and Turn, 1990). To date, research suggests that (1) user demand for data access through remote querying of relational data bases is inevitable and (2) modern data bases give rise to special problems in protecting confidentiality that require new disclosure limitation techniques.

RECENT RESEARCH ON DISCLOSURE LIMITATION

Until recently agencies had little theoretical justification for the statistical disclosure limitation tools they employed (see Cox, 1986; Duncan and Pearson, 1991). The tools of this field are not only statistical but also come from the fields of mathematics, computer science, numerical analysis, linear and integer programming, and operations research (see Brackstone, 1990; Greenberg 1990, 1991). Much of the research on disclosure limitation has taken place in federal agencies, especially the Census Bureau (Bailar, 1990). Recently, statistical disclosure limitation has begun to attract the attention of university researchers as a field of inquiry. Below we describe a few recent studies of statistical disclosure limitation techniques.

Systematic Frameworks

Duncan and Pearson (1991) describe some general techniques for limiting disclosures from microdata through a process of matrix masking. A statistical agency would disseminate a transformed file rather than the original file. By a process of matrix multiplication, the records can be transformed, the attributes can be transformed, or both. By a process of matrix addition, the individual data values can be displaced. Such matrix masking makes uses of well-known disclosure limitation methods. Among record-transforming masking techniques are aggregation across records, suppression of certain records, release of statistics for ordinary least squares regression, release of a sample of records, and multiplication of records by random noise. Among displacing masking techniques are addition of random noise and addition of deterministic noise. In his discussion of the Duncan and Pearson paper, Cox (1991) suggests how certain generalizations of matrix masks can also make use of other disclosure limitation methods, such as random rounding, grouping, and truncation.

Papers Commissioned by the Panel

To aid its deliberations, the panel commissioned a series of papers dealing with a range of issues bearing on confidentiality and data access (see Appendix A for a list of the papers). Below we briefly identify the contributions of the commissioned papers that dealt most directly with statistical disclosure limitation.

Fuller (1993), in his paper *Use of Masking Procedures for Disclosure Limitation*, examines the confidentiality protection provided by adding random error to data elements. Noting the importance of researchers' being able to analyze the resulting masked data, he examines the costs of data masking as a function of type of masking, degree of masking, and type of analysis. For a range of situations, Fuller provides appropriate statistical estimation procedures based on measurement error methodology.

Jabine (1993b), in his paper *Statistical Disclosure Limitation: Current Federal Practices and Research*, summarizes the statistical disclosure limitation practices of 18 agencies based primarily on their responses to a 1990 request from the panel for information about agency confidentiality and data access policies and practices. His paper also provides an update on the statistical procedures used by the agencies that were included in the 1978 Statistical Policy Working Paper 2.

Lambert (1993), in her paper *Measures of Disclosure Risk and Harm*, develops a decision-theoretic model for the actions of a data snooper in identifying a target record. She also examines a variety of measures of disclosure harm and relates her discussion to a larger literature.

Little (1993), in his paper *Statistical Analysis of Masked Data*, discusses a broad range of masking methods, including randomized response, release of subsamples of records, suppression of cells in a cross-tabulation, deletion of sensitive values, deletion followed by imputation of values, addition of random noise, rounding, grouping or truncation, transformation, slicing files into subsets of variables, slicing and recombination to form synthetic records, reduction to aggregate sufficient statistics, and microaggregation. He develops a likelihood theory for masked data files that combines elements of Rubin's (1976) theories for treatment assignment and missing data and Heitjan and Rubin's (1991) theory for coarsened data.

Keller-McNulty and Unger (1993), in their paper *Database Systems: Inferential Security*, synthesize research that has been conducted by computer scientists and statisticians on problems of data security and confidentiality. Computer scientists have focused on data release through sequential queries to a data base; statisticians have focused on the aggregate release of data.

In his discussion of the commissioned papers at the panel's March 1991 Conference on Disclosure Limitation Approaches and Data Access, Rubin broached the idea of applying multiple imputation methodology (see Rubin, 1987; Little and Rubin, 1987) to create artificial (synthetic) microdata files.[11] In this mode, federal statistical agencies would not release any actual data from subjects. The clear appeal of this notion is that there is no possibility of identity disclosure in disseminating synthetic data. However, the notion gives rise to important questions: To what extent can synthetic data sets created by using techniques such as multiple imputation and data swapping satisfy user needs? What would be the legal and research standing of inferences drawn from them?

Shielding Organizational Data

For the most part, statistical disclosure limitation techniques have been developed for data on persons and households. The task of protecting the confidentiality of organizational data—for example, economic data on establishments—is more difficult because organizational data are decidedly skew on key dimensions. Federal statistical agencies are thus reluctant to release public-use microdata files on organizations. Some research in this area has begun. Wolf (1988), for example, examines a technique of microaggregation that creates pseudo-records by combining information from similar records. He applies it to the Census Bureau's Longitudinal Research Development file (an earlier version of the Longitudinal Research Database), which consists of a longitudinal file of manufacturing establishment microdata records collected through the Annual Survey of Manufactures and the Census of Manufactures for the years 1972-1981. He examines the utility of the masked data by comparing characteristics of the distribution of the masked data with the corresponding characteristics of the original data.[12]   Other work in this area includes Govoni and Waite (1985), McGuckin and Nguyen (1990), and Spruill (1983).

Findings and Recommendations

Many of the statistical agencies included in the panel's review have standards, guidelines, or formal review mechanisms that are designed to ensure that (1) adequate analyses of disclosure risk are performed and (2) appropriate statistical disclosure limitation techniques are applied prior to release of tables and public-use microdata files. The standards and guidelines, however, exhibit a wide range of specificity: Some contain only one or two simple rules; others are much more detailed. Examples of more detailed formal documentation or procedures include those of the Census Bureau (for microdata), the Energy Information Administration (for tabulations only), the National Center for Health Statistics, and the 1977 Social Security Administration guidelines, which are still in effect. Other statistical agencies have far less formal procedures. This variation over agencies in the comprehensiveness of disclosure review has little justification in terms of agency mission. Further, unfulfilled opportunities exist for agencies to work together and learn from one another, perhaps pooling resources to investigate the strengths and weaknesses of various statistical disclosure limitation techniques.

Based on its findings, the panel endorses the following recommendations from Statistical Policy Working Paper 2 (Federal Committee on Statistical Methodology, 1978) and then makes Recommendation 6.1:

Recommendations from Statistical Policy Working Paper 2

All federal agencies releasing statistical information, whether in tabular or microdata form, should formulate and apply policies and procedures designed to avoid unacceptable disclosures (pp. 41-42:part of Recommendation B1).

To insure compliance with its disclosure-avoidance policies and procedures, each agency that releases statistical information should establish appropriate internal clearance procedures. There should be a clear assignment of individual responsibilities for compliance (p. 43:Recommendation B6).

The . . . [Statistical Policy Office, OMB] should encourage agencies that release tabulations and microdata to develop appropriate policies and guidelines for avoiding disclosure, and to review these policies periodically. To the extent feasible, . . . [this office] should help agencies to obtain technical assistance in the development of disclosure-avoidance techniques (p. 43:Recommendation B8).

The . . . [Statistical Policy Office, OMB] should conduct periodic training seminars for Federal agency personnel who are responsible for developing and applying statistical disclosure-avoidance procedures (p. 43:Recommendation C2).

Since the panel convened, the federal statistical agencies have initiated some activities consonant with the above recommendations. In particular, in 1991 OMB's Statistical Policy Office took the lead in organizing an interagency committee to coordinate research on statistical disclosure analysis. This Subcommittee on Disclosure Limitation Methodology was begun as an initiative of the directors of the major statistical agencies.

Recommendation 6.1 The Office of Management and Budget's Statistical Policy Office should continue to coordinate research work on statistical disclosure analysis and should disseminate the results of this work broadly among statistical agencies. Major statistical agencies should actively encourage and participate in scholarly statistical research in this area. Other agencies should keep abreast of current developments in the application of statistical disclosure limitation techniques.

As discussed above, statistical disclosure limitation methods can hide or distort relations among study variables and result in analyses that are incomplete or misleading. Because of this possibility, policy researchers have expressed serious reservations about the use of statistical disclosure limitation techniques (e.g., Smith, 1991). Further, data masked by some disclosure limitation methods can only be analyzed accurately by researchers who are highly sophisticated methodologically. Based on these findings, the panel makes the following recommendation:

> **Recommendation 6.2** Statistical agencies should determine the impact on statistical analyses of the techniques they use to mask data. They should be sure that the masked data can be accurately analyzed by a range of typical researchers. If the data cannot be accurately analyzed using standard statistical software, the agency should make appropriate consulting and software available.

The panel believes that no one procedure can be developed for all statistical agencies. Further, confidentiality laws governing particular agencies differ, as do the types of data collected and the needs of data users. In light of these findings, the panel endorses the following recommendations contained in Statistical Policy Working Paper 2:

> Because there are wide variations in the content and format of information released, the Subcommittee does not feel that it is feasible to develop a uniform set of rules, applicable to all agencies, for distinguishing acceptable from unacceptable disclosures. In formulating disclosure-avoidance policies, agencies should give particular attention to the sensitivity of different data items. Financial data, such as salaries and wages, benefits, and assets, and data on illegal activities and on activities generally considered to be socially sensitive or undesirable require disclosure-avoidance policies that make the risk of statistical disclosure negligible. . . .

> Agencies should avoid framing regulations and policies which define unacceptable statistical disclosure in unnecessarily broad or absolute terms. Agencies should apply a test of reasonableness, i.e., releases should be made in such a way that it is reasonably certain that no information about a specific individual will be disclosed in a manner that can harm that individual (p. 42:part of Recommendation B1).

> Special care should be taken to protect individual data when releases are based on complete (as opposed to sample) files and when data are presented for small areas (p. 42:Recommendation B2).

Given the potential difficulties that certain statistical disclosure limitation techniques can cause for analysts, it is important that federal statistical agencies involve data users in selecting such procedures. As Greenberg (1991:375) notes, "survey sponsors and data users must contribute to the decision making process in identifying areas in which some completeness and/or accuracy can be sacrificed while attempting to maintain as much data quality as possible." In the past, agency staffs have been essentially the sole determiners of which statistical disclosure limitation techniques are to be employed prior to releasing tables and microdata files.

Recommendation 6.3 Each statistical agency should actively involve data users from outside the agency as statistical disclosure limitation techniques are developed and applied to data.

Finally, over the past 30 years various agencies have released public-use microdata files successfully. Marsh et al. (1991a) make a compelling case for the release of public-use microdata files. (Note also Collins, 1992, for a cautionary viewpoint and Marsh et al., 1992, for a rejoinder.) Based on experience, such data dissemination has met a two-pronged test: (1) the microdata files have been useful to researchers and policy analysts and (2) confidentiality has been protected. Based on this finding, the panel makes the following recommendation:

Recommendation 6.4 Statistical agencies should continue widespread release, with minimal restrictions on use, of microdata sets with no less detail than currently provided.

We note that expansion of the number and richness of public-use microdata files to be disseminated would be better justified if all users were subject to and made aware of sanctions for disclosure of information about individually identifiable data providers (see Recommendation 5.3).

RESTRICTED ACCESS: ADMINISTRATIVE PROCEDURES TO PROTECT CONFIDENTIALITY

Procedures for providing restricted access to data typically establish eligibility requirements for access and impose a variety of conditions covering the purposes for which the data can be used, which organizations and individuals can have access, the location of access, physical security measures, and the retention and disposition of initial and secondary data files. Written agreements are usually required, and criminal or contractual penalties are often attached to noncompliance with the conditions of access.

Arrangements for providing restricted access to federal data for statistical purposes are not uncommon. In a paper prepared for the panel, Jabine (1993a) provides 19 examples, most of them current, and his list was intended only to illustrate various types of access that are allowed, not to provide an exhaustive summary. He also gives six examples of instances in which access could not be obtained to data that would have had important statistical uses.

The characteristics of interagency data-sharing agreements tend to be different from those associated with arrangements for restricted access by external users. The former are more likely to involve sharing of individual records with explicit identifiers, for purposes such as developing sampling frames and enhancing data bases. The latter typically are designed to permit access to potentially identifiable records for statistical analysis. These two types of access are discussed in the next two subsections.

INTERAGENCY DATA SHARING

We begin this subsection by presenting examples of agreements that have been developed to permit interagency sharing of identifiable, or potentially identifiable, personal records for statistical purposes. Some of the examples involve transfers of administrative records; others involve transfers of data collected in statistical surveys. Most of the examples are taken from Jabine (1993a). Following the examples, we discuss some of the general issues they illustrate.

This subsection does not include any examples of *unsuccessful* attempts to develop interagency data-sharing arrangements for statistical purposes. The absence of such examples does not mean that all or even most proposals for interagency sharing are successful. For some kinds of data, statutory restrictions make sharing impossible; in other instances, agencies' policies and their interpretations of confidentiality statutes have thwarted requests by other agencies for access to their data. The very limited ability of federal agencies to share business lists for statistical purposes (see Chapter 8) illustrates the kinds of barriers that exist.

Examples of Interagency Data Sharing

Bureau of Labor Statistics Access to Nonpublic Microdata from the Current Population Survey The main sponsor and funding agency for the monthly Current Population Survey (CPS) is the Bureau of Labor Statistics (BLS). The survey data are collected by the Census Bureau. Because the sample of households is based in part on address listings from the decennial censuses, all CPS data are subject to the confidentiality provisions of Title 13 of the U.S. Code, which means that only Census Bureau employees (including special sworn employees) can have access to individually identifiable information.

Such limitations on access have long been a source of discontent on the part of agencies sponsoring household surveys conducted under the provisions of Title 13. Sponsors believe they are unduly restricted in their ability to perform detailed analyses of the survey data and to use the survey materials for intermediate purposes that might involve data linkages or follow-up contacts with survey respondents to collect additional data. Nonetheless, BLS has opted to continue to take advantage of the sampling efficiency that results from the use of decennial census address lists for its CPS sample. In February 1990, the Census Bureau and BLS executed a formal five-year "Memorandum of Understanding on the Use of Nonpublic Current Population Survey Microdata by the Bureau of Labor Statistics."[13] Under the agreement, BLS users of nonpublic CPS microdata (which consist of microdata with geographic area identifiers and no topcoding of income items, but without explicit identifiers) must be special sworn employees of the Census Bureau. The data may be used for "longitudinal matching of Current Population Survey records, general statistical research [methodological research related to the survey design and operations], and improvement and expansion of general tabulations." No provisions are made, however, for linking CPS records with records from other sources or for follow-up contacts of any kind with CPS respondents. The agreement and attached statement of policies provide for strict security measures by BLS staff, periodic on-site inspections by the Census Bureau, and regular reviews of the benefits of the sharing arrangement.

Linkage of Records from the Departments of Defense and Health and Human Services This example also covers restricted access to data for statistical purposes. However, it is somewhat unusual in that the purpose of the record linkage was to provide statistical tabulations needed to determine the feasibility of a subsequent linkage for nonstatistical, compliance purposes. The agencies that participated were the Office of the Inspector General (OIG) in the Department of Health and Human Services and the Defense Manpower Data Center (DMDC) in the Department of Defense.

The purpose of the match was to determine how many military and civilian employees of the Defense Department might be in arrears on court-ordered child support payments. Based on the findings, OIG would determine whether to proceed with a full-scale records match for compliance purposes. The files to be linked were 1987 and 1988 Tax Intercept Files in the custody of the Family Support Administration of the Department of Health and Human Services and DMDC's personnel files for military and civilian employees of the Defense Department. To accomplish the linkage, OIG sent a tape to DMDC containing the Social Security numbers and names of persons potentially delinquent on child support payments. The latter agency matched this tape against its personnel files and provided OIG with a tabulation of the number of matches by category of Defense Department employment.

The arrangements were formalized by an exchange of letters between officials of the two agencies.[14] The main conditions agreed to were that DMDC would not use the OIG records for any purpose other than the specified match and that it would return the OIG data file when the match was completed. One of the letters noted that the match would not be subject to federal matching standards established by the Computer Matching and Privacy Protection Act of 1988 (P.L. 100-503) because that act does not cover matches performed solely for statistical purposes.

The number of matches found in the OIG-DMDC matching study was sufficient for the agencies to reach a decision to proceed with an ongoing matching operation for compliance purposes. No Defense Department employees whose child support payments were in arrears were immediately affected because their records had been matched in the statistical study. However, many of them may have been subject to disciplinary action as a result of the subsequent matching operations for compliance purposes.

The 1973 Exact Match Study What may have been the most ambitious and complex statistical record linkage study, involving both survey and administrative records, that has yet been undertaken occurred in the 1970s. The 1973 Exact Match Study was a joint undertaking of the Social Security Administration (SSA) and the Census Bureau. As part of the study, the Internal Revenue Service (IRS) furnished selected tax information from 1972 individual income tax returns to the Census Bureau for matching to CPS records (see Kilss and Scheuren, 1978). The primary goal of the study was to provide a broad data base for addressing such policy issues as the redistributive effects of changes in income and payroll taxes and alternative Social Security benefit structures. Specific uses included evaluating the quality of CPS income reporting, conducting labor force participation and earnings analyses using CPS income and demographic data and SSA earnings histories, and developing lifetime earnings models.

The study linked survey records for persons in the March 1973 Current Population Survey, including the income supplement, with their earnings and benefit information for several years from SSA data files and IRS information from their 1972 tax returns. There had been earlier administrative data linkages to the CPS data, starting with the March 1964 round, but the scope of the 1973 study exceeded that of any previous one. The study was designed to take advantage of the possibilities that had been opened up by advances in computer matching techniques and by the achievement of close-to-universal coverage by the IRS and SSA record systems (Kilss and Scheuren, 1984).

The data products from the 1973 Exact Match Study included several public-use (unrestricted access) microdata files containing linked survey and administrative record data. The files were widely used by researchers and provided the basis for numerous published analytic and methodologic reports and papers (Kilss and Scheuren, 1978, list 41 reports and papers).

Although the end products of the study were available to all users, the intermediate stages in their development required restricted access arrangements among the three agencies involved. Kilss and Scheuren (1984) summarize the manner in which the confidentiality requirements of the three agencies were met. None of the linkages was performed at the IRS. For linkages performed at SSA (to extract earnings and benefit data for sample persons), limited extracts of CPS records were used and those records were processed only by SSA employees who had been given appointments as special sworn employees of the Census Bureau.

The primary personal identifier used to link records from the different sources was the Social Security number, which respondents to the CPS had been asked to provide—with assurance that their numbers would be used only for statistical purposes. The

SSA did not provide administrative data to the Census Bureau for the small number of CPS respondents who declined to provide their Social Security number.

One concern of those responsible for the study was the possibility that an SSA or IRS employee could, in theory, use the linked data to identify one or more individuals in the public-use file and then use the survey information in those individuals' records for administrative purposes. To minimize this possibility (often called the *reidentification problem*), income items were topcoded (that is, values above specified levels were replaced by codes indicating that they exceeded those levels) and the release of the most detailed public-use file, which included the tax return data, was delayed until the end of the period for which the IRS retained the same tax return information for all persons in its electronically accessible administrative files.

Could the same agencies collaborate on a study of this scope and utility for research on income distribution today? Probably not. Although the period for which the IRS maintains computerized files of individual income tax data is still about the same, the returns are kept indefinitely on microfilm or microfiche, so that the reidentification problem would not disappear completely. Moreover, the Census Bureau, as a matter of policy, no longer releases public-use microdata files that link census or survey and administrative data for individuals. Even if these difficulties could be overcome, it would probably be difficult to marshal the resources necessary to carry out an interagency linkage study of this magnitude.

Census Bureau Use of IRS and SSA Personal Records To carry out their respective responsibilities for the collection of federal taxes and the administration of Social Security benefit programs, the IRS and SSA have developed extensive personal record systems that now cover large segments of the U.S. population. Over the years, the Census Bureau has used those records in several ways to enhance its demographic censuses and surveys and to evaluate the quality of census and survey data.

Census Bureau uses of IRS and SSA administrative data can perhaps be best illustrated by explaining how the data serve as basic inputs to the Census Bureau's program of intercensal population estimates for small areas. The Census Bureau tracks trends in internal migration between censuses by matching individual taxpayer record extracts for successive years from the IRS Individual Master File. The migration data from the matched extracts serve as inputs to the estimates of the total population of states, counties, and other government units. The tax files do not include information on the age, sex, or race-ethnic classification of individual taxpayers, but this information can be obtained from the SSA's NUMIDENT file, which contains the basic demographic data obtained in connection with the issuance of Social Security numbers. The Census Bureau has used these and other subsidiary inputs to produce estimates of population for states and metropolitan areas by race and age.

As explained in Chapter 5, the Internal Revenue Code allows certain statistical uses of tax return information by the Census Bureau. Specific uses are spelled out in some detail in a series of Treasury Department regulations that identify the content of the records to be transferred, the uses to which they can be put, and the security measures that must be adopted to protect the confidentiality of information turned over to the Census Bureau. The information from the SSA's NUMIDENT file is transferred to the Census Bureau under a general agreement between the two agencies that provides for limited sharing of information in both directions for joint statistical projects (see Jabine, 1993a:example 6).

The future of the Census Bureau's program to develop population estimates for states and counties by age, race-ethnicity, and sex has been clouded by a recent development. Under arrangements negotiated between SSA and state registrars of vital statistics, birth certificates and Social Security numbers are now being issued jointly at the time of birth in most states. For the births covered by these arrangements, SSA no longer obtains data on race/ethnic classification. Unless SSA finds another way to get such information, which it has used only for statistical analyses of its programs, the gradual increase in the proportion of persons for whom it lacks race-ethnic information will degrade the Census Bureau's ability to include race-ethnic status in its small-area population estimates program.

Discussion

An obvious requirement for interagency data sharing is that the statutory confidentiality requirements of all of the agencies involved must be observed. A second requirement is that the transfer of data among agencies must be consistent with statements made to data providers when the data were obtained from them. When these requirements are not the same for all of the agencies involved, those that are most stringent govern the arrangements.

In the case of the Census Bureau, the law says that only sworn Census Bureau employees, who are subject to criminal penalties for improper disclosure, may have access to the data. Thus, in any sharing arrangement involving Census Bureau data, employees of other agencies can have access to the data only after taking an oath as special sworn employees of the Census Bureau. The use of the special sworn employee provision is further circumscribed by the requirement that it only be used in connection with activities that are part of the bureau's statutorily defined mission.

Statistical uses of IRS administrative records for purposes not related to tax administration are limited to the agencies and purposes specified in the Internal Revenue Code. The Tax Reform Act of 1976 (P.L. 94-455) restricted such uses to other units of the Treasury Department, the Census Bureau, and the Bureau of Economic Analysis, in each case for particular purposes. A subsequent amendment (P.L. 95-210) added the National Institute of Occupational Safety and Health to the list of eligible recipients (P.L. 95-210, § 6103(j) and 6103(m)(3)). The IRS has engaged in some sharing of records with agencies other than those mentioned specifically in the code, but only for studies it considers to be related to tax administration.

In general, data sharing among federal agencies other than the Census Bureau and IRS for statistical purposes is less constrained by legislation. However, statistical agencies that receive some of their data from the states under federal-state cooperative programs (e.g., BLS and NCHS) must comply with confidentiality provisions of state law, which vary among states. In some instances, potential users of identifiable data obtained by a federal agency under such cooperative arrangements have had to apply separately to each state for permission to have access to its data. A federal-state cooperative program is also central to the data collection activities of the National Agricultural Statistics Service (NASS). However, NASS uses of the data are controlled by federal rather than state law because the data collection, while jointly financed, is federally controlled (specified statistical products are provided to the states).

Developing arrangements for interagency data sharing can be a complex and time-consuming process, especially if more than two agencies are involved or if novel applications of the data are planned. New initiatives are likely to pose new legal, ethical, administrative, and policy questions. The expected benefits in terms of cost savings or better quality data must be substantial to justify the level of effort and perseverance needed to find acceptable answers. It helps if the proposed data-sharing arrangements offer benefits to all of the parties concerned.

EXTERNAL DATA USERS

The availability of high-speed computers and sophisticated analytic techniques and software have generated vastly increased appetites for federal statistical data. The statistical agencies have tried to satisfy the demand by issuing more detailed tabulations and public-use microdata sets, but not surprisingly, they have succeeded only in whetting user appetites further. Continued efforts to meet increasing demands from users are important; many users have the capacity to conduct sophisticated research on important matters of public interest.

For many of the data sets that users want, the risk of disclosure is great enough that some form of restricted access is the only option for release. Several modes of restricted access for external users have been developed by statistical agencies. Some of the important features of these access modes are eligibility criteria, location of access, cost and convenience for agencies and users, and methods of protecting confidentiality. As in the previous subsection, we present examples of different modes of restricted access by external users. We also present two examples of failures to gain access to data sets. We follow the examples with a discussion of their key features and the comparative advantages of different modes of access.

Examples of Restricted Access by External Data Users

ASA/NSF Fellows Since 1978, the National Science Foundation (NSF) has funded and the American Statistical Association (ASA) has administered a program designed to promote the exchange of ideas and techniques between federal government statisticians and academic users of federal statistical data. Five agencies, the Bureau of Labor Statistics, the Census Bureau, the National Center for Education Statistics, the National Institute of Standards and Technology, and most recently, the National Science Foundation (as a host agency), have participated in the program, which enables senior research fellows and associates from universities to undertake research studies at one of the host agencies for a period of up to one year. The National Agricultural Statistics Service has a similar fellows program, administered by ASA, but paid for entirely with agency funds rather than jointly by the National Science Foundation and the agency.

The fellows work on research topics of joint interest to themselves and their host agencies. They have essentially the same access to agency data bases and computer facilities as regular employees doing similar work, and they are subject to the same confidentiality requirements and penalties for improper disclosure of individually identifiable information. At the Census Bureau, for example, the ASA/NSF/Census fellows receive appointments, take oaths as special sworn employees, and are subject to the same Title 13 confidentiality provisions, including penalties for violations, as regular employees.

The ASA/NSF fellows program has provided user access to data not available in unrestricted public-use files for a substantial number of academic researchers. From the start of the program through the end of 1991, 72 fellows and 54 associates had worked at the first four agencies listed above, about three-fourths of them at the Census Bureau. The primary restrictions are that access is available only at the agency's central facility, for a limited term (although fellows sometimes revisit agencies on a less formal basis), and only for projects that the host agency deems to be of interest. A more serious problem is that NSF funding for large numbers of fellows is expected to end soon, and it is unlikely that the other agencies will be able to support similar numbers out of their own operating funds.

Remote On-line Access: The Luxembourg Income Study The Luxembourg Income Study is an international cooperative research project providing remote access to microdata sets from household surveys conducted by member countries. The project is designed "to promote research on the distribution of income . . . and the general economic situation of households and families in an international context" (Cigrang and Rainwater, 1990:1). The project is supported by the Government of Luxembourg and the Center for Population, Poverty, and Policy Studies, also in Luxembourg.

At present, microdata sets from 14 countries, with explicit identifiers removed, reside in the Luxembourg Income Study data base system maintained at the Government of Luxembourg's computer center. Microdata sets from the United States, Canada, and Australia had previously been issued by those countries as public-use files, but the data sets for the remaining countries had either been available with restrictions or not at all.

The data base system is designed mainly to provide remote access to registered users through an EARN/BITNET computer mail network. Use of the data is restricted to academic and policy analysis research. Remote users submit job requests in the SPSS-X statistical language, specifying variable names used in the system. Dedicated batch-processing computers execute the requests and the outputs are forwarded to users over the computer mail network. To prevent disclosure of individual records, incoming job requests and statistical outputs are subjected to automated reviews and those that fail the review are given to the Luxembourg Income Study staff for further review. For all of the microdata sets, exact income amounts, some of which may have been taken from administrative sources, are rounded.

Once users receive the statistical outputs, they are not subject to further restrictions on use or publication, other than the general requirement that use for commercial purposes is prohibited. As of mid-1990, the data base contained 22 data sets from the 14 member countries, had about 150 registered users, and was averaging about 50 job requests a day.

Release in Encrypted CD-ROM Format The passage in 1988 of Public Law 100-297 (the Hawkins-Stafford amendments to the General Education Provisions Act) led the NCES to undertake a comprehensive review of its policies for protecting the confidentiality of individual information included in releases of tabulations and microdata sets. It became clear that for some of the microdata sets that had been released previously without restrictions the risk of disclosing individually identifiable data was too high. Criteria and procedures were established for deciding which files could continue to be released with no restrictions on access and which could not. For the latter group, other modes of release were sought. One of these modes, the encrypted CD-ROM format, is the subject of this example (Wright and Ahmed, 1990). Another, licensing agreements for use at user sites, is the subject of the next example.

Under the encrypted CD-ROM format, users purchase a diskette containing an encrypted microdata set and software that can produce descriptive statistics from the encrypted data. Prior to release, agency staff evaluate the disclosure risks associated with the outputs that can be produced with the software provided on the diskette. Restrictions are built into the software to prevent the user from printing out unencrypted individual records or statistics that would tend to disclose individual information. It is unlikely that any users would attempt to de-encrypt the records because of the high cost that would be associated with such an effort.

In general terms, this mode of release can be considered either public-use or restricted access, depending on what conditions are imposed on recipients. Significant advantages for users are the relatively low cost of access and the ability to use the data at their own work sites. However, the only analyses they can perform are those for which the necessary programs are included on the diskette. At present, only elementary analytic techniques are supported, but work is proceeding to incorporate more complex types of analyses into the system.

This system has the potential for solving, at least in part, the reidentification problem described earlier in this chapter. Microdata sets containing linked survey and administrative data could then be released with very little risk that the custodians of the administrative records could reidentify individual records.

Release of Microdata under Licensing Agreements To meet the requirements of users whose needs cannot be satisfied with public-use or encrypted CD-ROM microdata sets, the NCES has developed a licensing procedure that allows eligible organizations or agencies to use its confidential data for research and statistical purposes at their own sites (see Wright and Ahmed, 1990). Some of the key features of the standard agreement, which was approved for use on a trial basis in November 1990, follow:

• All employees of the licensee who will have access to the data become special sworn employees of NCES. They are required to sign affidavits of nondisclosure and are subject to severe penalties for violation of their oath.

• The physical security of the identifiable data must be ensured by use of specified procedures. Representatives of NCES have the right to make unannounced and unscheduled inspections of the licensee's facility to evaluate compliance.

• All publications and other data products must be submitted to NCES for review. If there are evident reasons to be concerned about the possibility of disclosure, the products must also be submitted for review prior to any release.

• The research conducted under the license must be consistent with the statistical purposes for which the data were initially supplied to NCES and the data must be returned to the center or destroyed when the research is completed.

• If the licensee is a state agency or contractor thereof, the attorney general of the state must certify that the licensee cannot be required to make individually identifiable data available to a state agency or employee not covered by the agreement.

These licensing procedures permit somewhat wider restricted access than that currently provided by the Census Bureau under its special sworn employee provision. The NCES statutory provisions for the appointment of special sworn employees are identical, but the statutory definition of the latter's mission (in the Hawkins-Stafford amendments) places greater emphasis on the dissemination of data. Much of the research on educational policy issues takes place outside the federal government, and NCES has taken the position that a licensing system that allows researchers to work with restricted access files at their own site is an important element of its compliance with its mission statement.

By early 1992, NCES had issued about 30 licenses to users. The Statistical Policy Office, OMB, has announced that the licensing procedures and agreement will be submitted to a formal regulatory review, including publication in the *Federal Register* and comment by all interested groups.

Examples of Failure to Gain Access

SSA's Continuous Work History Sample The Social Security Administration established its Continuous Work History Sample (CWHS) system about 50 years ago to serve as a multipurpose longitudinal data base for program analysis and research on earnings, Social Security benefits, labor force behavior, internal migration, and other characteristics of the U.S. population. For a 1 percent sample of all persons who have been issued a Social Security number, the system contains their date of birth, sex, and race-ethnic classification (as stated earlier in this chapter, race-ethnic information is no longer being captured for most new births) from the Social Security number application form and longitudinal information on earnings and type and location of employment. The earnings information comes from employer annual wage reports (quarterly prior to 1978) submitted to the IRS, and the information on type and location of employment comes primarily from applications to the IRS for an Employer Identification number.

Prior to 1976, CWHS files were widely available and were used for research by other agencies and organizations on the subjects mentioned above. The CWHS system was a prime source of information for labor market and related research. The proceedings of a 1978 workshop on the uses of Social Security research files, for example, included more than 10 research papers based on CWHS data sets, mostly from nonfederal researchers (Social Security Administration, 1978). The Bureau of Economic Analysis also used CWHS data for its regional national income accounts and analyses of regional labor force characteristics.

To enable users to update their longitudinal CWHS files on a quarterly or annual basis, a numerical identifier was included with each record. Initially, the identifier was the actual Social Security number, but after a short time, the actual number was replaced by an encrypted number, based on a simple substitution cipher. Later, a more sophisticated transformation was introduced. It is also worth noting that the specific combinations of Social Security number ending digits used to select the 1 percent sample were published in a journal article many years ago, at a time when the effects of such an action on disclosure risks were not generally understood.

Prior to 1974, CWHS files were released without restrictions. However, concerns arose that in files containing county and detailed industry codes it would be possible to identify some employers, especially large ones. Further, employers with access to the file, making use of knowledge of the ending digits that had been used to select the sample, would be able to identify records for some of their own employees and to obtain information, for example, about their previous and other current employment. Starting in 1974, because of these concerns, all recipients were required to agree in writing not to redisclose their files without permission or to attempt to identify individual employers or employees from the file.

As explained in Chapter 5, the Tax Reform Act of 1976 severely curtailed the use of identifiable tax return information for statistical purposes by users outside the IRS. Both the employer information from Employer Identification number applications and the earnings data were considered to be tax return information, and thus, the release of CWHS files containing such data came under the new provisions of the Internal Revenue Code. In 1977, the IRS concluded that CWHS files could not be released in the same detail as previously to nonfederal users or to most of the federal agencies that had been using them, including the Bureau of Economic Analysis, which had, until that point, played a major role as a user and disseminator of CWHS files in convenient formats to other users (Carroll, 1985; Smith, 1989).

Since the 1977 termination of releases under the arrangements that had been used prior to the 1976 Tax Reform Act, there have been a few releases of CWHS files, under restricted conditions, to other federal agencies. Files with identifiers removed have recently been released to the Treasury Department's Office of Economic Policy and the Congressional Budget Office. Provisions of the 1976 Tax Reform Act permit both of these agencies to use tax return information under certain conditions, so one cannot anticipate similar releases to the many potential users who do not have this authority. One possibility for wider release would be to develop one or more versions of the CWHS containing less detailed information for characteristics like industry classification and geographic location of employment. However, SSA and the IRS have not been able to agree on a formula for doing this. Thus, agencies like the Bureau of Economic Analysis no longer have access to the microdata files. It seems fair to say that while the CWHS continues to be used for policy analysis by components of the SSA and a handful of other agencies, its availability to the broader community of users is only a small fraction of what it was prior to passage of the 1976 Tax Reform Act.

Access to Address Information in Federal Files for Medical Follow-up and Epidemiologic Studies Access to data for use in epidemiologic studies and user access to the results of such studies raise many complex issues. This example focuses on a single question: access to federal address information for use in locating and tracking respondents in long-term follow-up studies. Although a few federal agencies do have access to such information, access is so limited that it seems reasonable to put this example in the failure category.

The importance of epidemiologic follow-up studies is hard to exaggerate. Most people are exposed, in their work and other aspects of their lives, to a host of substances and environmental factors that may lead to adverse health effects. Some of these effects, such as cancer, may not show up until long after initial exposure. Thus, to determine relationships between exposures and effects and to identify the most serious environmental risks, it is necessary to follow groups of exposed persons for long periods, say 20 years or more, and to determine periodically the state of their health, and if they have died, the cause of their death. For many such studies the group of persons to be followed is not identified until well after the period of exposure, so that finding them is not a simple matter.

Within the federal system, the best potential source of current addresses for most of the population is the IRS, which has recent addresses and Social Security numbers for all tax filers and their dependents. The Social Security Administration and the Health Care Financing Administration have the current address and Social Security number for beneficiaries, who include virtually all persons aged 65 and over, but their coverage of persons under 65 is limited.

For death information, the National Death Index provides access to information on all registered deaths in the United States for 1979 and subsequent years. Because of restrictions imposed by the states on uses of their vital statistics data, NCHS, which is the custodian of the National Death Index, can tell researchers only which members of their study populations have died and the states where those deaths occurred. Researchers who want cause of death and other information appearing on the death certificate must contact the state where the death occurred to purchase a copy of the certificate. Another limitation of the National Death Index is that deaths prior to 1979 are not included. There was some discussion of extending the coverage of the National Death Index back to about 1965, but that was found to be infeasible.

The Social Security Administration releases information about date and place of death to the public from its own files, and epidemiologists can obtain this information about members of study populations they are tracking. However, section 205(r) of the Social Security Act, added in 1983 (P.L. 98-21), required the agency to establish a program of voluntary contracts with the states to obtain death certificate information. The purpose was to correct SSA records and remove decedents' names from its benefit rolls. With some exceptions (see Aziz and Buckler, 1992), SSA cannot provide epidemiologists and other researchers with the death information it obtains from the states through this program. It regularly releases death information it obtains through its own sources.

Prior to 1976, it was possible, at least in some instances, to obtain current name and address information from the IRS for use in follow-up studies. Such access was completely cut off by the 1976 Tax Reform Act; subsequent amendments made the information available again to the National Institute for Occupational Safety and Health on a limited basis and also for follow-up studies of veterans of military service. However, numerous other government and private organizations conducting follow-up studies do not have access to this relatively low-cost and effective means of tracking their study populations.

On a slightly different, but related subject, SSA cannot disclose, for use in epidemiologic follow-up studies, rosters of persons who have worked in a particular industry during a specified period. Such lists would be based on information from earnings reports and Employer Identification number applications, both of which are classified as tax return information and are therefore prohibited from disclosure by the 1976 amendments to the Internal Revenue Code. For periods of employment prior to 1978 there would also be difficulties because the manner in which the SSA's files are organized would make the development of such lists a costly process unless a list based on the 1 percent Continuous Work History Sample could serve the purpose of the study. Finally, SSA has little if any information on current addresses for nonbeneficiaries except on tax records that are subject to the Internal Revenue Code's restrictions on disclosure.

Discussion

These examples illustrate the wide spectrum of modes of external user access to federal statistical data, ranging from no access at all to completely unrestricted access. Legal requirements for confidentiality are not the only factors that influence statistical agencies' decisions on what modes of access are acceptable for particular classes of data and users. When the probability that individual records can be identified and the perceived sensitivity of the data items are high, the agencies are likely to impose greater restrictions on access by external users. An underlying consideration in all decisions is the possibility that a well-publicized violation of confidentiality might lead to widespread public resistance to participation in voluntary or even mandatory statistical data collection programs.

Users look for modes of access that are low cost and enable them to work at their own sites with a minimum of restriction and formality. When their needs cannot be met with public-use data sets, they will generally prefer to work under licensing agreements (Smith, 1991) or with encrypted CD-ROM diskettes, provided those modes will give them timely access to the kinds of data they want, in sufficient detail for their research. Modes of access that require working at agency sites or controlled remote access are not likely to be considered unless there are no alternatives and there are strong incentives to undertake the research.

ARCHIVING FEDERAL STATISTICAL DATA SETS

Our concern in this subsection is with arrangements whereby public-use and other versions of significant statistical data sets, largely in electronic form, are either maintained by statistical agencies or transferred by them to the National Archives and Records Administration (NARA) for preservation and future access for statistical and research uses. The potential interest in and value of secondary analyses of data files long after their original creation is much greater today than it was even 10 years ago given the expanded availability of computer power and new methods of analysis. Some data sets may have the potential for illuminating issues that were not even thought of when they were created. (An analogy would be the practice of freezing genetic material for future breeding and research uses.)

Unfortunately, researchers who have explored the possibility of secondary analyses of old data sets have often encountered serious obstacles. In many instances, the desired files have not been preserved in any form (David, 1980; David and Robbin, 1981). If the files do exist and are accessible, serious difficulties may still result from the lack of supporting documentation, outmoded storage media, and failure to retain the entire data content of files that were used for the original analyses. The question, then, is what can be done to make things easier for future secondary analysts and historical researchers who will want to work with data sets that are now in existence or about to be created?

Current Federal Archiving Procedures All federal agencies, including statistical agencies, operate under statutorily prescribed information management procedures that oblige them to notify the NARA of proposed schedules for disposition of their records. In turn, NARA reviews the proposed schedules and, when it considers the records to "have sufficient administrative, legal, research, or other value to warrant their further preservation by the United States Government" (Title 44 U.S.C. § 3303a (a)) may disallow the proposed destruction of the records. For records that have been in existence for more than 30 years, the archivist (director of the agency) may direct the transfer of such records to the National Archives.

In general, statutory restrictions on access to and use of records transferred to the National Archives expire after a period of 30 years. However, under certain conditions, by agreement between the archivist and the agency that transferred the records, such restrictions can remain in force for a longer period (Title 44 U.S.C. § 2108(a)). In addition, it is the usual policy of the National Archives to maintain access restrictions for 75 years when the data are about individuals and their earlier release by the agency that transferred the records could have been denied under Freedom of Information Act exemption 6, which covers "personnel and medical and similar files the disclosure of which would constitute a clearly unwarranted invasion of personal privacy" (Title 5 U.S.C. § 552(b)(6)).

The National Archives only accepts electronic files that are physically intact and have adequate documentation to enable researchers to read and make valid use of the data. The agency takes necessary precautions, such as reading files periodically and recopying them to new media, to ensure that the data remain accessible on current computers.

Archiving Census Bureau Records Arrangements for the archiving of Census Bureau records are fairly well developed. Economic census records, which identify the responding firms, can be used at the National Archives without any restrictions after the statutory period of 30 years has elapsed. Under a special 1952 agreement between the archivist and the Census Bureau, microfilm copies of the original population census records (which are of great interest to genealogists) that are transferred to the National Archives are kept confidential for 72 years, after which time they are made available to users.

About two years ago, another agreement between the archivist and the Census Bureau extended provisions of the 1952 agreement to records from the Current Population Survey and other demographic surveys conducted by the Census Bureau. The 72-year period of confidentiality does not apply to any public-use microdata files that are transferred to the National Archives, but it would apply to internal Census Bureau survey data files whose content had not been restricted to make them suitable for unrestricted public access. To date, no such internal survey files have been transferred to the National Archives, but the archivist has requested files of this type and it is likely that they will be transferred once appropriate security arrangements have been agreed on. To illustrate the kinds of issues that arise, archived electronic files must be copied periodically to ensure their preservation in usable form, and the Census Bureau believes that such copying should be done by special sworn employees who are subject to criminal penalties for improper disclosure of Census Bureau information.

The rapid replacement of paper records by electronic files as the primary storage medium and the prospect of further changes in data base technology pose many challenges and opportunities for NARA in its efforts to meet future research needs. Statutes and procedures developed for archiving paper records will require significant alterations. A panel established by the National Academy of Public Administration to review these questions issued a report in 1991, *The Archives of the Future: Archival Strategies for the Treatment of Electronic Databases*. The tenor of that panel's recommendations is clearly expressed by the following excerpt from the report:

> *NARA itself must take an active stance in seeking candidate databases to evaluate for inclusion as part of the National Archives* [emphasis in original]. Persuasive and aggressive oversight should be the ringing quality of NARA's role in guiding the preservation policies of all federal agencies. And time is of the essence. An outstanding characteristic of electronic records . . . is that there is a much briefer span of time in which to bring them under active preservation. NARA's authority prevents it from taking forceful action to guarantee preservation of records until 30 years have passed. Electronic records not brought under the control of a comprehensive and active preservation program are unlikely to survive more than a few years. NARA must seek additional authorities to sustain a viable program for bringing electronic databases into the National Archives (pp. 1-2).

The report recommended that the National Archives preserve data from 430 federal data bases in addition to more than 600 that the agency had already designated as archival. The National Archives is actively pursuing transfers from these data bases.

RESTRICTED ACCESS: FINDINGS AND RECOMMENDATIONS

Recommendation 6.5 Federal statistical agencies should strive for a greater return on public investment in statistical programs through carefully controlled increases in interagency data sharing for statistical purposes and expanded availability of federal data sets to external users.

Full realization of this goal will require legislative changes, as discussed in Chapter 5, but much can be accomplished within the framework of existing legislation.

The panel believes that some of the newer and more user-friendly restricted access techniques, such as the release of encrypted CD-ROM diskettes with built-in software and licensing agreements that allow users to use data sets at their own work sites, have considerable promise, and it commends the agencies and organizations that have pioneered the use of such procedures.

Recommendation 6.6 Statistical agencies, in their efforts to expand access for external data users, should follow a policy of responsible innovation. Whenever feasible, they should experiment with some of the newer restricted access techniques, with appropriate confidentiality safeguards and periodic reviews of the costs and benefits of each procedure.

Recommendation 6.7 In those instances in which controlled access at agency sites remains the only feasible alternative, statistical agencies should do all they can to make access conditions more affordable and acceptable to users, for example, by providing access at dispersed agency locations and providing adequate user support and access to computing facilities at reasonable cost.

The panel agrees with the views expressed in the excerpt (above) from the National Academy of Public Administration's report on the archiving of electronic data bases.

Recommendation 6.8 Significant statistical data files, in their unrestricted form, should be deposited at the National Archives and eventually made available for historical research uses.

This recommendation is intended to cover statistical data bases from censuses and surveys and those, like the Statistics of Income and Continuous Work History Sample data bases, that are derived from administrative records. We have purposely not been specific as to the content of such archived data bases and the length of time for which confidentiality restrictions should continue to apply. Some data bases, like the economic and population censuses, might include explicit identification of data providers. Others, especially those based on samples, might not include names and addresses, but would not be subject to statistical disclosure limitation procedures of the kind that are applied to produce public-use microdata sets for contemporary use.

NOTES

1. Statistical disclosure limitation techniques are often referred to as *disclosure control* or *disclosure avoidance*. We prefer *disclosure limitation* because it expresses more clearly the fact that zero disclosure risk is usually unattainable.
2. These and other conceptualizations of *disclosure* are explored in Duncan and Lambert (1989), Duncan and Pearson (1991), and Lambert (1993).
3. Called *samples of anonymized records*. See Collins (1992) and Marsh et al. (1991a, 1992).
4. For example, as recognized by the National Center for Health Statistics,

> Of course, all direct identifiers of study subjects, such as name, address, and social security number, are deleted from the public use files. Still, there are so many different items of information about any subject individual or establishment in our typical surveys that the set of information could serve as a unique identifier for each subject, if there were some other public source for many of the survey items. Fortunately there is not. But to minimize the chance of disclosure we take additional precautions; we make sure there are no rare characteristics shown on any case in the files, such as the exact bed-size of a large nursing home, or the exact date of birth of a subject, or the presence of a rare disease, or the exact number of children in a very large family. We either delete or encrypt the code identifying smaller geographical areas—places smaller than 100,000 in population—because anyone trying to identify a respondent will have his task greatly simplified if he knows the respondent's local area (Mugge, 1984:291).

5. Collins (1992) and Marsh et al. (1992) provide further discussion of the relationship between disclosure risk and uniqueness.
6. There are situations in which adding noise has no effect on certain important kinds of analyses. With, for example, the Health Care Finance Agency's Medicare data, releasing values like exact date of death can pose substantial disclosure risk. The common practice of coarsening the data to, say, year of death may limit the usefulness of survival analyses based on the data and make it impossible to draw good inferences about the efficacy of certain medical treatments. However, shifting all dates by a fixed amount, unknown to the data user, will substantially lessen disclosure risk while leaving most survival analyses unharmed, because survival analysis generally depends only on the elapsed time between various events.

7. Some researchers have begun to address these issues. Kamlet et al. (1985), for example, analyze the 1980 National Health Interview Survey, in which several averages are reported rather than individual-level data because of confidentiality restrictions. Typically, analysts of such data simply use the associated group-level information instead of the (unavailable) individual-level data. As Kamlet et al. note, however, this practice can produce inconsistent estimates and regression coefficients of the wrong sign. Kamlet and Klepper (1985) demonstrate how consistent estimators can be computed in special cases. Hwang (1986) deals with the errors-in-variables nature of data masked by adding noise. For such a case, Fuller (1993) illustrates how the data can be analyzed.

8. The material in this section is based largely on Jabine (1993b), a paper commissioned by the panel. Brackstone (1990) notes that the development and application of statistical disclosure limitation techniques to protect the confidentiality of data is a relatively new area of statistics that arose out of the practical problems statistical agencies faced. Early discussions include Bachi and Baron (1969) and Steinberg and Pritzker (1967). Bailar (1990) identifies the development of statistical disclosure limitation techniques to be one of the five major contributions of the Census Bureau. Also see Barabba and Kaplan (1975), Cox et al. (1985), and Greenberg (1990, 1991).

9. The seven agencies are the Bureau of the Census, Bureau of Labor Statistics, Internal Revenue Service, National Center for Education Statistics, National Center for Health Statistics, Social Security Administration, and the Statistical Reporting Service (now the National Agricultural Statistics Service).

10. Based on conversation between Thomas Jabine, a consultant to the panel, and Patricia Doyle of Mathematica at a meeting of the American Statistical Association/Survey Research Methods Working Group on the Technical Aspects of SIPP on May 21, 1992.

11. Published along with other discussion and commissioned papers in a special issue of the *Journal of Official Statistics* 1993(2). See Appendix A for a list of the papers.

12. For univariate dimensions, he checks percentiles, the mean, standard deviation, and skewness. For multivariate dimensions, he checks correlation coefficients and covariance matrices.

13. The memorandum was signed on February 2, 1990, by Barbara E. Bryant (Census Bureau) and Janet L. Norwood (BLS).

14. The letters were signed on October 20, 1988, by John A. Ferris (DMDC) and by Kenneth C. Scheflen (OIG) on November 22, 1988.

7

Statistical Data on Organizations

The idea of individual rights is well established in all societies and cultures of the world. Rights associated with collectives are, however, another matter.

Paul Reynolds, 1993

INTRODUCTION

The uses of statistics on businesses and other organizations are not as widely understood as are the uses of statistics on persons and households based on the population censuses, the Current Population Survey (source of monthly estimates of unemployment), the vital statistics compiled by the National Center for Health Statistics, and other household surveys and administrative record sources. Yet, economic statistics are critical to understanding the health of the economy and the direction in which the economy is moving. The U.S. national economic accounts, the retail and wholesale price indexes, the data on foreign trade and financial flows—all are based primarily on data collected from organizations. The generally favorable reception to the 1991 Boskin initiative to improve the quality of economic statistics (see Council of Economic Advisers, 1991) is evidence of the importance that policymakers and other users attribute to these kinds of economic data.

TYPES OF ORGANIZATIONS

Statistics on organizations (considered *legal* persons) cover all data subjects (units of analysis) other than natural persons or groups of natural persons, such as families or households. Occasionally, data for persons and organizations may be part of the same data set. For example, some surveys link information about the business activities of sole proprietorships with demographic information about the personal characteristics of the proprietors. Other surveys link information about such organizations as hospitals or schools with data on persons served by or working in those organizations.

There are many kinds of organizations, and the differences among them often determine the level of confidentiality accorded to their data. In the commercial sector there are three legal forms of ownership: sole proprietorship, partnership, and corporation. Nonprofit corporations, which are exempt from income taxation, are a special group. Among the for-profit corporations, those whose shares are publicly traded are subject to special reporting requirements, and the contents of their reports (e.g., to the Securities and Exchange Commission) are generally available to the public. A subset of for-profit corporations, especially utility companies, are granted exclusive rights to particular markets; in return, their financial and other data may be subject to even greater public scrutiny.

Many companies consist of several individual establishments, at different physical locations. Although data for the company as a whole may be readily available to anyone, the same is not necessarily true for employment, payroll, production, and other data for each establishment controlled by the company.

In the public sector, the general expectation is that most information about the activities of federal, state, and local agencies and units of government will be available to all. Public access to such data is facilitated by freedom of information and sunshine laws at the federal level and in many states.

DIFFERENCES BETWEEN DATA ON PERSONS AND DATA ON ORGANIZATIONS

Legislation

As noted in earlier chapters, information about organizations is not protected by the Privacy Act of 1974 (P.L. 93-579). If a statistical agency that has identifiable information about organizations is not governed by agency-specific confidentiality legislation, it must rely primarily on exemption 4 of the Freedom of Information Act (P.L. 89-487), which covers "trade secrets and commercial or financial information obtained from a person [interpreted to include legal persons—such as business organizations] and privileged or confidential," to deny *public* requests for access to identifiable records for organizations. The Freedom of Information Act, however, does not provide authority to deny requests from other parts of the government.

Most of the major federal statistical agencies have some form of legislation that allows them to protect the confidentiality of data on organizations that they collect and process. One exception is the Bureau of Labor Statistics, which, as explained in Chapter 5, has relied on a combination of regulations and lower court decisions to protect data that it obtains from businesses, either directly or through state employment security agencies.

For most of the economic censuses and surveys conducted by the Census Bureau, the confidentiality provisions in Section 9 of Title 13 of the U.S. Code apply. Those provisions protect the confidentiality of respondents' file copies of census and survey report forms, as well as the originals submitted to the Census Bureau. They do not apply to reports collected from state and local governments, because those reports, by their nature, contain only data available, at least in theory, to anyone. They also do not apply to the data compiled from official import and export documents in the Census Bureau's foreign trade statistics program. Section 301(a) of Title 13 makes the export data confidential unless the secretary of commerce determines that it is in the national interest to disclose them. The import data are not covered by Title 13 because they are collected by the Customs Service and only compiled by the Census Bureau. As a matter of policy, the import and export data are published in extensive detail by commodity and other variables, but without explicit identification of importers and exporters. The majority of data cells in the most detailed tabulations are based on fewer than five transactions.

Some additional aspects of confidentiality legislation and its effects on the ability of federal statistical agencies to protect data on organizations and to share or release their data for statistical and research purposes are discussed in connection with four case studies presented below.

Other Differences

In addition to the differences in confidentiality protection based on the type of organization involved and the statutory framework of the federal agency that collects the data, federal statistics on organizations differ from those on persons in several significant ways:

- Response to statistical surveys of organizations is more likely to be required by law. Mandatory response requirements do not guarantee complete response to such surveys because prosecution of survey nonrespondents is not a high priority for federal law enforcement units. They do have the effect, however, that many surveys of organizations do not require a true informed consent process, as detailed in Chapter 3.

- There are likely to be greater incentives for other federal agencies and individuals to desire access, for nonstatistical purposes, to individually identifiable statistical information about commercial organizations. As discussed below, agencies with regulatory and compliance roles might consider a survey of businesses a good source of leads to companies that are or may have been in violation of laws and regulations. Industrial spies might derive substantial material benefits by obtaining access to trade secrets and other information critical to a company's competitive position.

- For aggregate variables like production, payroll, and expenditures, the population distributions for organizations tend to be much more skewed than they are for most variables associated with persons. Especially at the subnational level, data for one or two large establishments can dominate a data cell. As a consequence, there have been virtually no releases of public-use microdata sets containing business data, and a considerable amount of masking is required even in the public release of aggregate statistics. The size of a firm also affects the dynamics of the data collection process. Small businesses are less likely to be users of the data collected from them, have less influence over the content of economic data collection programs, and are likely to be disproportionately burdened by paperwork requirements.

Content of Chapter

Most of the panel members have had limited experience with data on organizations and our time and resources did not permit a systematic review of all the confidentiality issues associated with such data. We therefore chose case studies as the vehicle for identifying and exploring selected issues that have come to our attention. The remainder of the chapter consists of four case studies. For each case study, we provide the relevant background information, discuss the main issues, and present our findings and recommendations.

THE ENERGY INFORMATION ADMINISTRATION VS. THE DEPARTMENT OF JUSTICE: A FURTHER EROSION OF FUNCTIONAL SEPARATION

BACKGROUND

Early in 1990, the Antitrust Division of the Department of Justice began an investigation into the sharp increases in the prices of home heating oil and other fuels that had occurred as a result of unusually cold weather in December 1989. Later in the year, the division also started an investigation of the increases in gasoline prices that followed the Iraqi invasion of Kuwait in August.

To aid its investigations, the Antitrust Division requested the Energy Information Administration (EIA), Department of Energy, to provide specified data on prices, production, and other variables, some in aggregate form and some for individually named companies or establishments. The Energy Information Administration was willing to provide the aggregate data, but it resisted the request for individual company records on the grounds that release would be contrary to its *Policy on Disclosure of Individually Identifiable Energy Information in the Possession of the Energy Information Administration*, which had been published in the *Federal Register* (45(177):59812-59816). The Antitrust Division's request did not meet any of the conditions, set forth in Section E of that policy, under which EIA would disclose individually identifiable information to other federal agencies. Further, EIA pointed out that it had notified survey respondents about its confidentiality policies and that its failure to abide by them could hurt its ability to collect complete, accurate, and timely data in the future.

Although other federal agencies requesting data from EIA had accepted its 1980 policy on disclosure, the Antitrust Division did not. After prolonged negotiations, the matter was referred to the Office of Legal Counsel in the Department of Justice, which ruled on March 20, 1991, that the Federal Energy Administration Act of 1974 (P.L. 93-275), one of the statutes on which the EIA policy on disclosure was based, required that EIA produce the information requested by the Antitrust Division. Subsequent to this ruling, the Energy Department brought the issue to the attention of Counsel to the President, C. Boyden Gray. Gray, although sympathetic to a prospective solution to EIA's problem, did not feel he could recommend to the President that he direct the Justice Department to withdraw its request in this instance. In the ensuing months, there were protracted negotiations on the precise nature of the data to be released. Eventually, the Justice Department closed the two oil-pricing investigations after receiving some aggregate data—but not company-specific proprietary data from EIA. The Justice Department, however, has indicated that it believes it is legally entitled to such data and will seek to obtain it if appropriate in future investigations (General Accounting Office, 1993).

With a few exceptions, the provisions of EIA's 1980 policy on disclosure had permitted disclosures of individually identifiable data to federal agencies outside the Energy Department only for statistical purposes. The March 1991 Justice Department ruling meant that that portion of the EIA policy on disclosure could no longer be sustained; identifiable records would have to be released to any agency that insisted on having them.

In August 1991, EIA sent a letter to all of the roughly 25,000 respondents to the surveys affected to notify them of the forced change in its policy. As of January 1992, EIA had received approximately 50 letters and 200 telephone calls with complaints or inquiries. By the end of 1992 there had been no observable effects on the completeness and timeliness of responses to the surveys. However, the real test will come if individually identifiable data are turned over to the Justice Department and the disclosures are publicized in trade journals or other media.

DISCUSSION

Is EIA a Statistical Agency?

The Committee on National Statistics (National Research Council, 1992b:2) has proposed the following definition of a federal statistical agency: "a unit of the federal government whose principal function is the compilation and analysis of data and the dissemination of information for statistical purposes." The committee also states that a federal statistical agency, to be effective, must protect the confidentiality of individual responses and must not disclose identifiable information for administrative, regulatory, or enforcement purposes.

The principal mission of EIA is statistical, and thus the agency may be said to meet the basic definition proposed by the Committee on National Statistics, but there are significant exceptions. The Department of Energy Organization Act (P.L. 95-91) requires EIA to gather data in support of regulatory and program needs of the Department of Energy. For those surveys that collect data already available to the public and for those that collect data for regulatory purposes, completed report forms are available for inspection by the public, and respondents are informed of this fact.

Clearly, EIA lacks the kind of confidentiality policy that the Committee on National Statistics considers essential for an *effective* federal statistical agency. Individually identifiable information can be disclosed and is sometimes required to be disclosed for nonstatistical purposes. The agency's 1980 policy on disclosure allows disclosures for nonstatistical purposes to other units of the Department of Energy, the Congress, the General Accounting Office, and when the information does not come under the exemptions in the Freedom of Information Act, to the public. Thus, the 1991 ruling by the Justice Department's Office of Legal Counsel was not a first breach in an otherwise airtight policy of functional separation of data. Rather, it might be looked at as another hole in an already leaky dike.

Officials in EIA are quite concerned about their inability to guarantee full confidentiality of information that they collect or acquire by other means for statistical purposes. They have tried more than once to obtain legislation to remedy the situation, but they have yet to succeed. In the meantime, because it cannot guarantee confidentiality, EIA has been unable to get access to other statistical agencies' lists of companies and establishments for use in its own surveys, and it must develop and maintain completely independent lists, at considerable cost.

Did EIA Mislead Respondents?

Most of EIA's survey respondents are companies or establishments and their response to most of its surveys is mandatory. Following final adoption of the 1980 policy on disclosure, the agency developed a standard notification statement for its mandatory company and establishment surveys, which included information about the conditions under which identifiable information might be released to the public in response to Freedom of Information Act requests, to courts and congressional bodies, and to other federal agencies. The provisions of the policy governing release to other federal agencies were not described in detail in the notification statement; respondents wanting full information had to obtain and study the complex 1980 policy statement in the *Federal Register*.

One can assume that many respondents did not bother to obtain the policy statement and therefore were not familiar with the conditions under which their individual data might or might not be released to other federal agencies. It cannot be said that respondents in this category were seriously misled, they were merely not fully informed. However, those who were familiar with the policy were confronted, when they received the August 1991 letter from EIA, with a sudden—and retroactive—change. They had clearly been misled by a statement representing a policy that EIA had believed it could follow but which turned out not to be fully supported by the relevant statutes.

Is the EIA's Problem Unique?

In a sense, every federal statistical agency operates under a different statutory and regulatory framework. However, as discussed in Chapter 5, the agencies may be classified roughly as haves and have-nots with respect to legislation that both allows and requires them to apply the principle of functional separation to all data in their possession. The Energy Information Administration is clearly one of the have-nots and is in an especially awkward position because its statutorily defined mission includes some collection of data for nonstatistical purposes. The Bureau of Labor Statistics (BLS) is also a have-not agency in terms of legal protection of confidentiality, but its mission is more clearly statistical and, as explained in Chapter 5, it has so far been able to maintain *de facto* functional separation.

The Intermodal Surface Transportation Efficiency Act (P.L. 102-240), passed late in 1991, included provisions to establish a separate Bureau of Transportation Statistics in the Department of Transportation. This legislation has weak confidentiality provisions, clearly putting the new agency in the have-not category with respect to adequate statutory protection of the confidentiality of data obtained for statistical purposes. Legislation, proposed but not passed in 1991, to establish a separate statistical agency in a Department of Environmental Protection had similarly weak confidentiality provisions.

FINDINGS AND RECOMMENDATIONS

Businesses are subject to many kinds of regulations and are also eligible for various benefits. Monitoring compliance with regulations and determining eligibility for benefits require substantial amounts of data for individually identifiable units. Such data are used to make decisions that directly affect individual businesses. They can also be used for statistical analyses, which are sometimes focused directly on the program for which the data were collected and sometimes may be entirely unrelated to it.

Some kinds of business data, however, are of interest only for statistical research and analysis. Such data can best be collected by statistical agencies that have the authority and mandate to ensure that the data are fully protected from disclosure and from any use whatsoever for nonstatistical purposes. The collection of data that have nonstatistical and statistical uses should be left to programmatic and regulatory agencies. Such data, with identifiers if needed, can be acquired by statistical agencies and used for statistical purposes, but once in the possession of a statistical agency, the data should be given the same confidentiality protection as data collected directly by the agency.

> **Recommendation 7.1** The principle of functional separation, which the panel endorsed in Recommendation 5.1(a), should apply equally to data for persons and data for organizations.

A similar position was adopted by the Conference of European Statisticians (1991). Its *Resolution on the Fundamental Principles of Official Statistics in the Region of the Economic Commission for Europe* states that "individual data collected by statistical agencies for statistical compilation, whether they refer to natural or legal persons [such as business organizations], are to be strictly confidential and used exclusively for statistical purposes" (p. 8).

As illustrated by the EIA example, a statistical agency's intention to operate under this principle is not sufficient.

> **Recommendation 7.2** Legislation that authorizes and requires protection of the confidentiality of data for persons and organizations should be sought for all federal statistical agencies that do not now have it and for any new federal statistical agencies that may be created (see also Recommendation 5.1).

An opposing argument is that, for the sake of efficiency, federal agencies needing data for nonstatistical purposes, especially if related to compliance of businesses with laws and regulations, should be permitted to acquire the data from any agency that has them. Such a policy would seriously threaten the quality of the nation's economic statistics. Businesses, knowing that their census and survey forms could be used for any purpose, would be less inclined to submit complete, accurate, and timely data. One has only to review the history of economic data in the socialist economies over the past 50 years to understand this. Why risk such consequences for the relatively small efficiencies that might be realized by compliance agencies in deciding which businesses should be the targets of their detailed investigations?

The EIA example also illustrates the need to exercise care in the development of statements that notify respondents to mandatory surveys about how their data will be used and who will have access to them.

> **Recommendation 7.3** Data providers, whether persons or organizations, should have ready access to as much information as they want about the uses of the information they are requested or required to provide to federal statistical agencies. They should be told who will have access to their data in individually identifiable form. Statements of the collecting agency's intentions should be clearly distinguished from statements describing what is authorized and required by statute.

INABILITY TO SHARE BUSINESS LISTS:
AN EMBARRASSMENT TO
THE FEDERAL STATISTICAL SYSTEM

BACKGROUND

The question of access to business lists for statistical purposes by federal agencies has a history covering more than half a century. It is a question that has important implications for the cost, quality, and internal consistency of the economic statistics produced by the federal statistical system. In essence, the problem is that there are significant barriers to interagency sharing of business lists among agencies in the decentralized federal statistical system.

Broadly speaking, business lists are lists of companies, establishments, employers, and other kinds of economic units. The lists contain identifiers, such as name, address, and Employer Identification number, and classifiers, such as a Standard Industrial Classification (SIC) code and size codes based on employment, wages, production, or other measures. A primary statistical use of business lists is the development and maintenance of sampling frames for censuses and surveys. In addition, the lists may be used as a means of achieving uniformity in the classifications, especially SIC codes, that are assigned to the same units by different agencies.

Major producers of economic statistics include federal statistical agencies and operating agencies with statistical units. In the first category, the Census Bureau, the Bureau of Labor Statistics, and the National Agricultural Statistics Service (NASS) have major programs. We also allude in this case study to the use of business lists by the Bureau of Economic Analysis (BEA) and the Energy Information Administration.

In the second category, the Internal Revenue Service (IRS), with its Statistics of Income program, and the Social Security Administration (SSA), with its Continuous Work History Sample, are of major importance. These two agencies maintain extensive business lists in connection with their tax and benefit programs, lists that have great potential value (only partially realized at this time) for statistical applications. We also refer here to the use of business lists by the Small Business Administration's (SBA's) Office of Advocacy, which has developed its own lists for use in surveys and studies of small businesses.

To what extent are business lists currently being shared? The Census Bureau in the early 1970s developed its Standard Statistical Establishment List (SSEL) to serve as a master list for use in all of its economic censuses and surveys. Direct use of the SSEL for intercensal surveys has been limited, however, because of the difficulty of keeping the list current between censuses. The Census Bureau also originally intended that the SSEL would be available for use by other statistical agencies. There have been several attempts, so far unsuccessful with one small exception, to obtain legislation that would make this possible. A report by the Economic Policy Council's (1987) Working Group on the Quality of Economic Statistics recommended that BLS and NASS be administratively designated, by the Office of Management and Budget (OMB), as the "central collection agencies" for nonfarm and farm business lists, respectively. However, this recommendation was never implemented.

The Census Bureau obtains inputs to the SSEL from several sources, especially the administrative lists of the IRS and SSA. Use of tax return information for this purpose is specifically permitted by the "statistical information" exception to the disclosure constraints of the Internal Revenue Code (see Chapter 5). The terms of this exception were negotiated between IRS and the

Commerce Department in the 1976 amendments that established the current disclosure policy of the Internal Revenue Code (Title 26 U.S.C.). However, those same provisions prohibit redisclosure, by recipients, of tax return information received for statistical purposes. For a particular establishment or employer whose identity was originally supplied by the IRS, the Internal Revenue Code allows the Census Bureau to contact the taxpayer, and any response returned to the Census Bureau is considered to be data collected under the authority of the Census Bureau (Title 13 U.S.C.) rather than tax return information.

There is little flow of business list information *from* the Census Bureau to other agencies. Exceptions are the occasional correction or updating of SIC codes on lists provided by other agencies, under the authority of a 1953 opinion issued by Attorney General McGranery (41 Op. A.G. 120), and the release of certain SSEL information to BEA, which has become possible as a result of legislation passed by the 101st Congress (Foreign Direct Investment and International Financial Data Improvements Act of 1990, P.L. 101-533). As part of the same legislation, BEA is required to share with BLS and the Census Bureau selected data on foreign direct investment that it collects from business enterprises.

There are a few other examples of business list sharing, but what is more to the point is the sharing that is not occurring. The National Agricultural Statistics Service shares its farm list information with the Census Bureau in preparation for each quinquennial census of agriculture, but Title 13 prohibits any reverse flow of information to NASS for use in its extensive program of current agricultural surveys. The Census Bureau uses farm tax return lists from the IRS as a major source of its sampling frame for the agricultural censuses, but the provisions of the Tax Reform Act of 1976 (P.L. 94-455) do not permit IRS or the Census Bureau to share the same lists with NASS. The result has been to increase substantially the cost to NASS of developing and maintaining the lists of farms that it needs for its data collection programs.

For a long time there had been no sharing of data for individual establishments or other units in either direction between the Census Bureau and BLS, the two agencies with the most extensive program of economic surveys for the nonagricultural sectors. However, changes are occurring. Late in 1990, in preparation for the 1992 economic censuses, the Census Bureau submitted a request to OMB for approval of several classification surveys to improve industry classification for new businesses. The OMB, within its authority under the Paperwork Reduction Act of 1980 (P.L. 96-511), denied the request by the Census Bureau to collect industry classification information because, in its view, such collection would duplicate surveys already conducted by the BLS. The OMB proceeded to work with BLS, the Census Bureau, and the IRS to resolve some legal questions about the sharing of business list information. Terms negotiated with the three agencies were incorporated in an order (authorized under 44 U.S.C. 3510) directing limited sharing of the data (see MacRae, 1990). A formal interagency agreement between BLS and the Census Bureau (signed by Barbara E. Bryant, Census Bureau, and Janet L. Norwood, BLS, April 19, 1991) implementing the OMB order was negotiated with the assistance and support of OMB. The matching of BLS and Census Bureau records, based primarily on Employer Identification numbers, is being carried out at BLS by BLS employees who are also special sworn employees of the Census Bureau. The emphasis in the list sharing is on the transfer of BLS's SIC codes to the Census Bureau. Under the McGranery opinion cited above, the Census Bureau's SIC codes could be transferred to BLS *for units already on BLS lists*, but BLS has not asked for the Census Bureau codes. It is not likely that information for unmatched units on either agency's list can be transferred to and used by the other agency. However, the agreement includes research to evaluate such discrepancies in coverage with a view to developing a coordinated data collection strategy, such as using a jointly sponsored data collection program, to resolve them.

The EIA and the SBA's Office of Advocacy require general and specialized business lists for most of their economic surveys, but neither has access to the Census Bureau's SSEL, BLS lists developed in connection with the federal-state Unemployment Insurance program, or the business lists that could be developed from the IRS/SSA administrative systems. Previous efforts to make the SSEL available to other agencies for statistical use have excluded EIA and SBA's Office of Advocacy because, as explained above for EIA, neither agency had the kind of statutory provisions that would guarantee that it could protect the shared list information from all access for nonstatistical purposes.

The proposal for improving the quality of economic statistics issued by Chairman Michael Boskin of the Council of Economic Advisers (1991:6) included as one of seven major elements the development of legislation to permit "limited sharing of confidential statistical information solely for statistical purposes between statistical agencies under stringent safeguards." Such legislation, as now envisioned, would provide a statutory basis for sharing business lists and other kinds of data among four major federal statistical agencies: the Bureau of Economic Analysis, Bureau of Labor Statistics, Census Bureau, and the National Agricultural Statistics Service. As of early 1993, the legislation had not yet been introduced.

PRACTICES IN OTHER COUNTRIES

The panel reviewed the policies and practices of several other developed countries with respect to statistical and other uses of business lists established and maintained by government statistical agencies. The review was based mainly on eight papers presented at two meetings of the International Roundtable on Business Survey Frames, an informal international group of government statisticians, which has met annually since 1986 to discuss statistical and other uses of business lists. Relevant papers from the 1989 meeting covered the business list confidentiality and access policies of Australia, France, Japan, the Netherlands, Sweden, and the United Kingdom. Papers from the 1990 meeting covered Finland and New Zealand. We obtained information about Canadian policies directly from Statistics Canada.

The nine countries whose policies the panel reviewed vary widely as to who may have access to business lists and the purposes for which they may be used. Insofar as we could determine, Finland, France, and Sweden place no restrictions on access to and uses of basic list information other than payment of fees and, in some instances, prohibition of release to third parties. The most restrictive country was Japan, which allows access to its complete list only by other units of national and local government, solely for statistical purposes. Australia and the United Kingdom joined Japan in allowing access only to other units of government, but they permitted some kinds of nonstatistical uses. The Netherlands allows disclosure to other units of government and specified types of nongovernment entities, solely for statistical purposes. New Zealand makes list information available to any type of organization, but it prohibits release to third parties and some types of nonstatistical uses.

In Canada, the Statistics Act allows the disclosure of lists of businesses, by order of the chief statistician, as an exception to the general prohibition against disclosure contained in the law. A committee reviews requests for such information, using criteria set out in an internal Statistics Canada policy, and makes recommendations to the chief statistician, who has the discretion to grant or deny each request. For each request, the review committee considers the proposed uses of the lists and their potential impact. Lists may be released for the collection of statistical data if the proposed survey uses acceptable methodology, does not duplicate information already collected, and does not appear to jeopardize respondents' continued cooperation with Statistics Canada. Lists may also be released to assist data users in the analysis or interpretation of data, and for that purpose, they are sometimes included in industry publications, particularly for the manufacturing sector. Lists may include any or all of the following information: names and addresses; telephone numbers for statistical inquiries; official language preferred for statistical inquiries; services provided and products produced, manufactured, processed, transported, stored, purchased or sold; and size, expressed in terms of an employment size range (letter from Ivan P. Fellegi, chief statistician of Canada, to panel, January 26, 1993).

Three of the nine countries give units included in their lists the option to have their names excluded from some kinds of releases. The United Kingdom, in connection with one of its economic surveys, requests permission from manufacturers for their inclusion in a directory that is published at five-year intervals. Less than half of the units, in terms of employment, agree to have their information included. In Finland and the Netherlands, units may request to have their information excluded from any releases of directory information to other organizations. Neither country provided information on the number of such requests.

The most striking finding of this review was that none of the nine countries has business list policies as restrictive as those currently followed in the United States. All of the countries reviewed allow, *at a minimum*, access to the government's business lists by *all* units of national government (and generally local government units as well) for statistical purposes. Some allow unrestricted access to the lists for any purpose.

FINDINGS AND RECOMMENDATIONS

In 1939, the U.S. Central Statistical Board proclaimed the need for "a United States Business Directory or Official Mailing List which will show the name, address, and industrial classification of each important business enterprise" (Bureau of the Budget, 1961:1). Over the intervening years, other organizations and advisory groups too numerous to mention have recommended more sharing of business lists (see, e.g., American Statistical Association, 1980; Economic Policy Council, 1987), but until quite recently the trend has been in the opposite direction.

There is little doubt that significant savings and improvements in the quality and comparability of the economic data produced by BLS, the Census Bureau, and NASS could be realized if all three agencies had full access to the IRS/SSA administrative lists and to each others' lists. Further gains would accrue if other agencies that conduct economic surveys could be brought into the system.

The panel commends OMB's Statistical Policy Office for the steps it has been taking to promote limited sharing of business list information between BLS and the Census Bureau and to develop legislation that will permit further sharing of business lists, as recommended in the Boskin initiative.

> **Recommendation 7.4** There should be increased sharing of business lists for statistical purposes by federal and state agencies.

Detailed business lists, especially at the establishment level, that are developed by federal agencies for statistical uses should be protected against nonstatistical uses. Hence, federal agencies should have access only if they can guarantee such protection. Two potential statistical users, EIA and the SBA's Office of Advocacy, are currently unable to meet this requirement.

> **Recommendation 7.5** New legislation on sharing of business lists for statistical purposes should provide that government agencies that are now unable to guarantee protection against nonstatistical uses can have access to business lists if they acquire statutory authority for such protection in the future.

WAIVERS: WHOSE INFORMATION IS IT?

BACKGROUND

Statistical agencies sometimes request permission from survey respondents to use the latter's information in ways that depart from standard agency policies for the protection of confidentiality. For example, an agency might wish to

- transfer individually identifiable information for an organization to another agency for a statistical purpose,
- release tabulations without application of some of the masking techniques that would usually be used, or
- include identification information for respondents in a published directory of organizations.

Agencies may seek waivers from respondents for such purposes, either because the proposed uses of the latter's data would not usually be permitted by applicable statutes or regulations or because the uses would be contrary to announced agency policies. In terms of fair information principles, the process of requesting waivers, *if carried out according to accepted procedures for informed consent*, allows respondents greater control over how information about them is used.

Organizations may benefit in some ways from granting waivers requested by statistical agencies. For example, if a waiver permits two agencies to share an organization's data for statistical uses, the organization will not have to provide it to each one separately. If the waiver allows an agency to publish a tabulation with a production or sales data cell that is dominated by the organization, the latter may be in a better position to determine its market share. Below we present several examples of situations in which federal statistical agencies have asked organizations to waive confidentiality protections for their data.

EXAMPLES

In detailed tabulations of economic survey data, it is common for one or two data providers to dominate a single data cell. For example, one establishment in a county or state may account for a large proportion of total employment, payroll, production, or some other variable. As described in Chapter 6, most agencies have policies that suppress or mask such data cells when one or two units account for more than a specified proportion of the total. At least three federal statistical agencies sometimes seek waivers that will allow them to include such data cells, without the usual suppression or masking, in their publications. The National Agricultural Statistics Service has a formal standard for its state offices to use for obtaining permission from respondents in instances in which there are only one or two respondents in a cell or one respondent accounts for more than 60 percent of the value to be published. Written permission is required and must be updated every five years (National Agricultural Statistics Service, 1989). Consideration is being given to updating the permission every two or three years.

The Bureau of Labor Statistics has a cooperative program with state employment security agencies for the collection of periodic occupational employment statistics data. Frequently, a single company will account for a high proportion of the persons in particular occupations in its area. In such instances the state agency conducting the survey seeks waivers to allow publication of the affected data cells.

The Census Bureau has a Current Industrial Reports program for periodic collection, from manufacturers, of intercensal data on the production of a large number of specifically defined commodities. For some commodities, one or two manufacturers may dominate total production, even at the national level. The Census Bureau uses a waiver procedure to obtain permission from survey respondents to publish data for the affected commodities.

Until recently, the Census Bureau also used waivers for a different purpose: to share individually identifiable data about cotton ginning operations with NASS. As described in a July 18, 1990, memorandum to the panel from Frederic A. Vogel, an official of NASS,

> in the past, NASS has had access to individual gin reports to compile data for the monthly cotton production forecast. This data sharing activity was done with the concurrence of the cotton gins so they could eliminate duplicate reporting.

However, OMB's legal counsel ruled in 1990 that Census Bureau employees may not release individually identifiable information collected under Title 13, even when waivers have been obtained. It was OMB's position, based on the legislative history, that the provision of Title 13 (§ 8(a)) that permits transfer of copies of reports to authorized agents was intended to apply only to special situations involving a few individual respondents, not to large-scale transfer of records from a particular survey. Further, OMB counsel argued, the right to confidentiality under Title 13 constitutes a public right (as opposed to a private right) that cannot be waived by the respondent. In this particular instance, the difficulty was resolved by transferring responsibility for the cotton ginning survey program from the Census Bureau to NASS, which is not governed by Title 13.

The panel finds it somewhat incongruous that OMB's interpretation of Title 13 prevents the Census Bureau from using a waiver procedure to share data with NASS for statistical purposes, but that the Census Bureau is able to use a waiver procedure in its Current Industrial Reports program to permit the release of data cells whose publication would usually be contrary to the confidentiality provisions of Title 13. We believe that the use of waiver procedures for the kinds of statistical purposes illustrated in this section should be permitted, provided the consequences of granting waivers are clearly explained to respondents and they are not put under any kind of pressure to grant the permission requested.

> **Recommendation 7.6** The Office of Management and Budget's Statistical Policy Office should develop uniform guidelines for federal statistical agencies covering the purposes for which waivers of confidentiality protections by organizations are considered acceptable and the methods of obtaining waivers from respondents. Efforts should be made to amend the confidentiality statutes of federal statistical agencies that would otherwise be prevented from using waivers for generally accepted statistical purposes.

With respect to waivers for the publication of data cells dominated by one or two large organizations, there may be some circumstances in which smaller organizations contributing to the same cell, especially if they are few in number, should also be asked for permission to publish the data for that cell. If there are only one or two smaller organizations, they may not want their large competitors to have more precise information about them than would usually be available. The written policies we reviewed did not include any provision for preventing that.

USER ACCESS: GETTING A BETTER RETURN ON INVESTMENTS IN ECONOMIC STATISTICS

BACKGROUND

As we pointed out in the introduction to this chapter, organizations vary widely on many important characteristics, and thus individual organizations are often easily recognizable on the basis of a few data items and classifiers, especially if their geographic location is given. Consequently, federal statistical agencies have been unable, with few exceptions, to issue public-use microdata sets containing individual records, minus explicit identifiers, for companies, establishments, employers, and other organizational entities. Even for aggregate data on organizations, the same considerations restrict the amount of detail by location, type of economic activity, and other classifiers that can be published.

Substantial benefits have been realized by data users, statistical agencies, and society as a whole as a result of the wide dissemination of public-use microdata sets on persons. Comparable returns on investment in data collection have not been realized from the resources devoted to statistics on businesses and other organizations. Those data are an underutilized resource.

The same constraints carry over to hierarchical files containing data on persons and organizations. As explained in Chapter 6, an important reason why microdata from the Continuous Work History Sample, a 1 percent longitudinal sample of persons issued Social Security numbers, are no longer widely available to researchers is the concern that some large employers could be identified fairly easily on the basis of their industry classifications and geographic locations. Thus, employers having access to the file might be able to identify their own employees who were in the sample and learn about their work histories and current second jobs. Similar considerations apply to data from surveys conducted by the National Center for Education Statistics in which data are collected simultaneously for students, staff, and educational institutions.

In Chapter 6, we described several forms of restricted access to federal statistical data that are provided for external users: American Statistical Association/National Science Foundation (ASA/NSF) fellowships that allow researchers to work with data at federal agencies; remote on-line access with query restrictions, as in the Luxembourg Income Study; release of encrypted microdata in CD-ROM format; and various types of licensing agreements that provide access for users at their work sites, but place restrictions on the uses that can be made of the data and often include penalties for failure to abide by the terms of the agreement.

To some extent, these kinds of arrangements have been providing greater access to data for organizations over the past few years. Some of the ASA/NSF fellows, including those who have worked at the Census Bureau's Center for Economic Studies, have had access to microdata for establishments and enterprises. Through contracts for joint research studies the Center for Economic Studies has also provided access to such data, at the Census Bureau, to several researchers from nonprofit organizations. McGuckin (1992), in a discussion paper issued by the Center for Economic Studies, proposes that some economic microdata sets be made available to researchers, working as special sworn Census Bureau employees, at the Census Bureau's regional offices. He also recommends a broad interpretation of the requirement that research studies relying on this mode of data access be of joint interest to the Census Bureau and the researchers.

The National Agricultural Statistics Service and the Economic Research Service of the Department of Agriculture have established a research enclave that makes it possible for researchers to have limited access, in Washington, D.C., to microdata on farms from the two agencies' annual Farm Costs and Returns Survey. The National Agricultural Statistics Service has also developed administrative procedures that allow some researchers to have restricted access to statistical data at its state offices. The National Center for Education Statistics has become an active proponent of dissemination of data by means of encrypted CD-ROM diskettes and licensing agreements, and some of the data released in those ways are for schools.

Despite these developments, external users still have difficulty obtaining access to federal statistical data on organizations. This is particularly true for data on nonagricultural establishments and other economic units, for which many of the data sets that would be of most interest to researchers are maintained by the Census Bureau.

FINDINGS AND RECOMMENDATIONS

The panel's general findings and recommendations about procedures for giving external users restricted access to federal statistical data were presented in Chapter 6. In brief, we expressed our belief that a greater return on public investment in statistical programs would be possible through carefully controlled expansion of the availability of federal data sets to external users. We encouraged statistical agencies to develop and use some of the newer data dissemination techniques, such as the use of encrypted CD-ROM diskettes and licensing agreements, with appropriate confidentiality safeguards and periodic reviews of costs and benefits.

We believe there is a need for substantially expanded user

access to federal statistical data about organizations, especially business establishments and other economic units.

Recommendation 7.7 Federal statistical agencies that collect data on organizations should make a special effort to improve access for statistical research and analysis by external users and, if necessary, should seek legislation that will permit them to develop licensing arrangements that allow such users to have access at their work sites, subject to penalties for violating the conditions under which they are allowed access to the data.

8

Managing Confidentiality and Data Access Functions

Technology always moves ahead of sound management principles.
Stuart Sutton, 1991

The effective functioning of the federal statistical system requires responsible policies toward data providers and data users. Managers of federal statistical programs must give constant, careful attention to confidentiality and data access issues. However, new data collection and processing technologies, novel types of surveys, and innovative statistical uses of administrative records bring with them questions for which statutes, regulations, and policy statements do not always provide definitive answers.

The general principles and recommendations in this report are broadly focused. In the course of this study, the panel has identified many more questions than it could expect to provide detailed answers for. We have tried to provide useful guidelines, but we have not tried to give specific answers to questions such as the following:

• How much detail should be included in aggregate statistics and microdata sets that are released to the public with no restrictions on their use?

• Under what conditions should a proxy respondent be allowed to provide data for another person or household without the latter's informed consent?

• Under what circumstances are passive waivers acceptable?

• To what extent should lists of businesses compiled by federal statistical agencies be made publicly available?

• What conditions should be included in interagency agreements for sharing identifiable data for statistical purposes?

• What kinds of informed consent procedures are appropriate for telephone surveys?

Agencies in the federal statistical system have established policies and procedures for reaching administrative decisions about these and other confidentiality and data access questions. Are those decision mechanisms adequate? If not, how might they be improved? In this chapter we look at internal agency staffing and organization of information management activities and at government-wide mechanisms for standardizing and coordinating policies and practices. We also examine the extent to which the decision processes of federal statistical agencies incorporate the views of data providers and data users. We discuss the relevant decision mechanisms, such as data protection boards, that have been established in other countries, and we explore their possible relevance for the U.S. statistical system.

MANAGEMENT OF CONFIDENTIALITY AND DATA ACCESS QUESTIONS IN THE FEDERAL STATISTICAL SYSTEM

WITHIN STATISTICAL AGENCIES

The documentation provided to the panel by federal statistical agencies included several examples of policy manuals, policy memorandums and standards related to statistical disclosure limitation procedures, informed consent procedures, and other aspects of confidentiality and data access. The most comprehensive formal codification of these issues by any of the agencies that responded to our request for information was in two publications of the National Center for Health Statistics (NCHS): the *Policy Statement on Release of Data for Individual Elementary Units and Special Tabulations* (1978; first published in 1969) and the *NCHS Staff Manual on Confidentiality* (1984; first published in 1978). The *Policy Statement* is addressed primarily to data users and focuses on various ways of gaining access to NCHS microdata. The basic policy statement is as follows:

> Within prevailing ethical, legal, technical, technological and economic restrictions, it is the policy of the National Center for Health Statistics to augment its programs of collection, analysis, and publication of statistical information with procedures for making available, at cost, transcripts of data for individual elementary units—persons or establishments—in a form that will not in any

way compromise the confidentiality guaranteed the respondent (National Center for Health Statistics, 1978:4).

The NCHS *Staff Manual* presents the agency's policies for the protection of confidentiality. It includes information and rules covering legal requirements and penalties, employees' responsibilities, promise of confidentiality to respondents, treatment of requests for information, physical protection of records, disclosures that may be permitted, avoidance of unintentional disclosures through published data, maintenance of confidentiality in the release of microdata files, and requirements placed on contractors.

Several agencies have prepared written guidelines for the application of statistical disclosure limitation procedures in the release of tabulations and microdata. Some of the guidelines contain only one or two simple rules; others are much more detailed. Agencies with more detailed formal documentation of procedures include the Census Bureau (for microdata), the Energy Information Administration (EIA; for tabulations only), NCHS, and the Social Security Administration (SSA). The panel found that agency guidelines gave much less attention to other aspects of confidentiality and data access, such as the development of interagency data-sharing agreements and the content of informed consent and notification statements for surveys.

Two agencies, the Census Bureau and the National Center for Education Statistics (NCES), have internal committees that review all proposals for releases of new microdata sets. The Census Bureau's Microdata Review Panel has a formal charter and guidelines, as well as a standard prospectus that must be completed by all divisions sponsoring new microdata releases. Key elements of the Microdata Review Panel's evaluation criteria were published in the *Federal Register* (46(72):22017) at the time the panel was formally established in 1981. The Microdata Review Panel has no outside members; however, the Census Bureau is considering an arrangement for periodic review of the panel's policies and decisions by outside advisors selected to represent data providers and data users.

The NCES's Disclosure Review Board was created more recently, in 1989. The board's primary function, like that of the Census Bureau panel, is to determine whether microdata sets proposed for release pose an acceptably low risk of disclosure of individually identifiable data. The board consists of NCES staff members and a Census Bureau representative.

Several federal statistical agencies have external advisory groups, and they sometimes ask them for their views on confidentiality and data access questions. The Census Bureau has asked several of its advisory groups to review its plans for the application of statistical disclosure limitation procedures to decennial census data. About 1980, when EIA was developing its confidentiality policies, it asked the American Statistical Association's (ASA's) Committee on Energy Statistics to review drafts of policy statements on more than one occasion. More recently, EIA has sought advice from the same committee on how to deal with the consequences of the Justice Department's request for identifiable records (discussed in Chapter 7).

Statistical agencies have also drawn on the Committee on National Statistics to help them address specific problems. In the late 1970s, a panel established by the committee in response to a request from the Census Bureau undertook research to obtain information on "how people in the United States currently feel and behave in their roles as respondents, or intended respondents, in household censuses and surveys" (p. viii). The main findings from that panel's report, *Privacy and Confidentiality as Factors in Survey Response* (National Research Council, 1979), were discussed in Chapter 3 of this report.

Prior to the start of this panel's study, the Committee on National Statistics and the Social Science Research Council organized two workshops at the request of federal agencies. The first workshop, sponsored by the National Institute on Aging, explored the legal and ethical aspects of a proposed follow-up survey of surviving members of the sample panel for the SSA's Longitudinal Retirement History Survey. The second workshop, sponsored by the National Science Foundation (NSF), explored various options for improving researchers' access to microdata from two of NSF's scientific and technical personnel data systems, the Doctorate Records File and the Survey of Doctorate Recipients.

During the term of this study, the panel conducted a workshop on confidentiality and data access issues for the National Center for Education Statistics, which had been seeking advice from several groups on how best to collect data and serve the needs of data users under the terms of new agency confidentiality legislation that had been passed in 1988. All three of these workshops brought together agency staff, data users, and experts on information law, statistical disclosure limitation procedures, and other relevant topics. Several members of the panel participated in one or more of the workshops.

The panel did not conduct a review of detailed management and organizational issues, such as where confidentiality and data access functions are placed within statistical agencies or the titles, grade levels, and qualifications of the individuals who play major roles. Based on our general knowledge of these matters, however, we can make a few broad statements. First, only a handful of statistical agencies have a staff person whose primary role is to deal with such issues as informed consent, release of microdata, interagency data-sharing agreements, and other aspects of confidentiality and data access. The development and application of statistical disclosure limitation techniques is frequently assigned to mathematical statisticians in a unit responsible for methodological research and consulting assistance to operating units. In some of the smaller statistical agencies, there are no specialists on confidentiality issues, and the relevant questions are dealt with on an ad hoc basis by operating staff, some of whom have little or no pertinent background or experience.

ACROSS STATISTICAL AGENCIES

The Office of Management and Budget's (OMB's) original Statistical Policy Division, the interim successor—the Office of Federal Statistical Policy and Standards in the Department of Commerce—and OMB's current Statistical Policy Office have played a role in developing and monitoring government-wide standards and policies regarding protection of confidentiality and access to federal statistical data. Two of the early Statistical Policy Working Papers issued by the Federal Committee on Statistical Methodology covered relevant topics: No. 2, *Report on Statistical Disclosure and Disclosure-Avoidance Techniques* (1978), and No. 5, *Report on Exact and Statistical Matching Techniques* (1980). Working Paper 2 and the interagency seminars based on it were instrumental in raising the level of awareness of federal statisticians to the need for more careful application of statistical disclosure limitation techniques when releasing aggregate data or microdata.

Subsequent to the start of this panel's study, the head of the Statistical Policy Office has taken steps to review, with agency representatives, such issues as informed consent, statistical disclosure limitation procedures, interagency data-sharing, and licensing procedures for data access for external users. Early in 1992, the office formed an interagency committee to exchange information on current statistical disclosure limitation practices and on recent technical developments. (Early in 1993, this committee became the Subcommittee on Disclosure Limitation Methodology of the Federal Committee on Statistical Methodology.) The office is planning a formal review, with public comment, of the data user licensing procedures that are now being used on a trial basis by NCES.

As explained in Chapter 7, the Statistical Policy Office has been instrumental in persuading the Census Bureau and the Bureau of Labor Statistics to begin sharing business lists that until now have been developed and maintained independently. In addition, it is coordinating the development of proposed legislation that would permit list sharing for statistical purposes among four of the major federal statistical agencies: the Bureau of Economic Analysis, the Bureau of Labor Statistics, the Census Bureau, and the National Agricultural Statistics Service.

The Statistical Policy Office has also been working for some time on a revision of the OMB Circular, *Guidelines for Federal Statistical Activities*. One can expect, on the basis of an early draft published for public comment, that the final version of these guidelines will cover some of the issues studied by the panel, such as the content of informed consent and notification statements and the conditions under which record matching for statistical purposes is appropriate.

The Statistical Policy Office reviews all data collection requests developed by the Census Bureau and the Bureau of Economic Analysis. Data collection requests submitted to OMB by other federal agencies, including those for statistical purposes, are reviewed by OMB clearance officers who are not part of the Statistical Policy Office. The Statistical Policy Office provides advice on statistical data collections to the clearance officers on request, and on its own initiative it frequently makes recommendations concerning proposals sponsored by statistical agencies. Forms-clearance reviews provide an opportunity to examine informed consent and notification statements, but currently the OMB reviewers do not work from any written guidelines, aside from the Privacy Act regulations, about what should be included in such statements. This may change when the OMB circular mentioned above is issued.

In addition to the interagency committees and other formal coordination mechanisms established by OMB's Statistical Policy Office, there are many other ways in which employees of federal statistical agencies exchange information about the policies and procedures they use to deal with confidentiality and data access questions. Many surveys and other statistical programs involve two or more agencies and require joint efforts to develop appropriate methodologies. Official statisticians from different agencies often participate in discussions of confidentiality and data access matters at meetings of organizations like the Committee on National Statistics and the Council of Professional Associations on Federal Statistics. Managers and technicians from various statistical agencies have frequent contacts through their active participation in national and local professional associations, as described in the next subsection.

THE INFLUENCE OF PROFESSIONAL SOCIETIES

The American Society for Access Professionals is an organization whose membership consists primarily of federal government employees whose functions include activities related to agency compliance with the requirements of privacy and freedom of information statutes. The society organizes an annual symposium in the fall and sponsors tutorial sessions each spring to update its members on changes in privacy and freedom of information legislation and case law. A few of the society's members are from federal statistical agencies, and some of the presentations at their annual symposiums have covered the application of information legislation to research and statistical activities.

As outlined below, the American Statistical Association has been actively involved in addressing confidentiality and data access issues:

• Two ASA committees, the Ad Hoc Committee on Privacy and Confidentiality and the Ad Hoc Committee on Professional Ethics, have developed guidelines relevant to census and survey activities, especially in the area of informed consent (see discussions in Chapters 3 and 4). The association now has a permanent Committee on Privacy and Confidentiality. Over the years, several members of this committee have been employees of federal statistical agencies. The current chair was Gerald Gates of the Census Bureau. As described in Chapter 3, the committee has developed an informational brochure, *Surveys and Privacy.*

• The journals and proceedings of ASA have included numerous articles on statistical disclosure limitation theory and methods and other aspects of confidentiality and data access. Several panel discussions have been held on these topics at annual and other meetings.

• From time to time other ASA committees, such as the

Census Advisory Committee and the Committee on Energy Statistics, have advised federal statistical agencies on confidentiality questions.

Other U.S. professional associations, including the American Association for Public Opinion Research, the American Psychological Association, and the American Sociological Association, have developed codes or guidelines for their members, some portions of which are relevant to the conduct of surveys and experimental research. And as mentioned in Chapter 3, the International Statistical Institute's (1986) *Declaration on Professional Ethics* included extensive guidelines for the content of informed consent procedures.

On the data access side, meetings of organizations like the Association of Public Data Users provide another forum in which agency statisticians and data users can exchange views. Also, data users tend to be well represented on the various advisory committees to federal statistical agencies, especially the ones that deal with substantive rather than methodological issues.

ALTERNATIVE MODELS FOR MANAGING CONFIDENTIALITY AND DATA ACCESS QUESTIONS: A LOOK AT OTHER COUNTRIES

The issues that the panel has studied are not peculiar to the United States. As a natural consequence of the coming of the information age, they have arisen in all of the countries that have led the way in the development of modern data collection, processing, storage, and dissemination methods. The panel would be remiss if it failed to ask what can be learned from other countries that have also been grappling with how to manage confidentiality and data access questions.

The mechanisms described in this section go well beyond purely statistical and research uses of data about persons. The Privacy Act in the United States and the data protection boards established in other countries have jurisdiction over administrative and statistical uses of individual records. A key question, for official statisticians, is how well these mechanisms take into account the differences between statistical and other uses of personal data.

Flaherty (1989:viii) has undertaken "a comparative examination of the passage, revision, and, especially, implementation of data protection laws at the national and state levels" in Canada, the Federal Republic of Germany, France, Sweden, and the United

States. His review, plus materials the panel obtained directly from Statistics Canada, provide the main basis for our discussion of what has happened in countries other than the United States. Also helpful were papers by Dalenius (1979) and Durbin (1979) in the *Journal of the Royal Statistical Society* and discussants' comments on those papers.

In the United States, the responsibility for oversight of compliance with the requirements of the Privacy Act of 1974 was assigned to OMB. In contrast, in each of the four other countries that Flaherty studied, data protection legislation provided for the establishment of a commissioner or board, with a considerable degree of independence from the executive branch of the government, to monitor compliance with the fair information practices mandated by the legislation. The structure, scope of authority, and functions of those independent units vary. Canada has separate privacy and information commissioners. Both have jurisdiction only over records and information in the public sector and both function mostly in an ombudsman/advisory mode, although they may take certain cases to the Federal Court of Canada when agencies do not follow their advice.

The Swedish Data Inspection Board has jurisdiction over record systems in the public and private sectors, but only those maintained in electronic form. Initially, all new electronic record systems had to be licensed by the board. This proved to be unwieldy, and the procedure was changed to require registration, rather than licensing, of new systems, with some exceptions. The board has broad regulatory powers over all electronic record systems; for example, almost all record linkages are subject to its regulation.

The Federal Republic of Germany has an independent federal data protection commissioner, as well as data protection offices in the states. The federal and state commissioners have jurisdiction over record systems in the public sector only and operate mainly in an advisory capacity. They maintain registers of record systems, respond to complaints, and have the authority to conduct investigations or audits of compliance with the fair information practices mandated by law.

France has a National Commission on Informatics, Data Banks and Freedoms (CNIL), whose functions extend well beyond protection of the privacy and confidentiality interests of individuals. The CNIL is an independent agency and operates under the direction of a group of part-time commissioners. It has broad authority to regulate processing of automated personal data in the public and private sectors, carry out inspections, rule on complaints, maintain a register of data processing activities, and assist persons to gain access to their own data.

What impact have these independent boards and commissions had on the collection and use of data about individuals for statistical and research purposes? In Sweden, which pioneered formal data protection activities at the national level, the Data Inspection Board initially focused considerable attention on the central statistical agency, Statistics Sweden. An early ruling of the board prevented Statistics Sweden from using imputation for persons not responding to the Swedish labor force survey. Another ruling prohibited the use of proxy respondents in the same survey; in other words, persons asked to participate in the survey could respond to the questions only for themselves, not for other members of their families or households. This ruling was appealed and it was decided that proxies could be used for objective data items only, provided the proxy respondent was closely related to the data subject (Dalenius, 1979).

Other rulings requiring the removal of identifiers placed severe constraints on the conduct of longitudinal surveys and record linkages for statistical purposes. In the early 1980s, a widely publicized debate between the heads of the Data Inspection Board and Statistics Sweden about proposed uses of administrative records in the national census of population eventually led to a government decision to conduct a more traditional census. According to Flaherty (1989), the two agencies are by now able to reach understandings on most issues, but some minor ones remain outstanding.

Like the U.S. Privacy Act, the Swedish Data Act allows individuals to inspect their own records in government record systems. Unlike the U.S. act, however, the Swedish act does not allow any exceptions for statistical record systems. As a consequence, Statistics Sweden has "faced a major financial and administrative burden of replying to requests for access from individuals. There were 67,000 such requests during the first four years" (Flaherty, 1989:152).

In the mid-1980s important privacy issues were raised by Project Metropolitan, a longitudinal research data base maintained at the University of Stockholm that linked information from many sources, much of it highly sensitive, for 15,000 persons born in the Stockholm area in 1953. About 1980, after the researchers had adopted recommended data protections, the Swedish Data Inspection Board licensed the data base, showing "a high degree of tolerance for the linkage of a large amount of sensitive personal information" (Flaherty, 1989:154). However, in 1986 the project came to the attention of the data subjects and the general public, and a major debate ensued. The debate finally led to the board's requiring the removal of all identifiers from the system, so that no further data from other sources could be linked to the existing records.

It is more difficult to define the role of the German data protection commissioners in connection with the controversies that led to a four-year delay in carrying out the scheduled 1983 census of population for the Federal Republic of Germany. The federal commissioner's office had warned the federal Statistical Office that potential problems with data protection were associated with the census procedures, but the Statistical Office did little to respond. Nevertheless, in March 1983 the commissioner's office issued a press release stating that "people's fears about the census were unfounded, and that adequate safeguards were in place" (Flaherty 1989:81). Continued public concern and legal challenges to the census, however, forced postponement, and it was not until after the passage of new census legislation in 1986 that the census was finally undertaken in 1987, still in a very controversial atmosphere. According to Flaherty, these difficulties occurred, at least in part "because the strong data protection laws and statistical laws currently in place are not well enough known to the general public, and because public anxieties about surveillance practices using administrative data are so great" (p. 83).

Flaherty does not detail any specific instances of actions by the privacy commissioner of Canada having direct effects on the programs of Statistics Canada. However, he does describe measures that have been introduced to reduce substantially the administrative uses of Canada's Social Insurance number (comparable to the Social Security number in the United States). As a consequence, there may be a reduction in the number and scope of administrative record systems that can readily be used for research studies and statistical analyses that require linking of records from different sources. Nevertheless, Statistics Canada has an active and successful program to produce current demographic data from administrative sources, and it is possible that this system may at some time take the place of the more traditional kind of population census.

From other sources, it is clear that the former privacy commissioner of Canada, John Grace (in an interesting change of hats, he became the information commissioner in 1990), had serious doubts about record linkages and longitudinal studies for research purposes, although he did not entirely rule them out (Grace, 1988, 1989). He believed that they should be limited in scope and only undertaken with strong justification and full knowledge by the data subjects. Statistics Canada, perhaps due in part to Grace's views, has taken a cautious approach to record linkage activities. A formal policy statement (Statistics Canada, 1986) describes the potential benefits of such activities, but it also lists a fairly rigorous set of conditions that must be satisfied before they can be undertaken. A series of agency guidelines issued over the past few years has set out requirements for notifying survey respondents of plans to link administrative record data with their survey information or to release nonpublic-use microdata to other agencies. The guidelines provide specific examples of language that can be used in the notifications, taking into account the mode of data collection.

U.S. PROPOSALS FOR AN INDEPENDENT PRIVACY PROTECTION BOARD

Although most drafts of the Privacy Act of 1974 provided for the establishment of a permanent privacy protection commission, the provision was eliminated just prior to final passage of the act. Consequently, responsibility for oversight of the act's fair information provisions devolved on OMB.

Recently, however, there has been growing interest among U.S. privacy advocates in the possible application of at least some features of the Canadian and European models in the United States (see Rotenberg, 1991). Bills to establish an independent data protection board in the executive branch of the government were introduced by Representative Robert Wise in 1989 and 1991. The 1991 bill, which would have taken the form of an amendment to the Privacy Act, provided for a board whose functions would have been largely advisory. The board would have been required to prepare guidelines under the Privacy Act and other information statutes and to issue periodic compilations of agency record system notices. It would have had authority to investigate compliance with the Privacy Act and report on violations, to review existing and proposed data protection legislation, investigate complaints about violations of data protection rights, and request agencies to take action on matters affecting data protection. Although no legislation had been passed by early 1993, there is sufficient interest in these issues that future enactment is possible.

There does not seem to be any corresponding interest or activity, at least in any organized sense, aimed at furthering the ability of data users to gain access to federal data for research and statistical purposes. Paul Reynolds (1993), in a paper prepared for the panel's Conference on Disclosure Limitation Approaches and Data Access, presented a detailed proposal for the issuance of "federal data base research certificates," which would be issued to organizations presenting worthy research proposals to a "federal data base review board." The certificates would provide access to data maintained by any federal agency (with their approval), immunity from any legal subpoena, and substantial penalties for researcher disclosure of individual information.

FINDINGS AND RECOMMENDATIONS

AGENCY STAFFING AND MANAGEMENT OF CONFIDENTIALITY AND DATA ACCESS FUNCTIONS

The panel has noted several instances, some of them recent or current, of federal agency practices that reflect inadequate knowledge of and attention to confidentiality and data access issues. As discussed in Chapter 3, some informed consent and notification statements have been inadequate in terms of accuracy, completeness, and comprehensibility. And as noted in Chapter 6, some agency standards for statistical disclosure limitation are rudimentary and do not take full advantage of current knowledge and experience in this area.

Recommendation 8.1 Each federal statistical agency should review its staffing and management of confidentiality and data access functions, with particular attention to the assignment within the agency of responsibilities for these functions and the background and experience needed for persons who exercise these responsibilities.

Currently, there is a dearth of opportunities (such as the seminars that were conducted following the 1978 publication of Statistical Policy Working Paper 2) for federal statisticians to obtain training in fair information practices and related subjects.

Recommendation 8.2 Statistical agencies should take steps to provide staff training in fair information practices, informed consent procedures, confidentiality laws and policies, statistical disclosure limitation procedures, and related topics.

Possible sites for such training include the new Joint University of Maryland-University of Michigan Program in Survey Methodology (National Research Council, 1992a; University of Maryland et al., 1993) and the U.S. Department of Agriculture Graduate School.

The panel believes that it is highly desirable for data providers and data users to participate in or have greater input into agency decisions on data protection and data access policies and procedures. The existing institutions and mechanisms that we have described are useful, but not entirely adequate. Especially for data users, there are inadequate means to appeal adverse decisions by federal statistical agencies.

Recommendation 8.3 Statistical agencies should establish mechanisms for allowing and encouraging greater external inputs into their decisions on confidentiality protection and data access.

One possibility would be to establish data review boards, with external members representing data subjects and data users, in all federal statistical agencies that release substantial amounts of data to the public. Trade-offs between confidentiality protection and data access exist whether data releases are in aggregate or microdata form, and thus both kinds of releases should be subject to review by such boards.

Alternatively, existing agency advisory committees could be asked periodically to review agency policies and practices for confidentiality protection and data access. For the latter approach to be effective, committee membership should be balanced to provide representation of data subjects and data users.

INTERAGENCY COORDINATION

The Office of Management and Budget and, in particular, its Statistical Policy Office, have an important role in coordinating federal data protection and access activities. The Statistical Policy Office, although handicapped by having a very small staff, has recently undertaken some important initiatives, such as its efforts to promote and facilitate business list sharing for statistical purposes and to bring agency officials together to review and evaluate new data access procedures.

The OMB Circular, *Guidelines for Federal Statistical Activities*, which is being revised, has the potential to provide an impetus for improved agency practices in such areas as informed consent and notification statements, application of statistical disclosure limitation techniques, and record linkages for statistical purposes.

> **Recommendation 8.4** The Statistical Policy Office should give high priority to proceeding with the development and issuance of the OMB *Guidelines for Statistical Activities*, with the full participation of the federal statistical agencies and the public.

The policy directives and memorandums issued by Statistics Canada might provide useful models for the treatment of such topics as informed consent and record linkage.

DATA PROTECTION BOARD

Unlike other advanced industrial societies, the United States does not have an independent advisory board or commission charged with promoting effective implementation of the Privacy Act and other information legislation. There have been recent proposals by privacy advocates and legislators to create such a body.

> **Recommendation 8.5** The panel supports the general concept of an independent federal advisory body charged with fostering a climate of enhanced protection for all federal data about persons *and* responsible data dissemination for research and statistical purposes. Any such advisory body should promote the principle of functional separation and have professional staff with expertise in privacy protection, computer data bases, official statistics, and research uses of federal data.

The experience of other countries has shown that data protection agencies can be a source of additional oversight for statisticians and researchers, subjecting their activities to greater scrutiny, promoting balance in data protection and data dissemination, and generating public debate. In some instances, new restrictions have been imposed on practices that do not appear to pose a threat to the confidentiality of individual data. Nevertheless, the panel believes that creating a positive climate for enhanced data protection and data dissemination requires assurances from many different quarters that legitimate protective policies and procedures are in place and are being followed.

An independent advisory board, with appropriate professional staffing, could constitute a regular source of expertise on a wide spectrum of privacy issues, including those related to research and statistics. It could give advice, serve as a sounding board for data protectors and data users, and offer legitimacy to responsible initiatives by both groups. The advisory board could provide support for responsible access to personal data as needed to realize the fundamental goals of democratic accountability and constitutional empowerment, which we introduced in Chapter 1. A professionally competent, respected advisory body could also act as a mediator when there are differences of opinion among data providers, privacy advocates, data users, and statistical agencies. Orderly evaluation and resolution of such differences by an impartial ombudsman could reduce the likelihood of their escalating to the point at which they seriously disrupt key data collection and dissemination activities.

Data protectors can and should be important allies of official statisticians and the general public in the achievement of an appropriate balance between the privacy interests of individuals and societal needs for research and statistical data about a complex society. In particular, data protectors can help statistical agencies resolve difficult issues in the areas of informed consent, confidentiality, data access, and record linkage.

An advisory body could also promote harmonization of disparate interpretations of federal regulations under the Privacy Act of 1974 or other legislation covering all or part of the federal statistical system. It could disseminate information about innovative techniques to permit the exchange of data for statistical uses without diminishing the protection offered to individuals, and it could provide oversight of agency practices in maintaining and disseminating sensitive information.

Recommendations

For the reader's convenience, we present all the panel's recommendations, keyed to the chapters in which they appear.

CHAPTER 3
DATA SUBJECTS

Recommendation 3.1 Federal statistical agencies should follow a flexible, multilayered approach to informing data providers of the conditions under which they are being asked to provide information.

Recommendation 3.2 Basic information given to all data providers requested to participate in statistical surveys and censuses should include

(a) for data on persons, information needed to meet all Privacy Act requirements. Similar information is recommended for data on organizations, except that the requirement to inform providers about routine uses (as defined by the Privacy Act) is not applicable.

(b) a clear statement of the expected burden on the data providers, including the expected time required to provide the data (a requirement of the Office of Management and

Budget) and, if applicable, the nature of sensitive topics included in the survey and plans for possible follow-up interviews of some or all respondents.

(c) no false or misleading statements. For example, a statement that implies zero risk of disclosure is seldom, if ever, appropriate.

(d) information about any planned or potential *non-statistical* uses of the information to be provided. There should be a clear statement of the level of confidentiality protection that can be legally ensured.

(e) information about any planned or anticipated record linkages for statistical or research purposes. For persons, this notification will usually occur in conjunction with a request for the data subject's Social Security number.

(f) a statement to cover the possibility of unanticipated future uses of the data for statistical or research purposes.

(g) information about the length of time for which the information will be retained in identifiable form.

Recommendation 3.3 In keeping with the objective of giving individuals control over their own information whenever societal needs do not clearly take precedence, data subjects or data providers should be allowed to waive certain aspects of confidentiality protection that would usually be accorded to the information they provide. Agencies should take special care to ensure that any such waivers are based on fully informed consent.

Recommendation 3.4 Statistical agencies should undertake and support continuing research, using the tools of cognitive and survey research, to monitor the views of data providers and the general public on informed consent, response burden, sensitivity of survey questions, data sharing for statistical purposes, and related issues.

Recommendation 3.5 Federal statistical agencies should continue to develop systematic informational activities designed to inform the public of their ability to maintain the confidentiality of individually identifiable information, including use of legal barriers to disclosure and physical security procedures, and their intentions to minimize intrusions on privacy and the time and effort required to respond to statistical inquiries.

Recommendation 3.6 Agencies should be prepared to deal quickly and candidly with instances of "moral outrage" that may be directed at statistical programs from time to time as a result of actual or perceived violations of pledges of confidentiality given to data providers by data collectors. The agencies should be prepared to explain the purpose of specific data collection activities and the procedures used to protect confidentiality. They should accept full responsibility if a violation occurs and should announce measures to prevent future violations.

Recommendation 3.7 As part of the communication process, statistical agencies should work more closely with appropriate advocacy groups, such as those concerned with civil liberties and those that represent the rights of disadvantaged segments of the population, and with specialists on ethical issues and human rights.

CHAPTER 4
DATA USERS

Recommendation 4.1 Greater opportunities should be available for sharing of explicitly or potentially identifiable personal data among federal agencies for statistical and research purposes, provided the confidentiality of the records can be properly protected and the data cannot be used to make determinations about individual data subjects. Greater access should be permitted to key statistical and administrative data sets for the development of sampling frames and other statistical uses. Additional data sharing should only be undertaken in those instances in which the procedures for collecting the data comply with the panel's recommendations for informed consent or notification (see Recommendations 3.2 and 3.3).

Recommendation 4.2 Federal statistical agencies should seek to improve the access of external users to statistical data, through both legislation and the development and greater use, under carefully controlled conditions, of tested administrative procedures.

Recommendation 4.3 All federal statistical agencies should establish systematic procedures for capturing information on a continuing basis about user requests for data that have been denied or only partially fulfilled. Such information should be used for periodic reviews of agency confidentiality and data access policies.

Recommendation 4.4 *All* users of federal data, regardless of the formal conditions of access, should subscribe to the following principles for responsible data use:

(a) Conscientiously observe all conditions agreed to in order to obtain access to the data. Allow access to the original data set only by those permitted access under the agreed conditions of recipiency and ensure that all such persons are aware of the required conditions of use.

(b) Make no attempt to identify particular individuals or other units whose data are considered to be confidential.

(c) In the event that one or more individuals or other units are identified in the course of research, notify the organization that provided the data set, and do not inform anyone else of the discovered identities.

Recommendation 4.5 To promote knowledge of and adherence to the principles of responsible data use,

(a) Federal statistical agencies should ask all recipients of federal microdata sets to submit to the releasing agency, in writing, their agreement to observe the above principles, plus any other conditions deemed necessary for specific data sets.

(b) Professional societies and associations that have ethical codes, standards, or guidelines should incorporate these principles in them.

(c) The principles and the justifications for them should be included in academic and other training for disciplines whose members are likely to be users of federal statistical data.

CHAPTER 5
LEGISLATION

Recommendation 5.1 Statistical records across all federal agencies should be governed by a consistent set of statutes and regulations meeting standards for the maintenance of such records, including the following features of fair statistical information practices:

(a) a definition of statistical data that incorporates the principle of functional separation as defined by the Privacy Protection Study Commission,

(b) a guarantee of confidentiality for data,

(c) a requirement of informed consent or informed choice when participation in a survey is voluntary,

(d) a requirement of strict control on data dissemination,

(e) a requirement to follow careful rules on disclosure limitation,

(f) a provision that permits data sharing for statistical purposes under controlled conditions, and

(g) legal sanctions for those who violate confidentiality requirements (see Recommendation 5.3 for further discussion of this requirement).

Recommendation 5.2 Zero-risk requirements for disclosure of statistical records are, in practice, impossibly high standards. Regulations and policies under existing statutes should establish standards of reasonable care. New statutes should recognize that almost all uses of information entail some risk of disclosure and should allow release of information for legitimate statistical purposes that entail a reasonably low risk of disclosure of individually identifiable data.

Recommendation 5.3 There should be legal sanctions for all users, both external users and agency employees, who violate requirements to maintain the confidentiality of data.

CHAPTER 6
TECHNICAL AND ADMINISTRATIVE PROCEDURES

Recommendation 6.1 The Office of Management and Budget's Statistical Policy Office should continue to coordinate research work on statistical disclosure analysis and should disseminate the results of this work broadly among statistical agencies. Major statistical agencies should actively encourage and participate in scholarly statistical research in this area. Other agencies should keep abreast of current developments in the application of statistical disclosure limitation techniques.

Recommendation 6.2 Statistical agencies should determine the impact on statistical analyses of the techniques they use to mask data. They should be sure that the masked data can be accurately analyzed by a range of typical researchers. If the data cannot be accurately analyzed using standard statistical software, the agency should make appropriate consulting and software available.

Recommendation 6.3 Each statistical agency should actively involve data users from outside the agency as statistical disclosure limitation techniques are developed and applied to data.

Recommendation 6.4 Statistical agencies should continue widespread release, with minimal restrictions on use, of microdata sets with no less detail than currently provided.

Recommendation 6.5 Federal statistical agencies should strive for a greater return on public investment in statistical programs through carefully controlled increases in interagency data sharing for statistical purposes and expanded availability of federal data sets to external users.

Recommendation 6.6 Statistical agencies, in their efforts to expand access for external data users, should follow a policy of responsible innovation. Whenever feasible, they should experiment with some of the newer restricted access techniques, with appropriate confidentiality safeguards and periodic reviews of the costs and benefits of each procedure.

Recommendation 6.7 In those instances in which controlled access at agency sites remains the only feasible alternative, statistical agencies should do all they can to make access conditions more affordable and acceptable to users, for example, by providing access at dispersed agency locations and providing adequate user support and access to computing facilities at reasonable cost.

Recommendation 6.8 Significant statistical data files, in their unrestricted form, should be deposited at the National Archives and eventually made available for historical research uses.

CHAPTER 7
STATISTICAL DATA FOR ORGANIZATIONS

Recommendation 7.1 The principle of functional separation, which the panel endorsed in Recommendation 5.1(a), should apply equally to data for persons and data for organizations.

Recommendation 7.2 Legislation that authorizes and requires protection of the confidentiality of data for persons and organizations should be sought for all federal statistical agencies that do not now have it and for any new federal statistical agencies that may be created (see also Recommendation 5.1).

Recommendation 7.3 Data providers, whether persons or organizations, should have ready access to as much information as they want about the uses of the information they are requested or required to provide to federal statistical agencies. They should be told who will have access to their data in individually identifiable form. Statements of the collecting agency's intentions should be clearly distinguished from statements describing what is authorized and required by statute.

Recommendation 7.4 There should be increased sharing of business lists for statistical purposes by federal and state agencies.

Recommendation 7.5 New legislation on sharing of business lists for statistical purposes should provide that government agencies that are now unable to guarantee protection against nonstatistical uses can have access to business lists if they acquire statutory authority for such protection in the future.

Recommendation 7.6 The Office of Management and Budget's Statistical Policy Office should develop uniform guidelines for federal statistical agencies covering the purposes for which waivers of confidentiality protections by organizations are considered acceptable and the methods of obtaining waivers from respondents. Efforts should be made to amend the confidentiality statutes of federal statistical agencies that would otherwise be prevented from using waivers for generally accepted statistical purposes.

Recommendation 7.7 Federal statistical agencies that collect data on organizations should make a special effort to improve access for statistical research and analysis by external users and, if necessary, should seek legislation that will permit them to develop licensing arrangements that allow such users to have access at their work sites, subject to penalties for violating the conditions under which they are allowed access to the data.

CHAPTER 8
MANAGING CONFIDENTIALITY AND
DATA ACCESS FUNCTIONS

Recommendation 8.1 Each federal statistical agency should review its staffing and management of confidentiality and data access functions, with particular attention to the assignment within the agency of responsibilities for these functions and the background and experience needed for persons who exercise these responsibilities.

Recommendation 8.2 Statistical agencies should take steps to provide staff training in fair information practices, informed consent procedures, confidentiality laws and policies, statistical disclosure limitation procedures, and related topics.

Recommendation 8.3   Statistical agencies should establish mechanisms for allowing and encouraging greater external inputs into their decisions on confidentiality protection and data access.

Recommendation 8.4   The Statistical Policy Office should give high priority to proceeding with the development and issuance of the OMB *Guidelines for Statistical Activities*, with the full participation of the federal statistical agencies and the public.

Recommendation 8.5   The panel supports the general concept of an independent federal advisory body charged with fostering a climate of enhanced protection for all federal data about persons *and* responsible data dissemination for research and statistical purposes. Any such advisory body should promote the principle of functional separation and have professional staff with expertise in privacy protection, computer data bases, official statistics, and research uses of federal data.

References

Adam, N.R., and J.C. Wortman
1989   Security control methods for statistical databases: A comparative study. *ACM Computing Surveys* 21:515-556.

Allison, J., and W.W. Cooper
1991   Data Disclosure and Data Sharing in Scientific Research. Paper presented at a Conference on Research Policies and Quality Assurance, Rome, Italy.

American Statistical Association
1977   Report of Ad Hoc Committee on Privacy and Confidentiality. *The American Statistician* 31(2):59-78.

1980   Business directories: Findings and recommendations of the ASA Committee on Privacy and Confidentiality. *The American Statistician* 34(1):8-10.

1983   Ethical guidelines for statistical practice: Report of the Ad Hoc Committee on Professional Ethics (with comments). *The American Statistician* 37(1):5-20.

1989   Ethical guidelines for statistical practice. *AMSTAT News* 1989(154):24-25.

1991   *Surveys and Privacy.* Committee on Privacy and Confidentiality. Washington, D.C.: American Statistical Association.

Andrussier, S.E.
1991   The Freedom of Information Act in 1990: More freedom for government; less information for the public. *1991 Duke Law Journal*:753-801.

Aziz, F., and W. Buckler
1992   The Status of Death Information in Social Security Administration Files. Paper presented at the Annual Meeting of the American Statistical Association, Boston.

Babcock, L., and J. Engberg
  1990   Are Local Labor Market Statistics Appropriate for Policy? Paper presented at the Annual Meeting of the Association for Public Policy and Management, San Francisco.
Bachi, R., and R. Baron
  1969   Confidentiality problems related to data banks. *Bulletin of the International Statistical Institute* 43:225-241.
Bailar, B.A.
  1990   Contributions to statistical methodology from the U.S. federal government. *Survey Methodology* 16(1):51-61.
Barabba, V.P., and D.P. Kaplan
  1975   U.S. Census Bureau Statistical Techniques to Prevent Disclosure—The Right to Privacy vs. the Need to Know. Paper presented at the 40th Session of the International Statistical Institute, Warsaw.
Beauchamp, T.L., R.R. Faden, R.J. Wallace, and L. Walters, eds.
  1982   *Ethical Issues in Social Science Research.* Baltimore: Johns Hopkins University Press.
Bethlehem, J.G., W.J. Keller, and J. Pannekoek
  1990   Disclosure control of microdata. *Journal of the American Statistical Association* 85:38-45.
Black, H.C., J.R. Nolan, and J.M. Nolan-Haley
  1990   *Black's Law Dictionary.* St. Paul, Minn.: West Publishing.
Boorstin, D.J.
  1973   *The Americans: The Democratic Experience.* New York: Random House.
Boruch, R.F., and J.S. Cecil
  1979   *Assuring the Confidentiality of Social Research Data.* Philadelphia: University of Pennsylvania Press.
Boruch, R.F., and W. Kehr
  1983   On Use of the Doctorate Records File and the Survey of Doctorate Recipients: Privacy and Research Utility. Report prepared for the National Science Foundation. University of Pennsylvania, Philadelphia.
Brackstone, G.B.
  1990   Comment on "Contributions to Statistical Methodology from the U.S. Federal Government." *Survey Methodology* 16(1):58-61.
Bureau of the Budget
  1961   Brief History of the Movement in the Federal Government for a Central Directory and of Related Efforts Aimed at Improving Quality and Comparability of Economic Statistics. Unpublished paper. Washington, D.C., Bureau of the Budget.
Bureau of the Census
  1982   *Evaluating the Public Information Campaign for the 1980 Census: Results of the KAP Survey.* Preliminary Evaluation Results Memorandum (PERM) No. 31. Washington, D.C.: U.S. Department of Commerce.
  1985   *How the Census Bureau Keeps Your Information Strictly Confidential.* Washington, D.C.: U.S. Department of Commerce.
Bureau of Labor Statistics
  1980   Responsibility for safeguarding sensitive information. *BLS Directive System.* Washington, D.C.: U.S. Department of Labor.
Burnham, D.
  1983   *The Rise of the Computer State.* New York: Random House.

Butz, W.P.
1985a Data confidentiality and public perceptions: The case of the European censuses. *American Statistical Association 1985 Proceedings of the Section on Survey Research Methods.* Washington, D.C.: American Statistical Association.
1985b The future of administrative records in the Census Bureau's demographic activities. Comment on Jabine and Scheuren, "Goals for Statistical Uses of Administrative Records: The Next 10 Years." *Journal of Business and Economic Statistics* 3(4):393-395.
Carroll, J.J.
1985 Uses of administrative records: A social security point of view. Comment on Jabine and Scheuren, "Goals for Statistical Uses of Administrative Records: The Next 10 Years." *Journal of Business and Economic Statistics* 3(4):396-397.
Cassel, C.M.
1976 Probability based disclosures. In T. Dalenius and A. Klevmarken, eds., *Personal Integrity and the Need for Data in the Social Sciences.* Stockholm: Swedish Council for the Social Sciences.
Cecil, J.S.
1989 Regulation of Federal Research Records: Fifteen Years Since the Privacy Act and the Freedom of Information Act. Paper presented at the Annual Meeting of the American Statistical Association, Washington, D.C.
1993 Confidentiality legislation and the United States federal statistical system. *Journal of Official Statistics* 9(2):519-535.
Cigrang, M., and L. Rainwater
1990 Balancing Data Access and Data Protection: The Luxembourg Income Study Experience. Paper presented at the Joint Statistical Meetings of the American Statistical Association, Anaheim, Calif.
Coles, T.R.
1991 Does the Privacy Act of 1974 protect your right to privacy? An examination of the routine use exemption. *American University Law Review* 40:957-1001.
Collins, M.
1992 The case for samples of anonymized records from the 1991 census. Letter to the Editor. *Journal of the Royal Statistical Society* 155(1):165-166.
Commission on Federal Paperwork
1977a *Confidentiality and Privacy.* 052-003-00458-5. Washington, D.C.: U.S. Government Printing Office.
1977b *Statistics.* 052-003-00454-2. Washington, D.C.: U.S. Government Printing Office.
Committee on National Statistics and Social Science Research Council
1989 Collaborative Research: A Proposal for a Panel on Confidentiality and Data Access. Committee on National Statistics and Social Science Research Council, Washington, D.C.
Conference of European Statisticians
1991 Resolution on the fundamental principles of official statistics in the region of the Economic Commission for Europe. *International Statistical Information Newsletter* 15(2):8.
Council of Economic Advisers (Executive Office of the President)
1991 FY 1992 Economics Statistics Initiative: Improving the Quality of Eco-

nomics Statistics. Press Release. Executive Office of the President, Washington, D.C.
1992   *Economic Report of the President.* Washington, D.C.: U.S. Government Printing Office.
Courtland, S.
1985   Census confidentiality: Then and now. *Government Information Quarterly* 2(4):407-418.
Cox, L.H.
1980   Suppression methodology and statistical disclosure control. *Journal of the American Statistical Association* 75:337-385.
1986   Confidentiality issues at the United States Bureau of the Census. *Journal of Official Statistics* 2(2):135-160.
1987   A constructive procedure for unbiased controlled rounding. *Journal of the American Statistical Association* 82(398):520-524.
1991   Comment on Duncan and Pearson. *Social Sciences* 6(3):232-234.
Cox, L.H., B. Johnson, S. McDonald, D. Nelson, and V. Vazquez
1985   Confidentiality issues at the Census Bureau. *Proceedings of the First Annual Research Conference.* Washington, D.C.: U.S. Department of Commerce.
Dahl, R.A.
1982   *Dilemmas of Pluralist Democracy: Autonomy vs. Control.* New Haven: Yale University Press.
Dalenius, T.
1977   Towards a methodology for statistical disclosure control. *Statistisk Tidskrift* 5:429-444.
1979   Data protection legislation in Sweden: A statistician's perspective (with comments). *Journal of the Royal Statistical Society* 142(3):285-298.
1988   *Controlling Invasion of Privacy in Surveys.* Stockholm: Statistics Sweden.
David, M.H.
1980   Access to data: The frustration and utopia of the researcher. *Review of Public Data Use* 8(4):327-337.
1991   The science of data sharing: Documentation. In J.E. Sieber, ed., *Sharing Social Science Data: Advantages and Challenges.* Newbury Park, Calif.: Sage.
David, M.H., and A. Robbin
1981   The great rift: Gaps between administrative records and knowledge created through secondary analysis. *Review of Public Data Use* 9:153-166.
Denning, D.E.
1980   Secure statistical databases with random sample queries. *ACM Transactions on Database Systems* 5:291-315.
Denning, D.E., and T.F. Lunt
1988   A multilevel relational data model. *Proceedings of the 1988 IEEE Symposium on Research Security and Privacy.* Los Alamitos, Calif.: IEEE Computer Society.
Desky, J.
1991   Government information and privacy: Who controls the data? *PA Times* 14(12):1,12.
Duncan, G.T., and D. Lambert
1986   Disclosure-limited data dissemination. *Journal of the American Statistical Association* 81(393):10-28.

1989   The risk of disclosure for microdata. *Journal of Business and Economic Statistics* 7(2):207-217.

Duncan, G.T., and S. Mukherjee
1991   Microdata disclosure limitation in statistical databases: Query size and random sample query control. *Proceedings of the 1991 IEEE Symposium on Research in Security and Privacy*. Los Alamitos, Calif.: IEEE Computer Society.
1992   Confidentiality Protection in Statistical Databases: A Disclosure Limitation Approach. Paper presented at the International Seminar on Statistical Confidentiality, Dublin.

Duncan, G.T., and R.W. Pearson
1991   Enhancing access to microdata while protecting confidentiality: Prospects for the future. *Statistical Science* 6(3):219-239.

Duncan, J.S., and W.C. Shelton
1978   *Revolution in United States Government Statistics 1926-1976.* 003-005-00181-6. Washington, D.C.: U.S. Department of Commerce.
1992   U.S. Government contributions to probability sampling and statistical analysis. *Statistical Science* 7(3):320-338.

Durbin, J.
1979   Statistics and the report of the Data Protection Committee (with comments). *Journal of the Royal Statistical Society* 142(3):299-306.

Economic Policy Council
1987   *Report of the Working Group on the Quality of Economic Statistics.* Washington, D.C.: Economic Policy Council.

Ellenberg, J.H.
1983   Ethical guidelines for statistical practice: A historical perspective. *The American Statistician* 37(1):1-5.

Equifax Inc.
1990   *The Equifax Report on Consumers in the Information Age.* A national opinion survey conducted for Equifax Inc. by Louis Harris and Associates and Alan F. Westin. Atlanta, Ga.: Equifax Inc.

Federal Committee on Statistical Methodology
1978   *Report on Statistical Disclosure and Disclosure-Avoidance Techniques.* Statistical Policy Working Paper 2. Subcommittee on Disclosure-Avoidance Techniques. Washington, D.C.: U.S. Department of Commerce.
1980   *Report on Exact and Statistical Matching Techniques.* Statistical Policy Working Paper 5. Washington, D.C.: U.S. Department of Commerce.
1993   Untitled draft statistical policy working paper dated July 1993. Subcommittee on Disclosure Limitation Methodology. Office of Management and Budget, Executive Office of the President, Washington, D.C.

Fellegi, I.P.
1972   On the question of statistical confidentiality. *Journal of the American Statistical Association* 67:7-18.

Fienberg, S., and J.M. Tanur
1989   Combining cognitive and statistical approaches to survey design. *Science* 243:1017-1022.

Flaherty, D.H.
1978   Final report of the Bellagio Conference on Privacy, Confidentiality, and the Use of Government Microdata for Research and Statistical Purposes. *Statistical Reporter* 78(8):274-279.

1979   *Privacy and Government Data Banks: An International Perspective.*
        London: Mansell Publishing.
1989   *Protecting Privacy in Surveillance Societies: The Federal Republic of
        Germany, Sweden, France, Canada, and the United States.* Chapel Hill:
        The University of North Carolina Press.

Frank, O.
1976   Individual disclosures from frequency tables. In T. Dalenius and A.
        Klevmarken, eds., *Personal Integrity and the Need for Data in the Social
        Sciences.* Stockholm: Swedish Council for the Social Sciences.
1979   Inferring individual information from released statistics. *Bulletin of the
        International Statistical Institute: Proceedings of the 42nd Session* (Book
        3). NEDA-APO Production Unit. Philippines: Philippene Organizing
        Committee.

Frankfurter, F.
1930   *The Public and Its Government.* New Haven: Yale University Press.

Fuller, W.A.
1993   Masking procedures for microdata disclosure limitation. *Journal of Offi-
        cial Statistics* 9(2):383-406.

Gates, G.W.
1988   Census Bureau microdata: Providing useful research data while protect-
        ing the anonymity of respondents. *American Statistical Association 1988
        Proceedings of the Social Statistics Section.* Alexandria, Va.: American
        Statistical Association.

General Accounting Office
1993   Energy Security and Policy: Analysis of the Pricing of Crude Oil and
        Petroleum Products. Report to Congressional Requesters, GAO/RCED-
        93-17. Washington, D.C.: U.S. Government Printing Office.

Govoni, J.P., and P.J. Waite
1985   Development of a public use file for manufacturing. *American Statisti-
        cal Association 1985 Proceedings of the Business and Economic Statis-
        tics Section.* Washington, D.C.: American Statistical Association.

Grace, J.W.
1988   *Annual Report, Privacy Commissioner, 1987-88.* Ottawa: Minister of
        Supply and Services Canada.
1989   The Use of Administrative Records for Social Research. Notes for an
        address to the Statistics Canada Workshop, Ottawa.

Greenberg, B.
1990   Disclosure avoidance research at the Census Bureau. *Proceedings, 1990
        Annual Research Conference.* Washington, D.C.: U.S. Department of
        Commerce.
1991   Disclosure Avoidance Practices at the Census Bureau. Statistical Policy
        Working Paper 20. Washington, D.C.: U.S. Department of Commerce.

Greenberg, B., and L. Voshell
1990a   *The Geographic Component of Disclosure Risk for Microdata.* Census/
        SRD/RR-90/13. Washington, D.C.: U.S. Department of Commerce.
1990b   Relating risk of disclosure for microdata and geographic area size. *American
        Statistical Association 1990 Proceedings of the Section on Survey Re-
        search Methods.* Alexandria, Va.: American Statistical Association.

Greenberg, B., and L.V. Zayatz
1992   Strategies for measuring risk in public use microdata files. *Statistica
        Neerlandica* 46(1):33-48.

Hauser, R.M.
  1991   What happens to youth after high school? *Focus* 13(3):1-13.
Heitjan, D.F., and Rubin, D.B.
  1991   Ignorability and coarse data. *Annals of Statistics* 19(4):2244-2253.
Hwang, J.T.
  1986   Multiplicative errors-in-variables models with applications to recent data released by the U.S. Department of Energy. *Journal of the American Statistical Association* 81:680-688.
Internal Revenue Service
  1984   *Taxpayer Attitudes Study Final Report.* Prepared for the Statistics of Income Division, by Yankelovich, Skelly and White, Inc. Washington, D.C.: U.S. Department of Treasury.
  1987   *1987 Taxpayer Opinion Survey.* Document 7292(1-88). Conducted for the Internal Revenue Service by Louis Harris and Associates, Inc. Washington, D.C.: U.S. Department of the Treasury.
International Statistical Institute
  1986   Declaration on Professional Ethics. *International Statistical Review* 54(2):227-242.
Jabine, T.B.
  1986   Selected guidelines for notification to survey participants. *American Statistical Association 1986 Proceedings of the Section on Survey Research Methods.* Washington, D.C.: American Statistical Association.
  1993a Procedures for restricted data access. *Journal of Official Statistics* 9(2):537-589.
  1993b Statistical disclosure limitation practices of United States statistical agencies. *Journal of Official Statistics* 9(2):427-454.
Jabine, T.B., J.A. Michael, and R.H. Mugge
  1977   Federal agency practices for avoiding statistical disclosure: Findings and Recommendations. *American Statistical Association 1977 Proceedings of the Social Sciences Section.* Washington, D.C.: American Statistical Association.
Juster, F.T.
  1991   Discussion. *American Statistical Association 1991 Proceedings of the Social Statistics Section.* Alexandria, Va.: American Statistical Association.
Kamlet, M.S., and S. Klepper
  1985   Mixing Individual and Group-Level Data. Working Paper. Department of Social Sciences, Carnegie Mellon University, Pittsburgh.
Kamlet, M.S., S. Klepper, and R.G. Frank
  1985   Mixing micro and macro data: Statistical issues and implication for data collection and reporting. In *Proceedings of the 1983 Public Health Conference on Records and Statistics.* Hyattsville, Md.: U.S. Department of Health and Human Services.
Keller-McNulty, S., and E.A. Unger
  1993   Database systems: Inferential security. *Journal of Official Statistics* 9(2):475-499.
Kilss, B. and F. Scheuren (with F. Aziz and L. DelBene)
  1978   1973 CPS-IRS-SSA Exact Match Study: Past, present, and future. In Social Security Administration, Office of Policy, *Policy Analysis with Social Security Research Files: Proceedings of a Workshop Held March 1978 at Williamsburg, Virginia.* Research Report No. 52, Office of Re-

search and Statistics. Washington, D.C.: U.S. Department of Health, Education and Welfare.

1984   The 1973 CPS-IRS-SSA Exact Match Study. In *Statistical Uses of Administrative Records: Recent Research and Present Prospects*. Vol. 1. Washington, D.C.: U.S. Department of Treasury.

Kim, J.
1990   Masking Microdata for National Opinion Research Center. Final Project Report. Bureau of the Census, Washington, D.C.

Lambert, D.
1993   Measures of disclosure risk and harm. *Journal of Official Statistics* 9(2):313-331.

Lave, L.B.
1990   Does the surgeon-general need a statistics advisor? *Chance: New Directions for Statistics and Computing* 3(4):33-40.

Lewis, P.H.
1991   Why the privacy issue will never go away. *The New York Times*, April 7:F4.

Little, R.J.A.
1993   Statistical analysis of masked data. *Journal of Official Statistics* 9(2):407-426.

Little, R.J.A., and D.B. Rubin
1987   *Statistical Analysis with Missing Data*. New York: John Wiley & Sons.

Locke, J.
1690/   *Two Treatises of Government*. Cambridge: Cambridge University Press.
1988

Lodge, F.Z.
1984   Damages under the Privacy Act of 1974: Compensation and deterrence. *Fordham Law Review* 52(4):611-636.

Louis Harris and Associates
1981   *The Dimensions of Privacy*. A survey conducted for the Sentry Insurance Company. New York: Garland Publications.
1983   *The Road After 1984: The Impact of Technology on Society*. A survey conducted for Southern New England Telephone. New Haven, Ct.: Southern New England Telephone.

MacRae, J.B.
1990   Provision of Standard Industrial Classification Information to the Census Bureau. Memorandum to the Director of the Bureau of the Census and the Commissioner of Labor Statistics. December 20. Office of Management and Budget, Washington, D.C.

Marsh, C., A. Dale, and C. Skinner
1991b   Safe data versus safe settings: Access to customized results from the British census. *Proceedings of the 48th International Statistical Institute*. Voorburg, Netherlands: International Statistical Institute.

Marsh, C., C. Skinner, S. Arber, B. Penhale, S. Openshaw, J. Hobcraft, D. Lievesley, and N. Walford
1991a   The case for a sample of anonymized records from the 1991 census: A request from the Economic and Social Research Council Working Party on the 1991 census. *Journal of the Royal Statistical Society* 154(2):305-341.

1992   Authors reply to letter to the editor by Martin Collins. *Journal of the Royal Statistical Society* 155(1):166-167.

Martin, M.E.
1974   Statistical legislation and confidentiality issues. *International Statistical Review* 42(3):265-281.

Marx, G.T.
1988   *Undercover: Police Surveillance in America.* Berkeley, Calif.: University of California Press.
1990   Technology and privacy. *The World and I.* September:523-541.

Matloff, N.S.
1986   Another look at noise addition for database security. *Proceedings of the IEEE Computer Society Symposium on Research in Security and Privacy.* Los Alamitos, Calif.: IEEE Computer Society.

McGuckin, R.H.
1992   Analytic Use of Economic Microdata: A Model for Researcher Access with Confidentiality Protection. Discussion paper for the Center of Economic Studies, U.S. Department of Commerce, Washington, D.C.

McGuckin, R.H., and S.V. Nguyen
1990   Public use microdata: Disclosure and usefulness. *Journal of Economic and Social Measurement* 16:19-39.

McGuckin, R.H., and G.A. Pascoe, Jr.
1988   The Longitudinal Research Database: Status and research possibilities. *Survey of Current Business* July.

Mugge, R.H.
1984   Issues in protecting confidentiality in national health statistics. *Review of Public Data Use* 12:289-294.
1993   Informed consent in U.S. government surveys. *Journal of Official Statistics* 9(2):345-360.

National Academy of Public Administration
1991   *The Archives of the Future: Archival Strategies for the Treatment of Electronic Databases.* A Report for the National Archives and Records Administration. Washington, D.C.

National Agricultural Statistics Service
1989   Policy and Standards Memorandum Number 12-89. U.S. Department of Agriculture, Washington, D.C.

National Center for Education Statistics
1989   Policies and Procedures for Public Release of Data. Draft. U.S. Department of Education, Washington, D.C.
1992   *NCES Statistical Standards.* NCES 92-021. Washington, D.C.: U.S. Department of Education.

National Center for Health Statistics
1978   *Policy Statement on Release of Data for Individual Elementary Units and Special Tabulations.* DHEW No. (PHS)78-1212. Washington, D.C.: U.S. Department of Health, Education and Welfare.
1984   *NCHS Staff Manual on Confidentiality.* DHHS No. (PHS) 84-1244. Washington, D.C.: U.S. Department of Health and Human Services.
1992a   *Catalog of Electronic Data Products from the National Center for Health Statistics.* DHHS Pub. No. (PHS)92-1213. Washington, D.C.: U.S. Department of Health and Human Services.
1992b   *New Public Use Data Tape Distribution Policy in NCHS' Division of Vital Statistics.* Washington, D.C.: U.S. Department of Health and Human Services.

National Research Council
  1979   *Privacy and Confidentiality as Factors in Survey Response.* Panel on
          Privacy and Confidentiality as Factors in Survey Response, Committee
          on National Statistics, Commission on Behavioral and Social Sciences
          and Education. Washington, D.C.: National Academy Press.
  1985   *Sharing Research Data,* S.E. Fienberg, M.E. Martin, and M.L. Straf, eds.
          Committee on National Statistics, Commission on Behavioral and Social
          Sciences and Education. Washington, D.C.: National Academy Press.
  1991   *Computers at Risk: Safe Computing in the Information Age.* System
          Security Study Committee, Computer Science and Telecommunications
          Board, Commission on Physical Sciences, Mathematics, and Applications.
          Washington, D.C.: National Academy Press.
  1992a   *Center for Survey Methods: Summary of a Workshop.* F.E. Wolf, ed.
          Committee on National Statistics, Commission on Behavioral and Social
          Sciences and Education. Washington, D.C.: National Academy Press.
  1992b   *Principles and Practices for a Federal Statistical Agency,* M.E. Martin
          and M.L. Straf, eds. Committee on National Statistics, Commission on
          Behavioral and Social Sciences and Education. Washington, D.C.: Na-
          tional Academy Press.
Newton, K.B., and D.C. Pullin
  1990   Reconciling a Policy Favoring Dissemination of Information with the
          Privacy Rights of Individuals and Institutions. Paper commissioned by
          the National Center for Education Statistics, U.S. Department of Educa-
          tion, Washington, D.C.
  1991   The Impact of Section 252 of the Excellence in Mathematics, Science and
          Engineering Act of 1990 on the Policies and Practices of the National
          Center for Education Statistics. Paper commissioned by the Panel on
          Confidentiality and Data Access, Committee on National Statistics, Com-
          mission on Behavioral and Social Sciences and Education, National Re-
          search Council, Washington, D.C.
Norwood, J.L.
  1990   Statistics and public policy: Reflections of a changing world. Presiden-
          tial Address. *Journal of the American Statistical Association* 85(409):1-
          5.
Office of Federal Statistical Policy and Standards
  1978   *A Framework for Planning U.S. Federal Statistics for the 1980's.* Wash-
          ington, D.C.: U.S. Department of Commerce.
Office of Technology Assessment (U.S. Congress)
  1989   *Statistical Needs for a Changing U.S. Economy.* Background Paper. OTA-
          BP-E-58. Washington, D.C.: U.S. Government Printing Office.
O'Neill, H.V., and J.P. Fanning
  1976   The challenge of implementing and operating under the Privacy Act in
          the largest public sector conglomerate — HEW. *Bureaucrat* 5:171-188.
President's Commission on Federal Statistics
  1971   *Federal Statistics: Report of the President's Commission on Federal
          Statistics.* Vol. 1. Washington, D.C.: U.S. Government Printing Office.
President's Reorganization Project for the Federal Statistical System
  1981   Improving the federal statistical system: Issues and options. *Statistical
          Reporter* 81-5:133-221.
Prewitt, K.
  1985   Public statistics and democratic politics. In J.J. Smelser and D.R. Gerstein,

eds., *Behavioral and Social Science: Fifty Years of Discovery.* Washington, D.C.: National Academy Press.

Privacy Protection Study Commission
1977a *Personal Privacy in an Information Society.* 052-003-00395-3. Washington, D.C.: U.S. Government Printing Office
1977b *The Privacy Act of 1974: An Assessment.* 052-003-00424-1. Washington, D.C.: U.S. Government Printing Office
1977c *Technology and Privacy.* Washington, D.C.: U.S. Government Printing Office.

Rainwater, L., and T.M. Smeeding
1988   The Luxembourg Income Study: The use of international telecommunications in comparative social research. *The Annals of the American Academy of Political and Social Science* 495:95-105.

Reynolds, P.D.
1993   Privacy and advances in social and policy science: Balancing present costs and future gains. *Journal of Official Statistics* 9(2):275-312.

The Roper Organization, Inc.
1980   *Roper Reports Research Service.* Issue 80-5, April 26-May 3.

Rotenberg, M.
1991   In support of a data protection board in the United States. *Government Information Quarterly* 8(1):79-93.

Rubin, D.B.
1976   Inference and missing data. *Biometrika* 63:581-592.
1987   *Multiple Imputation for Nonresponse in Surveys.* New York: John Wiley & Sons.
1993   Comments on confidentiality: A proposal for satisfying all confidentiality constraints through the use of multiple-imputed synthetic micro-data. *Journal of Official Statistics,* forthcoming.

Rubin, P.
1990   Applying the Freedom of Information Act's privacy exemption to requests for lists of names and addresses. *Fordham Law Review* 58:1033-1051.

Sagarin, E.
1973   The research setting and the right not to be researched. *Social Problems* 21:52-64.

Sande, G.
1983   Automated cell suppression to preserve confidentiality of business statistics. *Statistical Journal of the United Nations* 2:33-41.

Sartori, G.
1962/ *Democratic Theory.* Westport, Conn.: Greenwood Press.
1972

Scheuren, F.
1989   Statistical research problems in government. In B. Kilss and B. Jamerson, eds., *Statistics of Income and Related Administrative Record Research: 1988-1989.* Washington, D.C.: U.S. Department of Treasury.

Singer, E.
1978   Informed consent: Consequences for response rate and response quality in social surveys. *American Sociological Review* 43:144-162.
1979   Informed consent procedures in surveys: Some reasons for minimal effects on response. In M.L. Wax and J. Cassel, eds., *Federal Regulations: Ethical Issues and Social Research.* Boulder, Colo.: Westview Press.

1993   Informed consent and survey response: A summary of the empirical literature. *Journal of Official Statistics* 9(2):361-375.
Singer, E., H. Hippler, and N. Schwarz
1990   The Effect of Confidentiality Assurances on Survey Responses. Paper presented at the International Conference on Measurement Errors in Surveys, Tucson, Ariz.
Smith, C.M.
1989   The Social Security Administration's Continuous Work History Sample. *Social Security Bulletin* 52(10):20-28.
Smith, J.P.
1991   Data confidentiality: A researcher's perspective. *American Statistical Association 1991 Proceedings of the Social Statistics Section.* Alexandria, Va.: American Statistical Association.
Social Security Administration
1978   *Policy Analysis with Social Security Research Files: Proceedings of a Workshop Held March 1978 at Williamsburg, Virginia.* Research Report No. 52, Office of Research and Statistics. Washington, D.C.: U.S. Department of Health, Education and Welfare.
Spruill, N.
1983   The confidentiality and analytic usefulness of masked business microdata. *American Statistical Association 1983 Proceedings of the Section on Survey Research Methods.* Washington, D.C.: American Statistical Association.
Statistics Canada
1986   Policy on record linkage. *Policy Manual.* Ottawa: Statistics Canada.
Steinberg, J., and L. Pritzker
1967   Some experiences with and reflections on data linkage in the United States. *Bulletin of the International Statistical Institute* 42:786-808.
Sullivan, G., and W.A. Fuller
1989   The use of measurement error to avoid disclosure. *American Statistical Association 1989 Proceedings of the Section on Survey Research Methods.* Alexandria, Va.: American Statistical Association.
Tanur, J.M., ed.
1992   *Questions About Questions: Inquiries into the Cognitive Bases of Surveys.* New York: Russell Sage Foundation.
Tendick, P.
1991   Optimal noise addition for the preservation of confidentiality in multivariate data. *Journal of Statistical Planning and Inference* 27:342-353.
Turn, R.
1990   Information privacy issues for the 1990's. *Proceedings of the IEEE Symposium on Research in Security and Privacy.* Los Alamitos, Calif.: IEEE Computer Society.
U.S. Bureau of Labor
1889   *Fourth Annual Report of the Commissioner of Labor, 1888: Working Women in Large Cities.* Washington, D.C.: U.S. Government Printing Office.
U.S. Code Congressional and Administrative News
1976   *Legislative History,* P.L. 94-455. 4:2897-4284. St. Paul, Minn.: West Publishing Co.
U.S. Department of Health, Education, and Welfare
1973   *Records, Computers, and the Rights of Citizens.* Report of the Secretary's Advisory Committee on Automated Personal Data Systems. DHEW No.

(OS)73-94. Washington, D.C.: U.S. Department of Health, Education and Welfare.

U.S. Department of Labor
1972   *Control of Data and Information Collected by the Bureau of Labor Statistics.* Secretary's Order 39-72. Washington, D.C.: U.S. Department of Labor.

U.S. Department of Transportation
1992   Card establishes statistics bureau: Knisely will be deputy director. *U.S. Department of Transportation News.* Press Release, October 20.

University of Maryland, University of Michigan, and Westat, Inc.
1993   *The Joint University of Maryland - University of Michigan Program in Survey Methodology.* College Park: University of Maryland.

van Melis-Wright, M., D. Stone, and D. Herrmann
1992   *The Semantic Basis of Confidentiality.* Bureau of Labor Statistics, Statistical Note Series: Statistical Note 34. Washington, D.C.: Bureau of Labor Statistics.

Wallman, K.K.
1988   *Losing Count: The Federal Statistical System.* Washington, D.C.: Population Reference Bureau.

Wilson, O.H., and W.J. Smith, Jr.
1983   Access to tax records for statistical purposes. *American Statistical Association 1983 Proceedings of the Section on Survey Research Methods.* Washington, D.C.: American Statistical Association.

Wolf, M.K.
1988   Microaggregation and disclosure avoidance for economic establishment data. *American Statistical Association 1988 Proceedings of the Business and Economic Statistics Section.* Alexandria, Va.: American Statistical Association.

Wright, D., and S. Ahmed
1990   Implementing NCES' new confidentiality protections. *American Statistical Association 1990 Proceedings of the Section on Survey Research Methods.* Alexandria, Va.: American Statistical Association.

Appendix A

Study Procedures

This appendix describes the organization of the panel study and the procedures used by the panel to gather relevant background information, explore the issues, and develop its recommendations. This description covers two case-study workshops that were held prior to the formal convening of the panel, but made important contributions to the panel's work.

PANEL ORGANIZATION AND ACTIVITIES

The panel was jointly convened in 1989 by the Committee on National Statistics (CNSTAT) of the National Academy of Sciences-National Research Council and the Social Science Research Council (SSRC). Its goal was to provide recommendations to federal agencies to aid them in their stewardship of data for public policy decisions and research. The panel was comprised of experts in the fields of ethics, privacy, respondent issues, public policy, legislation, the history of the federal statistical system, and statistics. Supporting the panel's work was a staff consisting of a study director, two consultants, a senior project assistant, and a staff liaison from the Social Science Research Council. (See Appendix B for biographical sketches of panel members and staff.)

Funding for the study was provided by the National Science Foundation, the Bureau of the Census of the U.S. Department of

Commerce, the Bureau of Labor Statistics of the U.S. Department of Labor, the Internal Revenue Service Statistics of Income Division of the U.S. Department of Treasury, the National Institute on Aging of the U.S. Department of Health and Human Services, the National Center for Education Statistics of the U.S. Department of Education, and, through their general contributions to the work of the Committee on National Statistics, several other federal agencies.

The panel accomplished its work in several different ways. Prior to the first meeting of the panel, and as a foundation for the panel's work, the Committee on National Statistics and the Social Science Research Council sponsored two workshops: the Longitudinal Retirement History Workshop, held in September 1987, and the Workshop on Confidentiality of and Access to Doctorate Records, held in November 1988. In January 1991 the panel sponsored a workshop on confidentiality of and access to National Center for Education Statistics data. A conference on disclosure limitation approaches and data access was held in March 1991. The panel held nine deliberative meetings from November 1989 through January 1992. The panel also met with representatives from the federal statistical community, privacy advocates, and other concerned individuals and organizations. Finally, the panel commissioned papers to inform its deliberations, including several papers that served as background for the Workshop on Confidentiality of and Access to National Center for Education Statistics Data and the Conference on Disclosure Limitation Approaches and Data Access (see below).

The panel held nine meetings in Washington, D.C., between November 1989 and January 1992. Through presentations by agency representatives at these meetings, the panel was informed about the complexities and realities of the missions of the agencies and the role that those missions and environment play in agencies' efforts to protect confidentiality while permitting access to data for research. Agency representatives identified important aspects of confidentiality and data access and provided information on the subtleties of some of the problems they face in dealing with these issues. In addition, the panel held lengthy discussions with researchers, privacy advocates, and others about data sharing and record linkage, statistical disclosure limitation, administrative policies of the agencies, legislative problems and solutions, the needs of researchers, and the needs of the federal statistical agencies. The length, duration, and number of meetings was intended to encourage debate and ultimately develop consensus on the issues. Throughout these meetings, the panel was mindful of its goal to provide helpful recommendations to the federal statistical agencies.

At a June 1991 meeting, several privacy advocates were invited. The meeting focused on the public's interest, ethical issues, and cognitive research on informed consent and notification in relation to confidentiality and data access concerns.

CASE STUDIES

LONGITUDINAL RETIREMENT HISTORY WORKSHOP

The Longitudinal Retirement History Workshop, chaired by Jerry A. Hausman and held on September 18-19, 1987, was conducted at the request of the National Institute on Aging (NIA) and the Census Bureau. The National Center for Health Statistics provided additional support for the workshop.

The National Institute on Aging requested the workshop to help answer a question of whether its proposed reinterview of surviving panel members and spouses of decedents from the Longitudinal Retirement History Survey was feasible. Additional goals of the workshop were to learn some of the problems and issues in protecting confidential data, discuss the disclosure limitation practices of the Census Bureau, develop suggestions for methods to access confidential data for research, and provide information to NIA on how to achieve its goals while maintaining adequate protection of the data. Workshop participants were particularly interested in the legal, ethical, and policy questions surrounding the issues of recontacting the panel members, linking the data from the reinterview with the old data, and making the linked data files available to researchers for analysis.

After considering the questions above, the workshop participants outlined three possible courses of action. Two were deemed useful in a broad context: allowing access of researchers to microdata through their appointments as special sworn employees of the Census Bureau and the establishment of data resource centers where Census Bureau employees could process researcher requests. A third proposed course of action, one that was thought to be the most feasible for the follow-up of the Longitudinal Retirement History Survey, involved obtaining consent from the survey respondents to transfer data in existing files to another agency whose data are not subject to the conditions of Title 13 (see Chapter 5). The workshop participants also developed some ideas to help guide

the Panel on Confidentiality and Data Access, which at the time
had not yet been convened.

WORKSHOP ON CONFIDENTIALITY OF AND ACCESS TO DOCTORATE RECORDS

The Workshop on Confidentiality of and Access to Doctorate
Records, chaired by George T. Duncan and held November 4-5,
1988, was convened by CNSTAT and SSRC. The purposes of the
workshop were to determine if and how mechanisms for allowing
greater researcher access to data from the Doctorate Records File
and the Survey of Doctorate Records could be developed without
compromising the confidentiality of the data and to identify issues that would be important for the proposed Panel on Confidentiality and Data Access to address.

Workshop participants discussed various approaches for providing increased access to the Doctorate Records File and the Survey of Doctorate Records. Topics discussed included the creation
of public-use data files with all information that would allow
identification of the respondent removed; modification of statements of use; providing respondents an opportunity to approve or
disapprove of the proposed uses of the data; development of signed
agreements that clearly define users responsibilities in maintaining the confidentiality of the data; and providing remote access to
the data through a "gatekeeper," who would monitor access requests and ensure adherence to any confidentiality provisions associated with the remote access. The general conclusion of participants was that the tension between confidentiality and data
access could not be resolved by any one action.

WORKSHOP ON CONFIDENTIALITY OF AND ACCESS TO NATIONAL CENTER FOR EDUCATION STATISTICS DATA

The panel's Workshop on Confidentiality of and Access to
National Center for Education Statistics Data, chaired by William
M. Mason, was held in January 1991. The purposes of the workshop were to investigate confidentiality and access issues as they
apply to the National Center for Education Statistics (NCES) and
to obtain information for the panel's deliberations. Participants
from the educational research community, federal government,
education associations, and state departments of education were
invited to attend the workshop. Panel members also attended the
meeting.

During the workshop, participants discussed the evolution of confidentiality legislation covering the NCES particularly Section 3001(m) of the Augustus F. Hawkins-Robert T. Stafford Elementary and Secondary School Improvement Amendments of 1988 (the Hawkins-Stafford Act, P.L. 100-297) and Section 252 of the Excellence in Mathematics, Science and Engineering Act of 1990 (P.L. 101-589), which amended the confidentiality provisions of the General Education Provisions Act (P.L. 90-247). In a paper commissioned by the panel, Diana C. Pullin and Kenneth B. Newton discussed the impact of Section 252 on the policies and practices of NCES in permitting access to their data while respecting the confidentiality of respondents' identities. Discussion focused on the various data systems maintained by NCES, including the sources of the data and the type of data items in the data sets; NCES's confidentiality provisions; users' experiences before and after the Hawkins-Stafford Act; and NCES's statistical and administrative procedures to prevent the disclosure of individually identifiable information. Finally, participants assessed the issues and discussed possible changes in procedures, legislation, regulations, and interpretations that could increase access to data and protect the confidentiality of the data.

INFORMATION GATHERING

REQUEST FOR DOCUMENTATION

In fall 1990, the panel contacted approximately 40 federal agencies, requesting documentation of their policies and practices for ensuring the confidentiality of data that they collect and disseminate. The agencies were selected based on the number of their statistical activities and budgets for statistical programs. Information was requested on agencies' statutes, regulations, and internal guidelines; Privacy Act notices describing the nature of systems of records that it maintains (Title 5 U.S.C. § 552a(e)(4)); informed consent and notification procedures (for individuals and establishments); disclosure limitation techniques; access to non-public-use data, including the type of arrangements made for the access; instances of denied access; and other organizational arrangements and guidelines used to establish policies for protecting the confidentiality of data and reviewing requests for access to data. The panel also asked the agencies to provide information on their experiences as users of identifiable data.

The panel received extensive information on agencies' practices. The documentation was invaluable to its work in assessing the agencies' confidentiality and access practices and their future needs. The panel and staff conducted many follow-up contacts with the agencies. In addition, representatives from the agencies attended panel meetings. The text of the request appears as Attachment 1.

INVITATION FOR COMMENTS

In fall 1990, the panel also published an "Invitation for Comments" in a variety of professional journals and newsletters. The panel requested comments from users of federal statistics on access problems, suggestions for improving access, and information on persons or businesses harmed by disclosure of identifiable data. The "Invitation" provided an opportunity for concerned individuals to submit their comments, suggestions, and experiences for the panel's consideration. Approximately 20 responses were received. The text of the "Invitation for Comments" is included as Attachment 2.

CONFERENCE ON DISCLOSURE LIMITATION APPROACHES AND DATA ACCESS

Identification and examination of methods to maximize access to federal statistical data while maintaining the confidentiality of the respondents' identities were the foci of the Conference on Disclosure Limitation Approaches and Data Access, held in March 1991. Researchers, federal government employees, and panel members attended the conference, chaired by George T. Duncan. To understand the underlying issues, participants reviewed data dissemination policies of federal agencies and the effect of increasingly powerful technologies on the agencies' efforts to provide data and maintain confidentiality. To facilitate the discussion of the issues, the conference was divided into four sessions: basic issues, statistical disclosure limitation, computer issues, and assessment of current legislation and restricted access procedures.

The panel commissioned several papers to serve as background information for the conference. These papers were presented at the conference and are discussed in Chapter 6 of the report. They are published in a special issue of the *Journal of Official Statistics* (1993(2)).

COMMISSIONED PAPERS

The panel commissioned 11 papers to help its deliberations.

Paper commissioned for the Workshop on Confidentiality of and Access to National Center for Education Statistics Data

Kenneth B. Newton and Diana C. Pullin, "The Impact of Section 252 of the Excellence in Mathematics, Science and Engineering Act of 1990 on the Policies and Practices of the National Center for Education Statistics"

Papers commissioned for the Conference on Disclosure Limitation Approaches and Data Access

Session 1: Basic Issues
Diane Lambert, "Measures of Disclosure Risk and Harm"
Paul D. Reynolds, "Privacy Advances in Social and Policy Science: Balancing Present Costs and Future Gains"
Discussants: William Butz, Thomas Plewes, Eleanor Singer

Session 2: Statistical Disclosure Limitation
Wayne A. Fuller, "Use of Masking Procedures for Disclosure Limitation"
Roderick J.A. Little, "Statistical Analysis of Masked Data"
Discussants: Brian V. Greenberg, Donald B. Rubin

Session 3: Computer Issues
Sallie Keller-McNulty and Elizabeth A. Unger, "Database Systems: Inferential Security"
Discussants: Gerald Gates, Teresa F. Lunt

Session 4: Creative Solutions to the Disclosure Problem Under the Status Quo
Joe S. Cecil, "Confidentiality Legislation and the Federal Statistical System"
Thomas B. Jabine, "Procedures for Restricted Data Access"
Discussants: John P. Fanning, F. Thomas Juster, Nancy J. Kirkendall

Other papers

  Thomas B. Jabine, "Statistical Disclosure Limitation: Current
    Federal Practices and Research"
  Robert H. Mugge, "Informed Consent in U.S. Government Surveys"
  Eleanor Singer, "Summary of Informed Consent Literature for
    National Research Council Panel on Confidentiality and Data
    Access"

Most of the papers and discussants' comments appear in revised form in a special issue of the *Journal of Official Statistics
(9(2))*.

Attachment 1

COMMITTEE ON NATIONAL STATISTICS

NATIONAL ACADEMY OF SCIENCES
2101 Constitution Avenue, N.W., Washington, D.C. 20418

Panel on Confidentiality   CNSTAT: (202) 334-2550
   and Data Access   SSRC: (212) 661-0280

Request for Documentation of Policies and Practices

FROM: George T. Duncan, Chair

DATE: October 31, 1990

Federal agencies differ with respect to their statutes, regulations, and organizational arrangements that pertain to the confidentiality of and the access to statistical data that they collect and disseminate. The review of policies and procedures related to confidentiality and data access is one of the most important activities of our panel study. Therefore, we are asking you to assist the Panel on Confidentiality and Data Access in obtaining documentation on your agency's policies and practices.

The Panel plans to collect information in two steps:

• From a broad cross-section of federal statistical agencies and units, the Panel will request that each agency provide documentation related to its confidentiality and data access policies and practices; and

• Following the review of these materials, the Panel and staff will request meetings with key officials of a few agencies. The meetings will serve the purpose of adding to or clarifying information provided in the documents. They will also provide the Panel an opportunity to obtain information on topics for which there was no documentation.

The purpose of this memorandum concerns the first step: a request from the Panel to provide documentation about your agency's policies and practices. The Panel is primarily interested in obtaining documentation on policies and practices that pertain to the data your agency produces. In addition, the Panel would like to learn about your agency's experiences as a *user* of identifiable data from federal and non-federal sources. For instance, has your agency experienced difficulties or delays in accessing data produced by another federal agency? If so, what were the problems and how were they resolved? Examples of the relevant types of documentation are given below.

Please note that the Panel is asking your agency to provide *copies of existing documents.* We are not asking your agency to prepare additional written statements at this time. Since the documents collected from each federal agency will be used to develop the Panel's report and may be summarized in ways that can lead to the identification of an agency, they cannot be considered to be confidential.

To assist you in collecting this documentation, please consider the scope of this study: it includes publicly supported *statistical data collection activities* such as censuses, surveys, administrative record data (when used for statistical purposes), and epidemiological studies. We are interested in statistical data for both individuals and establishments. Data from clinical trials, while very important, will not be considered in this study. There are some special issues associated with clinical trial data that would require a separate study focusing on the bioethical aspects of confidentiality and data access.

I. DOCUMENTATION FOR DATA PRODUCED BY YOUR AGENCY

For data produced by your agency, we ask that you provide relevant documentation of your agency's confidentiality and data access policies and practices. We use the word "documentation" to refer to a broad array of *existing* materials, such as published technical papers, standards manuals, copies of consent forms, memoranda, policy statements, statutes, interagency agreements, etc., that are relevant to each of the topics below. Please remember that the Panel is interested in data collected from both individuals (except in clinical trials) and establishments. Note that the Panel has copies of all documents listed in the appendices and does not require additional copies.

1. **Statutes, regulations, agency guidelines**: Statutes, regula-

tions, agency guidelines (ex., National Center for Health Statistics' *Staff Manual on Confidentiality*), etc., that pertain to the confidentiality of and access to your agency's data. Please note that we are not interested in government-wide statutes and guidelines pertaining to data used for statistical purposes, such as the Privacy Act — the panel will contact the Office of Management and Budget for government-wide documents. However, if your agency has its own regulations or guidelines for compliance with government-wide statutes, we are interested in those.

2. **Privacy Act system of records notice**: We would like to obtain system of records notices for two or three of your agency's major systems that are used for statistical purposes. In addition, notices from other systems that have features of special interest for the panel study would also be appreciated.

3. **Respondent notification and consent procedures for both individuals and establishments**: The Panel would like to obtain examples, from questionnaires or other survey forms, of the respondent notification and consent procedures (RNCPs) used by your agency to collect data from both individuals and establishments. Note that the term RNCP, as used in this memorandum, refers to a wide range of notices provided by federal agencies to individuals and businesses. It includes, but is not limited to, informed consent statements or agreements, confidentiality notification statements, and privacy act notifications. Some topics of interest follow:

• How RNCPs differ for individuals and establishments, especially for agencies that collect information from both.

• The RNCP(s) used by your agency when it plans to link survey data with administrative record data (for example, when your agency plans to use Social Security Number for the linkage).

In addition, the Panel also requests agency documents that contain instructions for staff on how to write RNCPs.

4. **Disclosure limitation techniques**: Statistical methods and procedures are sometimes used to limit disclosure risk in the release of tabulations and microdata to the public, for example,

not releasing separate data for geographic areas with small populations. Some topics of interest are:

• The procedures that are used by your agency to limit disclosure risk.

• If relevant, how procedures differ for individuals and establishments.

5. **Facilitating access to non-public use data**: Some agencies have implemented special procedures to facilitate access to data that have not been released for public use. Some topics of interest to the Panel follow:

• Whether your agency has ever provided access to data that were not released for public use.

• If so, the type of arrangements used by your agency and its experience with such "special arrangements." Some examples include:

- allowing controlled access to specially sworn employees who are required to relocate to the principal office of your agency;

- allowing controlled access to specially sworn employees who work in regional offices of the agency; and

- employing special licensing agreements.

6. **Inability to facilitate access**: Documents from your agency of cases where access has been denied and the reason for denial. Documentation might be contained in correspondence or in published papers, e.g., G. Gates, "Census Bureau microdata: Providing useful research data while protecting the anonymity of respondents" in the *Proceedings of the Survey Research Section* (American Statistical Association, 1988).

7. **Organizational arrangements**: Existing documentation that describes organizational arrangements in your agency that are used (1) to establish confidentiality guidelines and (2) to review requests for access (for example, the Census Bureau's Microdata Review Panel). Essentially, the Panel is interested

in tracing the "standard flow" of a request for access to unpublished data through your agency.

II. DOCUMENTATION FOR ACCESSING IDENTIFIABLE DATA FROM FEDERAL AND NON-FEDERAL SOURCES

The second area of interest to the Panel concerns your agency's
experiences in accessing identifiable data from other federal agencies and non-federal sources — data to be used for statistical purposes. Specifically, we are interested in those experiences that
concern access to microdata which would not meet public-use
criteria.

Federal agencies may require identifiable data from other agencies
to (1) use as a frame for their surveys; (2) link with their own
survey data; and (3) do analyses. The Panel is interested in the
extent to which your agency had difficulty in obtaining such data
(documentation might be letters or published papers). The Panel
is also interested in knowing if special treatment was required for
these data, above and beyond the standards applied to microdata
produced by your own agency.

1. **Data from other federal agencies**: We are requesting information about your agency's experiences in accessing data from
other federal agencies, especially the barriers encountered. Topics
of interest include:

• The extent to which your agency uses data for statistical
purposes that are produced by other agencies.

• Cases in which your agency experienced "difficulties" in
accessing the federal data that it needed. For instance, barriers that a federal agency might experience are:

- an agency sponsors surveys but is unable to get fully detailed files from the collecting agency; or

- a federal agency or program experiences delays in getting
administrative data or business lists from other agencies —
data that are needed for use in its own statistical programs.

2. **Confidentiality and access issues for non-federal data**: A
federal agency sometimes serves an important role as a reposi-

tory of non-federal survey and/or administrative data. These non-federal data provide valuable sources of statistical information that supplement federal data. Some issues of interest to the Panel include the following:

• The extent to which your agency uses identifiable, non-federal records for statistical purposes (e.g., administrative data produced on the state-level).

• The provisions that exist concerning confidentiality to and access of these data, especially where agency policies for data that it produces differ from its policies covering non-federal data.

Finally, agency papers and/or publications that describe the preceding items, but which might also include the history of access to unpublished data or the history of changes to relevant confidentiality laws and regulations, would be most helpful.

If there is someone else the Panel should contact in your agency or program to obtain the documentation that we are requesting, please provide Virginia de Wolf, Study Director, (202-334-2550) with the name and telephone number. If you have any questions, please direct them to Virginia. We would appreciate receiving your agency's documentation by December 3, 1990. Thank you very much for your efforts in helping the Panel.

Attachment 2

PANEL ON CONFIDENTIALITY AND DATA ACCESS
Invitation for Comments

Many users of Federal statistics are aware of the balance that must be struck between protecting the confidentiality of information provided by persons and businesses for statistical purposes and the need to make publicly-collected data widely available for legitimate research and statistical uses.

In search of new ways to deal with this issue, the Committee on National Statistics and the Social Science Research Council, with support from several Federal agencies, have convened a Panel on Confidentiality and Data Access. As part of its two-year study, the Panel, which had its first meeting in December of last year, will be compiling relevant information from both producers and users of Federal statistics.

The scope of this panel study includes publicly-supported statistical data collection activities on individuals and establishments, such as censuses, surveys, administrative record data (when used for statistical purposes), and epidemiological studies. Data from clinical trials, while very important, will not be considered in this study. There are some special issues associated with clinical trial data that would require a separate study focusing on the bioethical aspects of confidentiality and data access.

Readers of this notice are invited to submit short statements on any or all of the following subjects:

Access problems. Specific examples of instances where Federal agency confidentiality laws or policies have made it impossible for you or your colleagues to obtain data needed in your work or caused excessive delays in arranging for access to the data. Please indicate the sources and specific kinds of data desired and the purposes for which the data were needed.

Suggestions for improving access. Have you had any experience in obtaining access to data not disclosed for general public use? How was this arranged? Do you have suggestions for improving data access with appropriate safeguards to maintain confidentiality and without undue risk of adverse effects on public cooperation with censuses and surveys?

Persons or businesses harmed by disclosure. Do you know of any instances in which persons or businesses were harmed by unlawful or unintended disclosure of information they provided to the government under the condition that the information was to be used only for statistical purposes? How did this happen? What were the consequences? (This category differs from the first two in that statements need not be based on your own personal experience.)

Please submit your statements to me c/o Committee on National Statistics, National Research Council, 2101 Constitution Avenue, NW, Washington DC 20418. If you have any questions, please call Virginia de Wolf, Study Director, on 202/334-2550. We look forward to hearing from you.

George T. Duncan, *Chair*
Panel on Confidentiality
and Data Access

Appendix B

Biographical Sketches

GEORGE T. DUNCAN is professor of statistics in the H. John Heinz III School of Public Policy and Management and in the Department of Statistics at Carnegie Mellon University. He previously held an academic appointment at the University of California, Davis, and was a Peace Corps volunteer in the Philippines in 1965-1967, teaching at Mindanao State University. His current research work centers on the decision processes of conflict resolution as they apply to privacy and information issues. He is a fellow of the American Statistical Association. He has been editor of the Theory and Methods Section of the *Journal of the American Statistical Association*. He received B.S. and M.S. degrees from the University of Chicago and a Ph.D. degree from the University of Minnesota, all in statistics.

JAMES T. BONNEN is professor of agricultural economics at Michigan State University. His current research interests include information systems theory, the design and management of statistically based policy decision systems, and agricultural research policy. Bonnen has served as chair of the National Research Council Panel on Statistics for Rural Development Policy (1979-1980), director of the President's Reorganization Project for the Federal Statistical System (1978-1980), president of the American Agricultural Economics Association (1975), member of the President's National

Advisory Commission on Poverty, and as senior staff economist with the President's Council of Economic Advisers (1963-1965). In 1981 he received the American Statistical Association's Washington Statistical Society's Julius Shiskin Award for Outstanding Achievement in Economic Statistics. He is a fellow of the American Agricultural Economics Association, the American Statistical Association, and the American Association for the Advancement of Science. He received a B.A. degree from Texas A&M University, an M.A. degree from Duke University, and a Ph.D. degree from Harvard University, all in economics.

JOE S. CECIL is a project director at the Federal Judicial Center. He is the author of numerous publications concerning legal standards affecting exchange of information for research purposes. Other areas of research interest include the use of scientific and technical evidence in litigation, variations in procedures employed by federal courts of appeals, and management of mass tort litigation. He received a J.D. degree from Northwestern University School of Law and a Ph.D. degree in psychology and evaluation research from Northwestern University.

MICHELE L. CONRAD is a senior project assistant with the Committee on National Statistics. Previously she was the senior project assistant for the Panel to Review Evaluation Studies of Bilingual Education, and she is currently working with the Panel on Census Requirements in the Year 2000 and Beyond. She received a B.A. degree from the University of Pittsburgh.

MARTIN HEIDENHAIN DAVID is professor of economics at the University of Wisconsin-Madison. His research has explored a variety of problems relating to taxation and transfer programs, involving extensive work in collecting, analyzing, and managing complex data and the design of information systems to support such data. His books include two that report on major data collection efforts, *Income and Welfare in the United States* (McGraw-Hill, 1962) and *Linkage and Retrieval of Micro-economic Data* (Lexington Books, 1974). He has served on the National Research Council (NRC) Panel on Statistics for Family Assistance and on the Panel on Research Strategies in the Behavioral and Social Sciences on Environmental Problems and Policies. He is a fellow of the American Statistical Association. He serves as adviser to the Statistics of Income Division of the Internal Revenue Service; a member of the Committee on National Statistics of the NRC; and a member of the Advisory Board of the German Socio-economic Panel Study, which is conducted by the Deutsches Institut fur Wirtschafts-forschung. He received an A.B. degree from Swarthmore College and M.A. and Ph.D. degrees from the University of Michigan.

VIRGINIA A. DE WOLF, who served as the panel study director, is currently a mathematical statistician at the Bureau of Labor Statistics. Previously she worked at the National Highway Traffic Safety Administration, the U.S. General Accounting Office, and the University of Washington (Seattle). She received a B.A. degree in mathematics from the College of New Rochelle, and a Ph.D. degree from the University of Washington (Seattle) in educational psychology with emphases in statistics, measurement, and research design.

RUTH R. FADEN is professor of health policy and management and director of the Program in Law, Ethics, and Health in the School of Hygiene and Public Health of the Johns Hopkins University, and she is also a senior research scholar at the Kennedy Institute of Ethics, Georgetown University. She serves as a consultant to numerous government and private agencies and is the author of books and journal articles on health policy, biomedical ethics, and health behavior. She also works on procedure-based rationing in medical care. She holds an M.A. degree in humanities from the University of Chicago, a M.P.H. degree from the University of California-Berkeley, and a Ph.D. degree in attitudes and behavior from the University of California, Berkeley.

DAVID H. FLAHERTY is a professor of history and law at the University of Western Ontario, London, Canada. He has had a long involvement with issues of personal privacy and information policy and has written several books on the issues of privacy and confidentiality, including *Privacy and Government Data Banks: An International Perspective* (Mansell, 1979) and *Protecting Privacy in Surveillance Societies: The Federal Republic of Germany, Sweden, France, Canada, and the United States* (University of North Carolina Press, 1989). He has testified before many U.S. and Canadian legislative committees on computer matching, the privacy implications of computer crime, and bills on freedom of information and protection of individual privacy. He also participated in the first oversight hearings on the Privacy Act of 1974, held by the House Subcommittee on Government Information of the U.S. Congress. In 1992-1993 Flaherty held appointments as a fellow at the Woodrow Wilson International Center for Scholars, a Canada-U.S. Fulbright fellow, a visiting scholar at Georgetown National Law Center, and a fellow of the Kennedy Institute for Ethics at Georgetown University. He received a B.A. degree from McGill University and M.A. and Ph.D. degrees from Columbia University.

THOMAS B. JABINE is an independent statistical consultant who specializes in sampling, survey research methods, and statistical policy. He was formerly a statistical policy expert for the Energy Information Administration of the U.S. Department of Energy, chief mathematical statistician for the Social Security Administration, and chief of the Statistical Research Division of the Bureau of the Census. He is a member of the International Statistical Institute and a fellow of the American Statistical Association, and he served as president of the Washington Statistical Society. He is the author of several articles on the confidentiality and data access policies and practices of federal statistical agencies and served as chair of the American Statistical Association Committee on Privacy and Confidentiality. With Richard P. Claude, he edited *Statistics and Human Rights: Getting the Record Straight* (University of Pennsylvania Press, 1992). He has a B.S. degree in mathematics and an M.S. degree in economics and science from the Massachusetts Institute of Technology.

F. THOMAS JUSTER is a research scientist at the Survey Research Center and professor of economics at the University of Michigan, Ann Arbor. His research includes the design of economic and social accounting systems, the analysis of saving and wealth accumulation patterns among U.S. households, the analysis of time allocation among households, and the development of measures of economic well-being. He has served on a number of National Research Council (NRC) committees, including the Committee on National Statistics, and he has chaired the NRC Committee on the Supply and Demand for Mathematics and Science Teachers and the American Economic Association Committee on the Quality of Economic Data. He is a fellow of the American Statistical Association and of the National Association of Business Economists. He received a B.S. degree in education from Rutgers University and a Ph.D. degree in economics from Columbia University.

GARY T. MARX is professor and chair of the Sociology Department at the University of Colorado at Boulder and director of the Center for the Social Study of Information Technology. Previously he taught at the University of California, Berkeley, Harvard University, and the Massachusetts Institute of Technology. He is the author most recently of *Undercover: Police Surveillance in America* (University of California Press, 1988) and of academic and popular articles on the social implications of information technology. His work has been translated into many languages, including Japanese and Chinese. He has worked on privacy and technology issues for the U.S. Office of Technology Assessment, the U.S. General Accounting Office, Senate and House Subcommittees, state and local governments, the Canadian House of Commons, and the Council of Europe. His current work focuses on technologies for extracting personal information and research on cross-border forms of social control. He received a Ph.D. degree from the University of California, Berkeley.

WILLIAM M. MASON is professor of sociology at the University of California, Los Angeles. He has held academic appointments at the University of Michigan, Duke University, and the University of Chicago. His research has been in the areas of research design, multilevel models, social demography, and political sociology; he is currently studying infant mortality in China. He has been a John Simon Guggenheim Foundation fellow and a fellow at the Center for Advanced Study in the Behavioral Sciences. He received a B.A. degree from Reed College and a Ph.D. degree from the University of Chicago.

WLODZIMIERZ OKRASA is a staff associate at the Social Science Research Council. He is currently developing a social science research laboratory for collaborative, comparative research in and about Eastern and Central Europe. He specializes in the methodology of social investigation, social statistics, and microeconomics. He has held appointments as an American Statistical Association research fellow and as a fellow of the British Academy and the Friedrich Ebert Stiftung. Previously he served as head of a research unit at the Institute of Economic Science at the Polish Academy of Sciences and as adviser to the president of the Polish Central Statistical Office. He has written and edited several books, including *Social Welfare in Britain and Poland*, with Julian Le Grand (London School of Economics, 1988). He received a Ph.D. degree in 1977 from the University of Warsaw.

ROBERT W. PEARSON is Director of Corporate and Foundation Relations at Barnard College. He previously served as Assistant Survey Director at the National Opinion Research Center at the University of Chicago and as staff associate at the Social Science Research Council (SSRC). While at SSRC, he worked with the panel and with committees on cognition and survey research, the comparative evaluation of longitudinal surveys, and research on the urban underclass. He received a B.A. degree from the University of Missouri, Columbia, and a Ph.D. degree in political science from the University of Chicago.

DONALD B. RUBIN is professor of statistics and chair of the Department of Statistics at Harvard University. Previously he was professor of statistics and of education at the University of Chicago and chair of the Statistics Research Group at the Educational Testing Service. His research has dealt with causal inference in experimental and observational studies, missing data and nonresponse in surveys, and applied Bayesian statistics, including computational methods. He has been coordinating and applications editor of the *Journal of the American Statistical Association* and is a past member of the National Research Council Committee on National Statistics. He is a fellow of a number of professional associations, including the American Academy of Arts and Sciences, the American Association for the Advancement of Science, the Institute of Mathematical Statistics, the American Statistical Association, and the International Statistics Institute. He received an A.B. degree from Princeton University and an M.S. degree in computer science and a Ph.D. degree in statistics, both from Harvard University.

ELEANOR SINGER is a senior research scholar at the Center for the Social Sciences at Columbia University. Her primary areas of work include public opinion and survey methods research, and she has conducted several studies of the impact of informed consent procedures and confidentiality assurances on survey participation rates and response quality. She is a past president of the American Association for Public Opinion Research and a former editor of *Public Opinion Quarterly*. With Stanley Presser, she edited *Survey Research Methods: A Reader* (University of Chicago Press, 1989). She received a B.A. degree from Queens College and a Ph.D. degree from Columbia University.

DAVID L. SZANTON is Executive Director of International and Area Studies at the University of California, Berkeley. He is an anthropologist with research interests in contemporary Southeast Asia. From 1975 to 1991 he organized and staffed numerous area and research planning committees at the Social Science Research Council in New York. He received a B.A. degree from Harvard College and a Ph.D. degree from the University of Chicago.

W.H. WILLIAMS is professor of mathematics and statistics at Hunter College in New York City. His current research interests are in the statistics of employment discrimination and the influence of language factors in mathematics learning. Previously he was in the Mathematics and Statistics Research Center at Bell Laboratories, Murray Hill, New Jersey, and he later headed a division of A.T.&T. responsible for econometric analysis of corporate financial structures. He has also been Executive Vice President of Louis Harris and Associates, the public polling firm, and president of Strategic Comaps, a firm that develops software for the credit and collections industry. He has had visiting appointments at the University of California, Berkeley, the University of Michigan, and the Census Bureau. He has published more than 50 papers and three books on statistical methods applicable to economic and business problems. He was educated at McMaster and Iowa State Universities.

Index